Making Civil Societies Work –
Zivilgesellschaft und gesellschaftliche Praxis

Potsdamer Textbücher Band 9

2006

Jochen Franzke (Hrsg.)

Making Civil Societies Work –

Zivilgesellschaft und gesellschaftliche Praxis

Universitätsverlag Potsdam

Bibliografische Information Der Deutschen Bibliothek
Die Deutsche Bibliothek verzeichnet diese Publikation in der
Deutschen Nationalbibliografie; detaillierte bibliografische
Daten sind im Internet über http://dnb.ddb.de abrufbar.

Potsdamer Textbücher *PTB*

Die Reihe wird herausgegeben von Erhard Crome,
Jochen Franzke und Raimund Krämer
im Auftrag des WeltTrends e.V. Potsdam.

Band 9
Making Civil Societies Work – Zivilgesellschaft und
gesellschaftliche Praxis / Jochen Franzke (Hrsg.).
- Potsdam : Universitätsverlag Potsdam, 2006
   (Potsdamer Textbücher ; 9)
   ISBN 3-939469-40-8
   ISBN 978-3-939469-40-7

*Dieser Band erscheint mit freundlicher Unterstützung durch den
Deutschen Akademischen Austauschdienst (DAAD).*

Satz: Rico Janke
Druck: BoD
Printed in Germany

© WeltTrends e.V., c/o Dr. Lutz Kleinwächter,
Großbeerenstraße 285, 14480 Potsdam

ISBN 3-939469-40-8
ISBN 978-3-939469-40-7

Inhalt

Vorwort ... 6

Ireneusz Pawel Karolewski
Civil Society and its Discontents ... 7

Sebastian Braun
Die Wiederentdeckung des Vereinswesens im Windschatten gesellschaftlicher Krisen
Konzepte, Kontroversen, Perspektiven ... 26

Lahouari Addi
Religion et Culture Politique dans le Monde Arabe ... 41

Benjamin Stachursky
Globale Normen, lokaler Aktivismus. *Advocacy* NGOs und die Sozialisierung der Menschenrechte von Frauen am Beispiel Ägyptens ... 63

Heidi Wedel
The Role of Civil Society Organisations for Democratisation. Lessons from Turkey ... 98

Leonardo Secchi
Agenda Building in Brazilian Municipalities: When and How Citizens Participate ... 109

Wenting Fei
Local Public Participation in Government Legislation and Decision-Making in China. The Case of Shanghai ... 125

Taghi Azadarmaki
Good or Bad Government – The Case Study of Iran ... 142

Jochen Franzke
Representation and Participation in New Unitary Municipalities
Cases from the German Federal State Brandenburg ... 154

Christoph Reichard
From Public Management to Public Governance
A Changing Perspective in the German Public Sector ... 170

Abstracts ... 182
Autoren ... 188

Vorwort

In vielen Staaten der modernen Welt wächst die Rolle der Zivilgesellschaft. Dieser Prozeß vollzieht sich in unterschiedlichen politischen Systemen, unter unterschiedlichen gesellschaftlichen Bedingungen und mit unterschiedlichen Geschwindigkeiten. Die Entwicklung der modernen Zivilgesellschaft und ihrer Ausprägungen in der Praxis international vergleichend darzustellen, ist daher eine gewaltige Aufgabe. Diese Publikation will einen Beitrag zur wissenschaftlichen Debatte über die Möglichkeiten und Grenzen zivilgesellschaftlichen Engagements der Bürger und ihrer Organisationen leisten.

Der vorliegende Band enthält neben einführenden Beiträgen Fallstudien aus sechs Ländern auf vier Kontinenten: der Türkei, dem Iran, Ägypten, Deutschland, China und Brasilien. In ihrer Gesamtheit zeichnen diese ein außerordentlich plastisches Bild der verschiedenen historischen Wurzeln von Zivilgesellschaften, ihrer differenzierten Rahmenbedingungen und der Schwerpunkte, die sich in der Realität der zivilgesellschaftlichen Prozesse in den verschiedenen Ländern zeigen. Gemeinsamkeiten und Unterschiede zivilgesellschaftlicher Entwicklung werden dabei sichtbar.

Die Idee zu dieser Publikation entstand im Rahmen der Hochschulkooperation zwischen der Universität Potsdam und der Universität Teheran. Einige Beiträge wurden in ersten Fassungen auf der Konferenz *„Social life, Civil Society, and Governance. Comparing Local Political Participation in a Global Society – Interdisciplinary Views"* vorgetragen, die im November 2004 in Potsdam stattfand.

Diese Publikation wurde zu unterschiedlichen Zeiten von einer Vielzahl von Kollegen unterstützt. Ihnen allen sei an dieser Stelle noch einmal ausdrücklich gedankt. Dr. Armin Triebel machte die Beiträge von Lahouari Addi, Taghi Azadarmaki, Benjamin Stachursky, Heidi Wedel und Sebastian Braun publikationsreif. Dr. Jochen Franzke bearbeitete die Beiträge von Wenting Fei, Leonardo Secci, Christoph Reichard und Ireneusz Pawel Karolewski. Ich bedanke mich weiterhin bei Azadeh Zamirirad, Ines Friedrich und Marcus Freitag für die Mitwirkung bei der aufwändigen redaktionellen Bearbeitung der Beiträge. Ausdrücklich bedanke ich mich bei der Redaktion der Zeitschrift für internationale Politik und vergleichende Studien „WeltTrends" für die technische Fertigstellung dieser Publikation.

Abschließend gilt mein Dank insbesondere dem Deutschen Akademischen Austauschdienst, der durch seine finanzielle Förderung diese Publikation erst ermöglicht hat.

Jochen Franzke als Herausgeber

Ireneusz Pawel Karolewski

Civil Society and its Discontents

For the last twenty years, the concept of civil society has probably attracted more scholarly attention than any other concept in social sciences. However, this concept is confronted with serious methodological challenges which cannot be ignored, particularly when one attempts to apply it in the context of different cultures. Some of those challenges will be addressed in this article. The article departs from the discussion of the sources of the broad interest in civil society and proceeds to the functional expectations about it. It tracks back the interest in civil society mainly in the search of scholars and political decision-makers for a new instrument of governance, particularly in the context of the debate on the defective state. The article claims that the concept of civil society, as it is frequently used in scientific and political debates, has specific cultural roots, which make a trans-cultural analysis difficult or perhaps even impossible. Subsequently, conceptual problems of civil society will be discussed. The article will address three aspects, namely the issue of what constitutes civil society, its autonomy and impact as well as the challenges with regard to the state. The final section will deal with aspects of a civil society analysis that should be taken into account. The central argument of the article is that in order to examine the impact of civil society on governance and democracy, it is recommendable to include three objects of analysis, namely the structure and functions of civil society (including also the possibly negative impact of it), the type of state co-existing with it as well as the character of the relationship between state and civil society.

1. Sources of Interest in Civil Society

Scholars' attention to civil society arose mainly from numerous expectations about it regarding its role as a potential agent of democracy and good governance. The primary context in which the interest in civil society came into being was the societal activity against authoritarian regimes in Eastern Europe in the 1980s. Hence, the democratising effects of civil society were believed to be specific, mainly with regard to regimes in the process of political transformation. Civil society was regarded as a democratic catalyst.

However, general expectations about civil society were nourished by two developments in the 1990s. *Firstly*, the popularity of the civil society concept was a consequence of the debate on the defective state launched in the 1990s by scholars such as Susan Strange

(Strange 1995, Cable 1995, Evans 1997, Keohane/Milner 1996). According to the defective state thesis, the state has been continually losing its capacity to produce efficient political outcomes. It was argued that the internationalisation of national economies and interdependence between the national states and societies render the national solution of governance problems virtually impossible. Consequently, the state command over the economy and society in terms of problem solving would have been continually diminishing since the 1970s. It also means that a gap between citizens' expectations and the problem solving capacity of the state emerged as a consequence. Since there were growing doubts about the capacity of the state to fulfil its governance tasks, political scholars proceeded to seek a new steering mode beyond the state. It was hoped that a new mode of governance could compensate for or substitute the decreasing state power. One of the modes was believed to be international institutions, regional or global in range, such as the European Union, the ASEAN, the Mercosur or the WTO (cf. Zürn 1998). The second mode was expected to be civil society (cf. Schuppert 2004).

Secondly, much hope was placed on civil society's capability to reduce the democratic deficit of the European Union. Since the EU has developed a great deal of regulation capacity, and it intervenes in the everyday life of European citizens[1], some scholars indicate a new form of European supranational statehood (less than a state, more than an international institution; cf. Kleger/Karolewski/Munke 2004). However, this statehood suffers from a democratic deficit, mainly because the citizens of Europe have little influence on the decisions taken at the European level. Civil society is supposed to compensate for the European democratic deficit by establishing new channels for citizens' participation. This expectation applies not only to the everyday politics of the European multi-level system (Heinelt 1998, Kaelble 2004), but also to the recent sessions of the European Constitutional Convention in which for the first time systematic hearings of civil society actors took place. Their role was to influence the agenda setting that was later debated by the representatives of European and national institutions (cf. Kleger 2004).

2. Functional Expectations about Civil Society

Civil society is primarily understood to be a sphere of self-organised, spontaneous and free groups of citizens. It is expected to fulfil certain functions with regard to democracy and governance. At first, the actors of civil society are supposed to associate primarily for the

---

[1] With regard to the EU, Giandomenico Majone (1993, 1996) coined the term ‚regulating state'.

sake of sociability. Thus, being of a collective nature, civil society constructs a cleavage that runs between the associated and the non-associated individual. Since civil society is constituted of associations, it is located on the intermediary level of society. It is expected to be self-organised and autonomous vis-à-vis the state. Otherwise it cannot fulfil its auxiliary functions. Thereupon, it is also independent of private economy, which encompasses enterprises and households. This double autonomy also implies that actors of civil society usurp neither the activities of the state nor those of private economy. Actors of civil society should not be willing to rule the entire political system or replace its agents. Nevertheless, civil society is expected to fulfil important functions concerning democracy and governance. Probably the most important expectation about civil society is the strengthening function with regard to the democratic performance of the state. Thus, the relation between state and society is envisaged as a non-zero-sum game in which one side does not lose, even if the other side wins. This perspective dates back to Alexis de Tocqueville (1835/40), who posited that the institutional structure of free associations is an indispensable safety belt against tyranny of the majority, which is the major potential pathology faced by democracies. Associations of civil society are schools of democracy, as they help develop virtues like solidarity and participation among the citizens. Citizens taking part in free associations are more likely to strive for the common good, which is essential for every majoritarian democracy. It stems from the expectation that in civil society individuals become socialised into community members.

However, the modern notion of civil society goes even further than the support of democracy. According to Robert Putnam (1993), civil society solves problems of collective action that stem from the inability of atomised actors to co-operate. Thus, civil society is expected to relieve the state from governance problems. Societal dilemmas like the tragedy of the commons, free-riding or prisoner's dilemma are considered major unsolved issues of governance. In all these dilemmas every citizen is better off when co-operating with each other than instead of acting unilaterally. But in the absence of a credible mutual commitment every individual has a rational incentive not to co-operate, which leads to a sub-optimal outcome for the community (cf. Morrow 1994). There is naturally a statist solution for these governance problems. The state can enforce co-operation between societal actors either by brute force or through the Hobbesian social contract in which societal actors voluntarily relinquish their decisional sovereignty to a central authority (Hobbes 1962). In the latter case, the state secures the necessary trust between the actors by its sheer efficiency of action. It supervises, monitors and enforces agreements and makes the violation of the contracts costly to the societal actors. However, a strong and contract-enforcing state is expensive to maintain, and it is always probable that it would turn authoritarian as a consequence of power concentration, thus endangering society itself. Against this background, civil society is supposed to solve the problems of societal co-operation in a different manner. Free associations such as choral societies, sports clubs or neighbourhood organisations are believed to produce social capital that enables voluntary co-operation (Putnam 1993; 1995). Social capital refers to mutual trust, norms of reciprocity and networks of civic engagement. It is a moral resource, which in contrast to economic capital increases through use, and becomes depleted whenever it is not used. Social capital can only be produced in the context of social activities and through repeated social exchange. Social trust between individuals makes them prone to co-operation, as it increases the credibility of participants. Horizontal social trust is based on norms of reciprocity, and it is expected to develop mainly in civil society.[2] Actors learn to trust others primarily in civil associations, as the contacts between them become embedded in a stable horizontal structure. In this structure, people are confident to trust others since they have less fear of exploitation than in an atomised and anonymous society. This structure facilitates social exchange and promotes general reciprocity, whereas social trust (trust between citizens) transforms into political trust (trust between citizens and the political elite). Consequently, civil associations are expected to become a tissue of a community. While civil society fosters trust, civic engagement and solidarity, it also is a measure of equality in comparison to asymmetric relations of hierarchy and dependence. Through civil society, citizens cease to be only spectators who vote, but instead develop their full civic potential.

Putnam (1993) states that social capital produced by civil associations shows positive effects on economic performance as well as on the quality of governance. In his comparative study of Northern and Southern Italian regions, he discovered that civic regions not only grew faster, but also had more effective public institutions. Consequently, he concludes that regions with few civic associations and more hierarchy tend to be less *civic*, and this lack of *civicness* is supposed to be self-enforcing. It can lead to a stable equilibrium whose features are disorder and stagnation. In his analysis of civil associations in the USA in the previous 30 years, Putnam (1995) concluded that American democracy is endangered, since many civil associations such as the Boy Scouts, parent-teacher associations and

---

[2] There is also a concept of vertical trust that develops in hierarchical social structures instead. But this, according to Putnam (1993), does not lead to ‚civility' necessary in democracies.

bowling leagues are in decline. According to him, weak civil society means weak state and weak economy.

Summing up, civic society is believed to support the market and the governance in fulfilling at least some of the economic and social tasks. For instance, Putnam (1993) describes horizontal rotating credit associations as an example of trust-producing civil society. In this sense, civil society is expected to be part of the economic system, even if it is situated outside the market. Since the activity of state ought to mainly consist of producing collective goods, civil society is expected to facilitate these tasks.

3. Cultural Roots of Civil Society

The rather general expectations regarding civil society ignore the cultural background of its concept, which poses a serious challenge to its universal application. The practices of civil society emerged initially in Europe during the first centuries of the last millennium in the city-state belt that stretched from London to Florence and Siena to the Netherlands. The consequence is not only the fact that the concept is deeply rooted in the European history of political thought, but also that it developed under the influence of a plethora of authors and naturally as a reaction to political and social changes on the European continent. During many centuries, different conceptual layers and thus expectations about civil society accumulated into a complex term, whose cultural focus is quite specific.

The notion of civil society in its political sense emerged relatively late, in the beginning of the 15th century. It had two major political connotations. Firstly, civil society was expected to protect citizens against the ruler's despotism. Thus, it was imagined as a space of freedom, which was guaranteed by the status of citizenship. The citizenship primarily encompassed individual freedoms such as the liberty of the person, freedom of speech, thought and religion as well as the right to own property and to establish associations. However, in the ancient and medieval period, civil rights were fused with political and social rights; hence citizenship entailed also political participatory rights (Marshall 1950). Against this background, civil society was a part of political society, and it did not begin differentiating as an autonomous sphere for about the next thousand years. Moreover, ancient and medieval civil societies were confined to one class, whereas the society of that period showed a high measure of inequality. In addition, civil society was accompanied by urbanity, given its origin in the city-states (Beyme 2000). However, since the 12th century, initially in England, the process of territorial expansion of civil rights has unfolded. Thus, civil society that previously had ended at the borders of the city-states received a territorial boost as a result of the establishment of nation-wide royal courts. It basically stemmed from the fact that civil rights became nationally executable, and they were no longer subject to local administration. Around the same time, a decoupling of civil rights from political and social rights started. Social rights became anchored in local communities, while political rights remained class-dependent. Nevertheless, it was civil rights that were to become the basis for the modern civil society. In the 19th century, civil rights inspired the expansion of political rights to broader parts of European societies, and thus civil society assumed a more political role. However, this manifested itself, as shown above, closely along the lines of development of European societies and therefore had a specific cultural context.

Conceptually, the most significant political definition of civil society can be found in John Locke's writings. In his „Second Treatise of Government" (1963), Locke uses the civil society concept synonymous with political society, which would come into being after the conclusion of the so-called social contract. In this sense, civil society, meaning society of citizens (that is, people with participatory rights), is irreconcilable with an absolutist regime. Only the civil government is capable of co-existing with civil society and vice versa. Nonetheless, civil society remains a sphere outside the state, or as Locke would put it, outside the government. In his liberal approach to politics, Locke envisages civil society as protection for the individual citizen and his pre-political, natural liberties against encroachment by the state. However, this is not the only hallmark of the relationship between state and civil society. Montesquieu (1748) supplemented this liberal and liberty-based, autonomy-accentuated notion of civil society with the concept of the spirit of law which enriched the civil society concept with the civilian element. According to this, the intermediary bodies of civil society mediate peacefully between state and society. Hence, the civil society concept not only depicts the status of civil rights or specifies the relationship between state and civil society, but it also outlines the specific mode of interaction between the societal actors as well as between the actors and the state. Thus, civil society embodies a non-military, pacific momentum (cf. Gosewinkel/Rucht 2004).

These specifically European cultural and societal roots of civil society challenge the general use of the concept, especially with regard to different cultural contexts. The frequent use of the civil society concept presupposes a specific model of society. It is a society that exhibits cultural homogeneity, atomisation and anonymity, which in turn is a depiction of an industrialised mass society, presented in writings of modern sociologists and philosophers. Moreover, the sociologist Ernest Gellner (1994, 1995) not only associates modern society on the macro-scale with an industrialised mass society, but also argues that this society produces „modular people". Modular people are culturally homogenous and rational. In addition, their society is based on double freedom: freedom from central political authority as well as freedom from ethnic or cultural associations that exert a tyranny of loyalty. Modular people can freely enter and exit associations of civil society without fear of being punished for their lack of loyalty. Loyalty in the modular society arises only in the situation-dependent context, meaning that modular people are indifferent regarding ethnic or religious loyalty. In such ideal-type society, it is quite easy to transform the social trust into political trust. If all people are exchangeable in terms of the role in society (that is what Gellner's concept of modularity presupposes), and if all modular people are similar in the functional sense (however, not necessarily in the sense of their common goals and preferences), it appears to be plausible to argue that individuals can generalise their specific experiences in civic associations into trust regarding the entire society and the government. However, this conclusion can only be made against the specific cultural and societal background in which civil society operates. One could go even further and argue that functions of civil society, assumed by Robert Putnam, can only be fulfilled in the cultural and societal context described by Ernest Gellner. Hence, the question whether civil society can find a general application remains open.

4. Conceptual Questions with Regard to Civil Society

Besides the problem of the universal application of the civil society concept, there are other methodological questions that arise from the study of civil society. The first major challenge is still how to define what civil society is.

4.1 What Constitutes Civil Society?

Many scholars disagree on what constitutes civil society as well as on its range within society, while the difference between political and civil society is not clear. Methodologically, there are at least two possibilities to define civil society.

Firstly, one could use the motivation to join civic associations as a criterion for definition. Robert Putnam himself states that joining associations is supposed to be for the *sake of sociability*. Therefore, we could examine the motivation of the participants to join free, spontaneous and autonomous associations. Regarding sociability, bowling clubs and choirs would belong to civil society, but not the rotating credit associations described by Putnam. Those are of a strictly economic nature and result from the economic needs of participants. Consequently, in terms of participant motivation, there is a considerable difference between a choir and a credit association or other common pool resources like grazing grounds, water supplies and fisheries, which are established and maintained by the citizens without any state initiative or support. Those associations are certainly free; however, they ought to be seen as a part of the economic system, not civil society, since their goal is to produce goods. Those associations may well ameliorate the economic performance of society, not necessarily as a result of the fact that they belong to civil society, but for a completely different reason: Production of goods is what causes economy to grow. Hence, we should differentiate civil society as constituted of purely sociable and community-based institutions from economic institutions, even if they are state-independent and market-independent.

Against this background, we shall distinguish between civil, political and economic society. Political society encompasses – among other things – parties and other political organisations that are not a component of the state, but aspire to become one. In contrast, civil society rather consists of associations, which give up any ambition to become a part of the state and whose goal is not to produce or distribute material goods. However, this does not mean that civil society is of an apolitical nature. Civil society may show direct political significance by assembling and channelling voices of different parts and layers of society. Hence, civil society not only fulfils a socialising function, thus having indirect political significance, but it also directly voices civil interests and grievances. These can be directed either towards the society itself, like in the case of the Polish Association against Crime, which attempts to enhance public awareness with regard to specific issues, or it is directed towards the state, like for instance the Russian Association of Soldiers' Mothers, whose goal is to enhance the awareness and sensibility of the state.

Economic associations in the form of common pool resources are based on the common economic interests of the participants. While these economic associations may very well include trust as a prerequisite for successful co-operation, the will to co-operate is not a result of social trust but has its source primarily in a similar utility definition of the participants. In contrast, ‚leisure time associations' such as choirs, which may foster *civicness* between participants, might also very well induce competition. An example could be the bowling clubs – admired by Robert Putnam – which operate in a league system, thus promoting competition. Consequently, it is hardly plausible to assume a causal link between leisure time associations, even if they do foster co-operation between their members, and the economic performance of society. Treating two different categories of associations as one seems to be quite misleading, since only economic associations might be able to fulfil economic tasks. Leisure time associations may even be counterproductive with regard to the quality of governance. An excessive participation in such organisations is time-consuming, and it certainly detracts from economic activity. If it reaches a critical level, civil society might bring damage to the economic performance of society. This is by no means a new insight. Thorstein Veblen (1912) developed his theory of the leisure class in the 19th century, a theory which was based on the idea of the proclivity of modern society to show unproductive conspicuous consumption and to focus on leisure. Albert Hirschman (1982) made a similar argument with regard to the time-consuming and unproductive extra-economic activities such as party and association meetings, parades etc.

Against this background, we shall conclude that different actor types may be in a contradictory relationship to each other. Leisure time associations could produce social capital but simultaneously harm the economic performance of society. Conversely, economic associations may promote economic growth; however, they rather need social capital as a prerequisite to function, and they do not necessarily produce any of it.

Furthermore, there is another aspect of the differentiation between associations for purely sociable purposes and those with economic goals. Associations founded as communities for production of collective goods are exclusive by definition. They exclude actors who do not contribute to the production of the goods in question. However, if those associations are exclusive, it is again hardly plausible to assume that they are able to establish generalised social trust without generating conflicts of commitment and loyalty. Free and spontaneous associations could turn into communities with exclusive identities, which would not necessarily socialise their members into good citizens. On the contrary, these associations could polarise society, instead of constructing general trust and solidarity. For instance, associations with strong deliberative features can exhibit this tendency. As Cass R. Sunstein (2003) argues, group polarisation is among the most robust patterns found all over the world. Drawing upon experimental literature from psychology, Sunstein argues that members of deliberating groups may engage in ‚enclave deliberation', in which they will not only reject alternative views, but also reinforce their initial position in a more extreme form. Members of deliberating groups always think of a certain number of arguments that underline their initial position. If a person hears like-minded people, she/he is likely to hear other arguments that support her/his initial position. Thus, the person will express her/his views less cautiously and move to a more extreme version of the initial position.

Secondly, another possibility of definition is outlining the concept of civil society in functional terms. Civil society could be conceptualised as a functional sphere of society, which can be entered and exited freely by any association that fulfils formal and functional criteria. In this sense, every self-organised and free association belongs to civil society once it fulfils the expected functions. Scholars distinguish five positive tasks in general which civil society is expected to carry out with regard to a democratic regime (Croissant et al. 2000): the protection function (it protects society from the state), the mediating function (it mediates between the political and social spheres), the socialising function (it socialises individuals into citizens), the community function (it bridges social cleavages) and the communication function (it provides a sphere of free debate and discourse outside of the state and the family). Since it is difficult to clearly distinguish between the civil, economic and political functions of civil society, civil associations could be conceived of as amphibian bodies, which can be active in different parts of the society and are sometimes only temporary (Taylor 1993). A trade union, for instance, could be considered such an amphibian body, operating in the interface between political and civil society, entering and leaving both spheres at different times.

4.2. Autonomy and Impact of Civil Society

Besides the problems of definition, there also exists a methodological difficulty regarding the proposition about the autonomy of state vis-à-vis civil society, which cannot be convincingly sustained. Civil society is incapable of functioning without the state, since it finds itself in a parasite-like relationship to it. Without a legal space for civil rights (even if it is limited), there cannot be civil society. If we use the broader definition of civil society (including independent economic associations), it becomes clear that citizens engaging in the production of common pool resources would need state loans or loan guarantees. In addition, if we apply the narrow definition (excluding economic associations), one must concede that philanthropic organisations, for example, are dependent on tax exemptions, churches need legal recognition (or at least state toleration) and professional associations are in need of state support for the licensing practices. The function of the state is also to protect weak groups against powerful ones and to restore the balance whenever it is needed (Walzer 1995). The idea of civil society implicitly requires balance and symmetry between civil associations. However, only the state is in the position to inhibit the dominance of some groups to the benefit of others. Thus, civil society requires a strong and responsive state. This is naturally an extremely challenging task, since the state itself is not free from ideological biases. Only in the liberal theory does the state remain simply a framework for society. In the political reality, state activity frequently results in a bias in favour of either enterprises or trade unions, either religious groups or ethnic groups, etc. Consequently, civil society ceases to be a space of equality as it is stipulated in the concept of citizenship and develops into an unequal civil society, characteristic of ancient or medieval ages.

Moreover, even if civil society makes a difference, it is unknown how significant it is. On the one hand, treating civil society as an antidote against all ailments of the state may be counter-productive. It could result in a new ideology of civil society. On the other hand, it is possible that such an ideology stems from a rational strategy, with which national governments attempt to cede their responsibility to non-governmental actors. However, this escapist strategy of relinquishing activities of the welfare state to actors of civil society indicates that civil society could become a stopgap of state elites unable to improve the economic performance with traditional macro-economic and structural policies. Against this background, civil society could serve as an instrument for depoliticising public space, which indicates nothing less than a dilution of political responsibility. A similar argument has been postulated with regard to European integration, which is supposed to help national governments avoid political responsibility by arguing that the EU is now responsible for many political decisions (cf. Milward 1992). There is a possible negative outcome of the process. Even though surrendering of the responsibility may ensue, there is naturally no guarantee that civil society will be capable of fulfilling the expectations. However, if civil society is unsuccessful in fulfilling the expected tasks, societal actors will hold the government responsible for the failure, since it is the only actor that can be punished politically. Consequently, the national government might not be able to escape political responsibility after all.

In conclusion, there is no certainty regarding the impact of civil society. Its influence could be neutral. Some religious groups such as the Amish people in the U.S. declare their retreat from social and political responsibility and live in isolation. In this case, it is hard to imagine how civil society would socialise individuals into citizens. Additionally, civil society may include actors who present a dangerous vision of civic responsibility that leads to uncivic behaviour, such as in the case of some militia groups in the United States. Furthermore, civil society can also challenge state power. The anti-state activity of civil society was particularly visible in Eastern Europe in the 1980s.

4.3. Challenge of Civil Society to the State

The communism crisis in the 1980s in Eastern Europe has been attributed mainly to the revolt of civil society against the communist state. In its totalitarian phase, the communist state was attempting to inhibit any spontaneous activity arising from civil society. Supported by the ideology of Marxism-Leninism, its aim was to suppress private property and market structures along with an annihilation of spontaneous, non-state public space. Consequently, civil society and the communist state found themselves in a systemic conflict (cf. Staniszkis 1992). Civil society was by definition a locus of pluralism, which developed as the antithesis of the collectivist party state. Every state collectivism, be it fascism or communism, seeks to absorb civil society in the name of an ideology, thus destroying its autonomy and spontaneous character. Only in the authoritarian phase of real existing socialism did the spontaneously growing Polish social movement, known as Solidarity, develop from the first independent trade union and challenge the prerogatives of the collectivist state. The Polish case shows an underlying paradox of civil society in its relationship to the state. While scholars of civil society highlight its benevolent functions for governance in democratic regimes, the Eastern European experiences emphasise the importance of civil society as a counterweight to the authoritarian state.

However, if the Eastern European type of civil society is strong enough to bring about a regime change, it could also undermine democratic governments. What would happen if civil society organises itself along social cleavages and polarises society? And what if civil society can oppose democratic governments as it can counterweight tyrannical regimes? As it is increasingly debated, civil society may very well apply radicalised methods and sympathise with undemocratic actors.

5. How can Civil Society be Analysed?

Firstly, one should notice that civil society possesses as equally dark and bright sides as any other central political category. Therefore, civil society depicts an ambivalent concept such as state or power. For instance, the state can on the one hand be viewed as a guarantee for citizens' freedom. On the other hand, it can be turned into an instrument of oppression and exploitation. By the same token, civil society may support state activity by socialising the individuals into citizens. It might work as a ‚laundry device', enriching individual preferences from egoistic preferences to civic ones (cf. Habermas 1996). However, this function of civil society depends on the type of state and civil society and their mutual relation. Civil society can turn into a destabilising force, particularly in weak and illegitimate states. In the worst-case scenario, it could cause disintegration of state structures and lead to civil war, a situation feared by Thomas Hobbes. Consequently, civil society is able to unfold its uncivic potential by becoming a militarised, uncivil society, as was the case in the former Yugoslavia or Rwanda.

Secondly, it is highly misleading to place many expectations on one instrument of governance, be it the market, the state or civil society. The choice of only one instrument could lead to the opposite, namely to a degeneration of governance capabilities of a society, since the dominance of one instrument of governance frequently rests on ideology. Yet, ideologies are fixed systems of political beliefs and therefore hardly suitable for societies in the process of change. On the one hand, the belief in state activity as an antidote against problems of governance has lead to collectivism and oppression. On the other hand, the belief in the market as a universal solution to problems of society might result in exploitation of weak actors by powerful ones. Consequently, civil society can also become an ideology. The dominance of civil society has its roots in the anarchist belief in the absolute self-steering capacity of societies. However, as Michael Walzer (1995) put it, one cannot choose civil society alone.

Thirdly, the nature and functioning of civil society depends on the relation between state and society. Every democratic system is in need of civil society but not necessarily in terms of improved economic performance. Democratic regimes should be responsive, not only with regard to material needs of society, but above all with regard to structural changes within the society.[3] It appears to be particularly necessary when the state is not able to reflect value changes in society. Consolidated democracies exhibit a high degree of rigidity, which is on the one hand a welcomed consequence of constitutionalism (constitutions are difficult to change, since they require a supermajority). On the other hand, the state, due to its rigidity, might be unable to respond to the value changes in society. For example, in the post-war democracies many impulses of change did not arise from within the state, which had apparently been too encapsulated, but from within the civil society. The pacifist and environmental movement in post-war Germany or the civil rights movement of Afro-Americans in the United States of the 1960s would have been largely ignored by the states of the countries if civil society had not voiced the societal change of values. Yet, it is exactly the responsiveness of the state vis-à-vis the civil society that guarantees the political survival of the state, since democratic states or states that claim to somehow follow the principle of popular

---

[3] See the concept of reflexive state by Heinz Kleger (1993).

representation rely (at least in the middle run) on some sort of democratic legitimacy.[4] Therefore, civil society could carry out the function of the transmission belt regarding the change in modern societies.

However, with regard to the functional dimension of civil society, different democratic regimes require differently vigorous civil societies. According to tendency, liberal states like the United States are more dependent on the civil society for their citizens' education or the functioning of the legal system. Since private education is pervasive in the U.S. and the legal system is precedence-based, a high level of activity by the civil society is vital for society and the political system. In contrast, republican states such as France rely strongly on state policies such as public education and steering by the elite for the functioning of democracy. Consequently, liberal regimes largely abstain from educating their citizens in correspondence to an a priori image of the citizen, and they renounce on the single concept of common good to be forged by the political elite. Therefore, of all things, civil associations have to fulfil the task of democracy schools. In turn, republican regimes cannot depend on the spontaneous and autonomous character of civil society, since it is not calculable and predictable enough with regard to the preconceived idea of citizenry.

However, the state should not only be responsive, but also strong in terms of legitimate monopoly of violence. This is necessary concerning the *uncivic* potential of civil society, mentioned above. Civil society is capable of preventing the state from functioning properly or it can even endanger the entire society. Only a state with the effective control of means of violence would be in the position to tame the dark side of civil society. Certainly, the concept of an effective state does not indicate repressive states such as Belarus. Instead, Spain would fit into it with its firm stance against Basque terrorism. Repressive states may very well use the uncivic potential of civil society against the society itself. This pattern can be found with tribal states such as Sudan, whose government uses actors of formerly civil society to destroy entire ethnic groups.

Fourthly, the criterion of responsiveness applies also to non-democratic states, whose interest is also to react to the demands of civil society. Otherwise, a too high perseverance of the regime might result in a violent revolution induced by civil society. There are probably *three variables* relevant to understanding the relationship between a non-democratic regime and civil society. The first has already been mentioned, namely the degree of regime perseverance

---

[4] Ernest Gellner (1994; 1995) represents an alternative position, arguing that political systems are dependent on material and cognitive growth for their survival.

to the societal demands of change (cf. Schmitter 1985). The second is the type of the regime's legitimacy. Traditional regimes, which are based on ethnicity or religion, might be far less responsive to civil society than those resting on a rational type of legitimacy rooted in welfare or modernity ideology. The third variable seems to be the degree of societal heterogeneity that confronts the regime. Heterogeneous civil society is less likely to challenge the regime, since it faces a plethora of collective action problems. Traditional regime legitimacy makes concessions to dissident demands less probable, as this kind of legitimacy rests on the idea of ultimate truth. Although communist regimes were not traditional in the Weberian sense, their legitimacy drew on Marxism-Leninism, which aspired to be the only correct interpretation of the course of history and civilisational progress. On that account, Ernest Gellner depicted Marxism as a secular religion (cf. Gellner 1995). Ethnic and religious cleavages enhance in turn the probability of uncivic potential of civil society, which in turn indicates a higher probability of tribal regimes to oppress or physically annihilate ethnic groups. Rational legitimacy as rooted in the capability of regimes to solve societal problems appears instead to be compatible with civil society, for the same reason as democratic regimes have to be responsive. Non-democratic regimes, which justify their rule in their capacity to establish welfare, are dependent on the information about dilemmas, problems, interests and worries of the society. Those regimes can also better cope with social heterogeneity, as they require the support of the majority of societal groups.

Fifthly, a responsive state is not the only prerequisite for the compatibility between state and civil society. In addition, reflexive civil society is required (cf. Kleger 1995). Reflexive civil society must be aware of its conflictual and uncivic potentials and able to limit itself, particularly whenever its activity endangers democracy. This is most important for two types of states: states experiencing disintegration of their institutions and states in the process of transformation. The former encourages the uncivic potential of civil society, which remains unchecked without solid institutions of state. For the latter, the role of civil society depends on the phase in which the transformation unfolds. Eastern European countries face a complex process of economic and political transformation (cf. Offe 1991). Economic transformation gave rise not only to a plethora of new associations, but also to new demands vis-à-vis the state. During the transformation, it was mostly trade unions and peasants, not choirs and bowling clubs, that took to the streets. However, frequent demonstrations and economic demands (which were essential for the breakdown of the communist regimes) run the risk of destabilising the neo-democracies and thus endangering the entire transformation (cf. Rohrschneider/Schmitt-Beck 2002). Therefore, reflexive civil society should be able to restrain itself, especially in the phase of democratisation when the newly established institutions are still not deeply rooted in the society. A hyperactivity of civil society in this phase might disturb the process of majority formation, which is necessary for a political continuity. An imperious civil society posing constant demands is a serious burden in a process of institutional transformation by increasing its costs for the population (cf. Schmitter 1995). However, vital civil society can also promote the consolidation of newly established democracy. Reflexive civil society can be conducive to recognition and reduction of defects that every democracy develops. Those are, in the case of transformation states, primarily pathologies of political capitalism such as collisions of political and economic power that result in corruption and nepotism (cf. Staniszkis 1999). Civil society can also help consolidate neo-democracies by providing the government information about societal problems to be solved, and in the first place about infringements of freedom by the society and state. Hence, a vital civil society is relevant in the phase of democratic consolidation, in which civil society stabilises expectations presented to the state, as it confronts the authorities with more aggregated and reliable information about the direction of reforms. It also provides an arena for articulation of popular will, which inhibits political alienation from the new political system as well as producing instruments that can be used in case of authoritarian deviation during the transformation process (Schmitter 1997).

6. Conclusion

We can conclude that the phenomenon of civil society requires a complex analysis, particularly if one attempts to examine it in a transcultural context. The roots of civil society are European, as is the belief in the benevolent impact of civil society on democracy, economy and governance. However, there are justified doubts about solely positive impacts of civil society. The dark side of civil society has manifested itself in recent political events worldwide, be it civil war in Yugoslavia, Rwanda or Congo.

In order to grasp the complexity of the phenomenon, one has to analyse it on three levels. Firstly, it is essential to question whether every free, spontaneous, state-independent and market-independent organisation belongs to civil society. The issue is particularly relevant with regard to the associations with economic character such as the rotating credit associations described by Putnam. The second level would touch upon the relationship between state and civil society. The thesis of this article is that the benevolent functions of civil society unfold only under the circumstances of responsive state and reflexive civil society. The third level of civil society analysis would examine the type of state in its relation to civil society. It makes a difference for the effects of civil society when it is confronted with a democratic state, an authoritarian state, a failed state or a state in transformation. Depending on those types of state, civil society can assume different functions, particularly those stemming from the dark side.

References

Beyme, Klaus von (2000): Zivilgesellschaft – Von der vorbürgerlichen zur nachbürgerlichen Gesellschaft?, in: Merkel, Wolfgang (ed.): Systemwechsel 5 – Zivilgesellschaft und Transformation, Opladen, pp. 51-70.
Cable, Vincent (1995). The Diminished Nation-State – A Study in the Loss of Economic Power, in: Daedalus 124 (2), pp. 23-53.
Croissant, Aurel/Lauth, Hans-Joachim/Merkel, Wolfgang (2000): Zivilgesellschaft und Transformation – Ein internationaler Vergleich, in: Merkel, Wolfgang (ed.): Systemwechsel 5 – Zivilgesellschaft und Transformation, Opladen, pp. 9-49.
Evans, Peter B. (1997): The Eclipse of the State – Reflections on Stateness in an Era of Globalization, in: World Politics 50, pp. 62-87.
Gellner, Ernest (1994): Bedingungen der Freiheit – Die Zivilgesellschaft und ihre Rivalen, Stuttgart.
Gellner, Ernest (1995): Nationalismus und Moderne, Berlin.
Gosewinkel, Dieter/Rucht, Dieter (2004): „*History Meets Sociology*" – Zivilgesellschaft als Prozess, in: Gosewinkel, Dieter et al. (eds.): Zivilgesellschaft – national und transnational, Berlin, pp. 29-60.
Habermas, Jürgen (1996): Between Facts and Norms, London.
Heinelt, Hubert (1998): Zivilgesellschaftliche Perspektiven einer demokratischen Transformation der Europäischen Union, in: Zeitschrift für Internationale Beziehungen 1, pp. 79-107.
Hirschman, Albert O. (1982): Engagement und Enttäuschung – Über das Schwanken der Bürger zwischen Privatwohl und Gemeinwohl, Frankfurt a.M..
Hobbes, Thomas (1962): Leviathan, New York.
Kaelble, Hartmut (2004): Gibt es eine europäische Zivilgesellschaft?, in: Gosewinkel, Dieter et al. (eds.), Zivilgesellschaft – national und transnational, Berlin, pp. 267-284.
Keohane, Robert O./Milner, Helen V. (eds.) (1996): Internationalization and Domestic Politics, Cambridge.
Kleger, Heinz (1993): Lernfähige Demokratie und reflexiver Staat, in: Voigt, Rüdiger (ed.): Abschied vom Staat – Rückkehr zum Staat?, Baden-Baden, pp. 443-458.

Kleger, Heinz (1995): Politische Theorie als Frage nach der Bürgergesellschaft, in: Berliner Debatte Initial 4/5.
Kleger, Heinz (2004) (ed.): Der Konvent als Labor: Texte und Dokumente zum europäischen Verfassungsprozess, Münster.
Kleger, Heinz/Karolewski, Ireneusz Pawel/Munke, Matthias (2004): Europäische Verfassung – Zum Stand der europäischen Demokratie im Zuge der Osterweiterung, 3. Auflage, Münster.
Locke, John (1963): Two Treatises of Government, Cambridge.
Majone, Giandomenico (1993): Deregulation or Re-regulation? Policymaking in the European Community since the Single Act, EUI Working Paper SPD 93/2.
Majone, Giandomenico (1996): Regulating Europe, London.
Marshall, T.H. (1950): Citizenship and Social Class, in: T.H. Marshall/Tom Bottomore: Citizenship and Social Class, London.
Milward, Alan S. (1992): The European Rescue of the Nation-State, London.
Montesquieu (1748/1957): De l'esprit des lois, Paris, Vol. 1.
Morrow, James D. (1994): Game Theory for Political Scientists, Princeton.
Offe, Claus (1991): Capitalism by Democratic Design? Democratic Theory Facing the Triple Transition in East-Central Europe, in: Social Research 58 (4), pp. 866-892.
Putnam, Robert D. (1993): Making Democracy Work – Civic Traditions in Modern Italy, Princeton University Press, Princeton.
Putnam, Robert D. (1995): Bowling Alone – America's Declining Social Capital, in: Journal of Democracy 6, pp. 65-78.
Schmitter, Philippe C. (1985): Speculations about the Prospective Demise of Authoritarian Regimes and its Possible Consequences (I), in: Revista de Ciència Politica 1, pp. 83-102.
Schmitter, Philippe C. (1995): The Consolidation of Political Democracies: Processes, Rhythms, Sequences and Types, in: Pridham, Geoffrey (ed.): Transitions to Democracy – Comparative Perspectives from Southern Europe, Latin America and Eastern Europe, Aldershot, pp. 535-569.
Schmitter, Philippe C. (1997): Consolidating the Third Wave Democracies, in: Diamond, Larry/Plattner, Marc F./Yun-Han Chu/Hung-Mao Tien, Baltimore, pp.239-262.
Schuppert, Gunnar Folke (2004): Governance-Leistungen der Zivilgesellschaft: Vom staatlichen Rechtsetzungsmonopol zur zivilgesellschaftlichen Selbstregulierung, in: Gosewinkel, Dieter et al. (eds.): Zivilgesellschaft – national und transnational, Berlin, pp. 245-264.
Staniszkis, Jadwiga (1992): The Ontology of Socialism, Oxford.
Staniszkis, Jadwiga (1999): Post-Communism – The Emerging Enigma, Warsaw.

Strange, Susan (1995): The Defective State, in: Daedalus 124 (2), pp. 55-74.
Sunstein, Cass R. (2003): The Law of Group Polarization, in: Fishkin, James/Laslett, Peter (eds.): Debating Deliberative Democracy, London, pp. 80-101.
Taylor, Charles (1993): Der Begriff der ‚bürgerlichen Gesellschaft' im politischen Denken des Westens, in: Brumlik, Micha/Brunkhorst, Hauke (eds.): Gemeinschaft und Gerechtigkeit, Frankfurt a.M., pp. 117-147.
Tocqueville, Alexis de (1835/40/1987): Über die Demokratie in Amerika, Zürich.
Veblen, Thorstein (1912): The Theory of the Leisure Class, New York.
Walzer, Michael (1995): The Civil Society Argument, in: Beiner, Ronald (ed.): Theorizing Citizenship, New York, pp. 153-174.
Zürn, Michael (1998): Regieren jenseits des Nationalstaates, Frankfurt a.M..

Potsdamer Textbücher *PTB 4*

Juan J. Linz:
Totalitäre und autoritäre Regime
Raimund Krämer (Hrsg.)

Die zweite Auflage mit dem neuen Vorwort, dem „Potsdam Paper II", ist exzellenter State of Art der vergleichenden Regierungslehre.

„Mit dieser Edition liegt ein klassischer Text der Politischen Wissenschaft nach 25 Jahren erstmals in deutscher Sprache vor."
Hanns-Georg Golz, Deutschland-Archiv 6/2000

„Das grundlegende Werk von Linz leistet für den Rückblick und als Hilfe zum Verständnis gegenwärtiger und künftiger Entwicklungen der Politik einen Beitrag von ungebrochenem Wert."
Karl Dietrich Bracher, FAZ vom 18.9.2000

Bestellungen beim Universitätsverlag Potsdam
ubpub@uni-potsdam.de

Sebastian Braun

Die Wiederentdeckung des Vereinswesens im Windschatten gesellschaftlicher Krisen

Konzepte, Kontroversen, Perspektiven

Es war vor rund einem Jahrhundert, als Max Weber, der in seiner programmatischen Rede auf dem ersten deutschen Soziologentag im Jahr 1910 eine Soziologie des Vereinswesens als fundamentale Aufgabe der Soziologie verstanden wissen wollte.

Daß die deutsche Soziologie Webers Forschungsanregungen nicht immer folgte, hat Siewert (1984: 180) rund 70 Jahre später kritisch bilanziert und pointiert interpretiert: „Es scheint, als blicke die ‚Zunft' nach wie vor ein wenig mitleidig auf die Niederungen der Vereinsforschung." Zu einer ähnlich skeptischen Einschätzung kam Mitte der 1990er Jahre auch Zimmer (1996), die seinerzeit eine grundlegende Arbeit über das Vereinswesen in Deutschland vorlegte. Auch sie beklagt die mangelnde Relevanz des Vereins in den deutschen Sozialwissenschaften, die diesen „als antiquierte, nicht mehr zeitgemäße Organisationsform beinahe schon zu den Akten gelegt hatte" (Zimmer, 1996: 11) und in erster Linie mit Spießigkeit und Vereinsmeierei assoziierte – nach dem altbekannten Motto: In seinem Verein, da richtet man sich's gemütlich und behaglich ein.

Wie behaglich es in Deutschland dann eigentlich zugehen müßte, lassen aktuelle Schätzungen nur erahnen. Demnach sind derzeit zwischen knapp der Hälfte und fast zwei Dritteln der Bevölkerung Mitglied in rund 500.000 bis 700.000 Vereinen. Allerdings ist es nicht die Behaglichkeit, sondern vielmehr das Unbehagen über längerfristige Entwicklungstendenzen in Deutschland, die in der gesellschaftspolitischen und sozialwissenschaftlichen Diskussion der letzten Jahre zu einem erheblichen Bedeutungsgewinn der assoziativen Lebenswelt beigetragen haben. Diese Entwicklungstendenzen werden zumeist als Krisen etikettiert, nämlich als Krise des Wohlfahrtsstaats, Krise der Arbeitsgesellschaft, Krise des sozialen Zusammenhalts und Krise der Demokratie. Vereine werden in all diesen Krisendiskursen als alternative Steuerungsressourcen und multifunktionale Akteure zur Bewältigung dieser disparaten, zugleich aber wechselseitig aufeinander bezogenen Krisenphänomene (wieder-) entdeckt. Der vorliegende Beitrag führt in aktuelle Ansätze ein, in denen Vereine als Hoffnungsträger zur Linderung der vier Krisenphänomene diskutiert werden.

1. Vereine im aktuellen Diskurs

1.1 Vereine und die Krise des Wohlfahrtsstaats

Die Debatte über die Krise des Wohlfahrtsstaats begann in der Bundesrepublik Mitte der 1970er Jahre. Unter dem Eindruck der ersten Ölkrise, die zu einer weltweiten Wirtschaftsflaute und steigenden Arbeitslosenzahlen führte, und des Berichts des *Club of Rome* über die „Grenzen des Wachstums" wurde nicht nur das Ende des seit dem Zweiten Weltkrieg anhaltenden Wirtschaftswachstums thematisiert, sondern auch das sozialdemokratische Modell vom „Staat als Hüter und Wächter des Gemeinwohls" (Naschold 1993) in Frage gestellt. In diesem Modell spielte die „aktive Bürgerschaft" eine untergeordnete Rolle: Nicht hohe Beteiligungsquoten und die „Inputs" der Bürger, sondern das staatliche Leistungsniveau und die „Outputs" des politisch-administrativen Systems galten als Maßstab für die Funktionstüchtigkeit des Gemeinwesens. Dieses wohlfahrtsstaatliche Arrangement wurde von verschiedenen Seiten kritisiert, wobei sich die Wiederentdeckung von anti-institutionellen sozialen Bewegungen und sozialem Pluralismus auf „links-alternativer" Seite mit Forderungen nach Entstaatlichung, Privatisierung und Subsidiarität auf „liberal-konservativer" Seite berührten.

Seitdem haben vor allem marktliberale Vorschläge zur Umgestaltung des Wohlfahrtsstaats an Bedeutung gewonnen. Deren Befürworter und Gegner sind sich zwar nach wie vor alles andere als einig; in einem Punkt ist ihre Argumentationsbasis aber ähnlich: Markt, Staat und der einzelne Bürger werden zumeist isoliert betrachtet, während gesellschaftliche Assoziationsformen – mit Ausnahme der Familie – nebensächlich sind. Genau in diese Lücke stoßen die Kritiker: Sie suchen nach einer grundsätzlichen Neuordnung der institutionellen Arrangements des Wohlfahrtsstaats und setzen dabei insbesondere auf Akteure der Wohlfahrtsproduktion jenseits von Markt und Staat sowie auf eine Stärkung von bürgerschaftlicher Mitwirkung und Selbsthilfe (vgl. Evers/Olk 1996). Wohlfahrtsrelevante Güter und Kostenvorteile, die durch unbezahlte (Laien-)Tätigkeiten insbesondere auch in Vereinen entstehen, werden mittlerweile quer durch das Parteienspektrum wiederentdeckt.

Diese Akzentverlagerung begründet auch die Popularität von Ansätzen, die seit längerem unter Begriffen wie *welfare-mix*, Wohlfahrtspluralismus oder gemischte Wohlfahrtsproduktion diskutiert werden – Ansätze, die vor allem den Unterschied zur Sozial*staatlichkeit* hervorheben: Der Bürger wird nicht nur als Klient und Konsument, sondern mit seinem alltäglichen Engagement als wichtige Säule im gesellschaftlichen Bedarfsausgleich betrachtet. Der Staat gilt zwar weiterhin als maßgeblicher Träger sozialer Dienste und Einrichtungen, in erster Linie soll er aber regulierende und moderierende Aufgaben übernehmen. Während Staat und Verwaltung bisher die Gewährleistungs-, Finanzierungs- und Vollzugsverantwortung bei der Herstellung öffentlicher Güter und wohlfahrtsrelevanter Leistungen innehatten, sollen sie sich nun auf die Gewährleistungsfunktion beschränken, die Vollzugs- und Finanzierungsverantwortung (zumindest teilweise) an freie Träger wie Vereine abtreten und damit zugleich „Gelegenheitsstrukturen" für bürgerschaftliches Engagement schaffen. „Vom schlanken zum aktivierenden Staat" lautet das Motto, das eine neue Verantwortungsteilung zwischen Staat und Gesellschaft vorsieht.

1.2 Vereine und die Krise der Arbeitsgesellschaft

Eines der offensichtlichsten Probleme des deutschen Wohlfahrtsstaats ist darin zu sehen, daß seit Mitte der 1970er Jahre eine wellenförmige, aber fortlaufende Zunahme von Personen zu konstatieren ist, die erwerbstätig sein möchten, aber keine (ihnen zusagende) Beschäftigung im Sinne einer unbefristeten, sozialversicherungspflichtigen und tariflich gebundenen Vollzeiterwerbstätigkeit finden. Während in den Nachkriegsjahrzehnten, der Blütezeit des Fordismus, das Zusammenspiel von keynesianischer Wirtschaftspolitik, sozialer Umverteilung, Ausbau des Wohlfahrtsstaats und Entwicklung der industriellen Beziehungen das Ziel der Vollbeschäftigung in greifbare Nähe rückte und sich unter diesen Rahmenbedingungen das so genannte Normalarbeitsverhältnis herausbildete, entpuppte sich diese Vorstellung bereits seit Mitte der 1970er Jahre als ein „kurzer Traum immerwährender Prosperität" (B. Lutz). Denn seit der ersten Ölkrise ist es nicht mehr gelungen, den rezessionsbedingten Anstieg von Arbeitslosigkeit im folgenden Wirtschaftsaufschwung auf das Ausgangsniveau zurückzuführen, womit sich Arbeitslosigkeit den Wellenbewegungen von Konjunktur und Rezession entzog.

Seitdem ist nicht nur eine Tendenz zur Verfestigung von Arbeitslosigkeit als dauerhafter Soziallage zu konstatieren, sondern auch ein deutlicher Anstieg atypischer Beschäftigungsverhältnisse und diskontinuierlicher Erwerbsverläufe, während der Anteil der Normalarbeitsverhältnisse, noch heute Kern sozialer Schutzregelungen im Arbeits- und Sozialrecht, kontinuierlich zurückgegangen ist. Parallel dazu expandierte die sich dem offiziellen Wirtschaftskreislauf entziehende „Schattenwirtschaft".

Vor diesem Hintergrund entfaltete sich Ende der 1970er Jahre eine Diskussion über Alternativökonomie, die das Phänomen der Arbeitslosigkeit im Kontext der lohnarbeitszentrierten sozialstaatlichen Sicherungssysteme thematisierte und auch den Schnittpunkt „zwischen Arbeitsamt und Ehrenamt" (Evers 1986) in den Blick nahm. Hinzu kamen vielfältige Beiträge aus der Frauenbewegung, die auf die ungleiche Bewertung verschiedener Tätigkeitsformen aufmerksam machte und die soziale Aufwertung unentgeltlicher Arbeiten forderte. In den Kontext dieser vielschichtigen Diskussionen der letzten Jahrzehnte sind die aktuellen Reformentwürfe einzuordnen, in denen Vereine als Hoffnungsträger zur Linderung der Krise der Arbeitsgesellschaft eine prominente Rolle spielen.

1.2.1 Von der „Arbeitsgesellschaft" zur „Tätigkeitsgesellschaft"

In einer ersten Argumentationsrichtung lauten die prominentesten Ansätze „Tätigkeitsgesellschaft" (Mutz 1997), „Bürgerarbeit" (Beck 1999) sowie – mit Abstrichen – das im Bericht an den *Club of Rome* entworfene „Mehrschichtenmodell produktiver Arbeit" mit „nichtmonetarisierten Werten" (Giriani/Liedtke 1998) und Rifkins (1997) „neuer Gesellschaftsvertrag", in dem Tätigkeiten in Vereinen eine maßgebliche Rolle spielen. Zwar setzen die Vertreter der einzelnen Ansätze unterschiedliche Akzente. Übereinstimmend gehen sie aber von einem grundlegenden Wandel der Arbeitsgesellschaft aus und betonen, daß Arbeit ihre individuelle und gesellschaftliche Integrationsfunktion nur dann beibehalten könne, wenn Tätigkeitsformen jenseits der Erwerbsarbeit aufgewertet würden.

Vor diesem Hintergrund wird insbesondere die normative Hierarchie in der Bewertung von Arbeitsformen kritisiert – eine Hierarchie, die sich im 19. Jahrhundert mit der Verallgemeinerung von Lohnarbeit ausbildete und die den Arbeitsbegriff weitgehend synonym mit wertschöpfender Erwerbsarbeit setzt, während z.B. unentgeltliches Engagement in Vereinen kaum mehr als Arbeit galt. Gefordert wird deshalb ein kultureller Wandel im Verständnis von Arbeit und eine flexiblere, den Lebenslagen und -situationen angepaßte Gestaltung des Erwerbssystems, das die bislang als abweichend geltenden Tätigkeitsformen einbezieht. Zwischen den verschiedenen Tätigkeitsformen müsse es, so die Forderung, größere Durchlässigkeiten und fließende Übergänge geben: „Die Menschen wären dann in kurzen oder langen Phasen erwerbslos, aber nicht arbeitslos, sie würden tätig sein und wären weiterhin über Arbeit in die Gesellschaft integriert", so lautet die These von Mutz (1997: 35) im Rahmen seiner – an Hannah Arendt angelehnten – Vision von einer Tätigkeitsgesellschaft.

1.2.2 Vereine als Hoffnungsträger für Erwerbsarbeitsplätze

Sämtliche dieser Ideen zum Umbau der Arbeitsgesellschaft konzentrieren sich bislang auf das freiwillige Engagement als einer alternativen Tätigkeitsform neben der Erwerbsarbeit, während Vereine eher am Rande thematisiert werden, obwohl sie auf empirischer Ebene die umfangreichsten Gelegenheitsstrukturen zu freiwilligem

Engagement eröffnen (vgl. Braun 2001a). Demgegenüber fokussiert eine zweite Argumentationslinie, in der Vereinen eine maßgebliche Bedeutung zur Linderung der Krise der Arbeitsgesellschaft zugesprochen wird, explizit die Beschäftigungspotenziale im Dritten Sektor. Es wird also nicht von der Idee einer grundlegenden Umgestaltung erwerbsarbeitszentrierter moderner Gesellschaften ausgegangen, sondern von der Fragestellung, ob und in welchem Umfang in Organisationen des Dritten Sektors zusätzliche Erwerbsarbeitsplätze geschaffen werden können.

Auslöser der darüber geführten Diskussion war das Johns Hopkins *Comparative Nonprofit Sector Project* (vgl. Priller/Zimmer 2001). Wie die Ergebnisse der deutschen Teilstudie zeigen, hat sich in Westdeutschland zwischen 1960 und 1990 die Zahl der Arbeitsplätze im erwerbswirtschaftlichen Sektor nur geringfügig verändert. Im staatlichen Sektor kam es hingegen nach einem deutlichen Beschäftigungswachstum in den 1960er und 1970er Jahren seit etwa Mitte der 1980er Jahre zu einer weitgehenden Stagnation, die seitdem in rückläufige Zahlen überging. Demgegenüber verzeichnete der Dritte Sektor ein dynamisches Beschäftigungswachstum bis in die 1990er Jahre hinein. Allein zwischen 1960 und 1990 wuchs das Beschäftigungsvolumen um 328% von 383.000 auf fast 1,3 Millionen Arbeitsplätze (1 Millionen Vollzeitäquivalente), die einen Anteil von 3,7% der volkswirtschaftlichen Gesamtbeschäftigung ausmachten. 1995 erreichte das Beschäftigungsvolumen im Dritten Sektor mit rund 2,1 Millionen Arbeitsplätzen (1,4 Millionen Vollzeitäquivalente) sogar einen Anteil von fast 5% an der Gesamtbeschäftigung.

Dieses Beschäftigungswachstum ist vor allem in der dynamischen Arbeitsplatzentwicklung in bestimmten Bereichen des Dritten Sektors begründet. 1995 befand sich fast jeder dritte Arbeitsplatz in den Kernbereichen wohlfahrtsstaatlicher Dienstleistungen: den Bereichen Gesundheitswesen und Soziale Dienste, die durch das Agglomerat der großen und staatlich hoch alimentierten Wohlfahrtsverbände dominiert werden. Demgegenüber verfügten andere Bereiche – wie jener der Kultur und Erholung, zu dem z.B. die fast 90.000 Sportvereine gehören – gerade einmal über rund 5% der Arbeitsplätze.

Gerade für diese lokale Vereinslandschaft, die bislang kaum verberuflicht ist und in erster Linie auf dem freiwilligen Engagement ihrer Mitglieder basiert, wird für die nähere Zukunft eine günstige Beschäftigungsentwicklung prognostiziert – und dies im Kontrast zu den beschäftigungsintensiven Bereichen Gesundheitswesen, Soziale Dienste sowie Bildung und Forschung. Folgt man diesen Ergebnissen, dann scheint die These, der Dritte Sektor könne einen Beitrag zur Linderung der Arbeitsmarktprobleme leisten, nicht für sämtliche Dritter Sektor-Organisationen gleichermaßen zu gelten, sondern in erster Linie für die lokalen Vereine in bestimmten gesellschaftlichen Bereichen.

1.3 Vereine und die Krise des sozialen Zusammenhalts

In den skizzierten Ansätzen zur Reformierung des Wohlfahrtsstaats und zur Neugestaltung der Arbeitsgesellschaft soll der engagierte Bürger durch seine Bereitschaft und Fähigkeit zur Selbstorganisation und aktiven Mitarbeit in Vereinen einen maßgeblichen Beitrag zur Lösung zentraler Gegenwartsprobleme leisten. In zahlreichen Gegenwartsdiagnosen wird allerdings ein ganz anderes Bild gezeichnet: Anstelle des engagierten Bürgers wird hier die fernsehglotzende Konsummonade in einer modernen Passivgesellschaft beschrieben, die das Vermögen zur sozialen Integration ihrer selbst verloren habe.

Seit den 1980er, insbesondere aber seit den 1990er Jahren ist die Diskussion über dieses Problem wieder zu einem sozialwissenschaftlichen Konjunkturthema geworden. Fürchteten schon die soziologischen Klassiker beim Übergang von traditionalen zu modernen Gesellschaften den Verlust des sozialen Zusammenhalts in egalitär-individualistischen Gesellschaften, so kulminierte die aktuelle Diskussion in der Frage, ob vermeintlich hoch individualisierte, postmoderne Gesellschaften überhaupt noch sozial integrierbar seien. Parallel dazu erlebten die alten Antipoden des Individualisierungsbegriffs – Anomie, Atomisierung und Vereinzelung – eine seit der industriellen Revolution nicht mehr gekannte Renaissance.

Robert D. Putnam, einer der derzeit am meisten nachgefragten Sozialwissenschaftler in der westlichen Welt, hat in diesem Kontext den Terminus *bowling alone* geprägt (Putnam 2000). Mit diesem Terminus versucht er, den Verlust des – so sein Schlüsselbegriff – „sozialen Kapitals" in modernen Gesellschaften in einer anschaulichen Metapher zusammenzufassen. Soziales Kapital soll dabei dreierlei bezeichnen: erstens soziales Vertrauen, das die zur gesellschaftlichen Koordination erforderliche Kooperation zwischen den Individuen erleichtere; zweitens die Norm generalisierter Reziprozität, die zur Lösung sozialer Dilemmata beitrage; und drittens Vereine, die soziales Vertrauen aufbauen, generalisierte Reziprozitätsnormen pflegen und somit maßgeblich zur (Re-)Produktion von sozialem Kapital in modernen Gesellschaften beitragen würden (vgl. Braun 2001b; Braun/Weiß 2005).

Vereine sind also ein Dreh- und Angelpunkt in Putnams Konzept von sozialem Kapital. Denn in diesen kleinen lokalen Vergemeinschaftungen bestünden, so Putnam, vielfältige *face to face -* Interaktionen und eine hohe interaktive Konnektivität zwischen den Mitgliedern, so daß sich identifikatorische und solidargemeinschaftliche Bindungen herausbilden würden. In der aktiven Mitgliedschaftsrolle erlerne man jene Tugenden und Verhaltensdispositionen, welche die Kooperation und das soziale Vertrauen innerhalb *und* außerhalb der Vereine erhöhten. Denn das in den Vereinen erworbene Vertrauen erstrecke sich als „generalisiertes Vertrauen" über alle gesellschaftlichen Bereiche und reduziere somit die Notwendigkeit zur sozialen Kontrolle. Abbau von sozialer Kontrolle hieße aber auch Reduktion von Kosten, und zwar im staatlichen ebenso wie im ökonomischen Sektor.

Mit dieser Argumentation hat Putnam einer traditionsreichen soziologischen Diskussion über den sozialen Zusammenhalt moderner Gesellschaften nicht nur eine bedeutende ökonomische Gedankenfigur hinzugefügt. Vielmehr hat er diese Diskussion auch mit einer klassisch politikwissenschaftlichen Debatte über die aktive Partizipation des Bürgers in einem demokratischen Gemeinwesen verbunden. Nach Putnam impliziert der Begriff soziales Kapital nicht nur gemeinschaftliche Bindungen, soziales Vertrauen und Reziprozitätsnormen, die sich allesamt in Vereinen (re-)produzieren und entscheidend zur sozialen Integration, aber auch zur wirtschaftlichen Performanz einer Gesellschaft beitragen. Das soziale Kapital sei auch „*closely related to what some have called ‚civic virtue'*" (Putnam 2000: 19). Da Putnam auch diese *civic virtue* im Niedergang begriffen sieht, seien moderne Gesellschaften ebenfalls in ihrer Existenz als demokratische Gemeinwesen gefährdet.

1.4 Vereine und die Krise der Demokratie

Diese Einschätzung korrespondiert mit den populären Diagnosen über den Zustand der Demokratie in Deutschland, die als bedroht, im Verfall begriffen oder krisenhaft beschrieben wird. Hintergrund dieser Vorstellungen ist insbesondere die Sorge, der Bürger sei eine aussterbende Spezies in der Menschheitsgeschichte, da die individuellen Orientierungen und Kompetenzen erodierten, die eine Demokratie als freiheitliches politisches System ermöglichen und stabilisieren würden.

Angesprochen ist damit eine normative Dimension von Demokratie, die vor dem Erfahrungshintergrund mit der deutschen Geschichte einen Allgemeinplatz darzustellen scheint: daß eine Demokratie ohne den *homo democraticus* zum Scheitern verurteilt sei. Als demokratieförderlich gilt hingegen der „mündige Bürger", der sich – über die formale Beteiligung an Wahlen hinaus – für das politische Gemeinwesen interessiert, in entsprechende Diskussions- und Entscheidungsprozesse einbringt und sich in Vereinen, den „Basiselementen der Demokratie" (Zimmer 1996), aktiv beteiligt.

Diese Argumentationsfigur spielte in der Bundesrepublik vor allem unter dem Eindruck der Studentenbewegung und des Regierungswechsels zur sozial-liberalen Koalition („mehr Demokratie wagen", W. Brandt) in den späten 1960er und 1970er Jahren eine maßgebliche Rolle. Hauptakteur war in diesem Kontext die Nachkriegsgeneration der *baby-boomer*, die vor dem Hintergrund des vieldiskutierten Wertewandels das Spektrum politischer Partizipationsformen erheblich erweiterten, für bürgerschaftliche Partizipations- und Gestaltungschancen sorgten und einen bislang ungebrochenen Gründungsboom von Assoziationen (*associational revolution*) auslösten. Im staatlichen Sektor ebbte die Reformeuphorie allerdings Ende der 1970er Jahre wieder ab; ihr vorläufiges Ende fand sie mit dem späteren Regierungswechsel zur liberal-konservativen Koalition.

Erst durch die in den letzten Jahren intensiver geführten Debatten über Legitimationsprobleme des etablierten Systems der Interessenvertretung und Effektivitätsprobleme staatlichen Handelns haben Forderungen nach einer „Rückkehr des Bürgers" und Fragen nach den Möglichkeiten und Grenzen von politischer Beteiligung und Bürgerengagement wieder höhere Aufmerksamkeit gewonnen. Unter dem Leitbild der Bürgergesellschaft entfaltete sich eine weit gespannte Diskussion über „eine Gesellschaft selbstbewußter und selbstverantwortlicher Bürger, eine Gesellschaft der Selbstermächtigung und Selbstorganisation" (Enquete-Kommission 2002: 76), in der das Verhältnis von Rechten und Pflichten neu auszubalancieren sei und in der die Bürger umfangreichere Verantwortung für das politische Gemeinwesen zu übernehmen hätten.

In diesem Kontext wurde auch der antiquiert klingende Begriff der „Bürgertugend" revitalisiert und mit dem Terminus der „freiwilligen Selbstverpflichtung" (Münkler 2002: 34) in ein moderneres Staats- und Gesellschaftsverständnis übersetzt. Dieser Begriff zeigt bereits an, daß es im Diskurs über die Bürgergesellschaft nicht nur um das Problem der juridischen Festlegung des Bürgerstatus geht, sondern insbesondere auch um die Qualifikationen und Dispositionen, über die ein Bürger verfügen sollte, um als solcher gelten zu können (z.B. politische Partizipationsfähigkeit und -bereitschaft, Gemeinsinn oder Gemeinwohlorientierung).

Diese Vorstellungen begründen auch die hohe Bedeutung, die dem lokalen Vereinswesen als maßgeblichem Bestandteil des institutionellen Kerns der Bürgergesellschaft zugesprochen wird. Denn die Vereine würden den Raum für plurale Identitäten schaffen und die Unterschiedlichkeit der Lebenswelten zum Ausdruck bringen, unmittelbare Möglichkeiten zu freiwilligem Engagement und politischer Partizipation eröffnen und somit als Schule der Demokratie fungieren. In dieser klassischen Argumentationsfigur, die von Alexis de Tocquevilles vor mehr als 150 Jahren verfasstem Reisebericht über die Demokratie in Nordamerika bis hin zur sozialwissenschaftlichen Forschung über die politische Kultur moderner Gesellschaften reicht, gelten Vereine als zentrales Element stabiler Demokratien, da sie in der sozialen Praxis die Verbindung von Mitgliedschafts-

und Staatsbürgerrolle ermöglichen würden. Mitgliedschaften, aktive Mitarbeit und politische Partizipation in Vereinen werden dabei mit der – im klassischen Republikanismus als „guter Bürger" bezeichneten – Figur des „kompetenten Bürgers" verbunden, der über kognitive, prozedurale und habituelle Fähigkeiten verfüge, um als politischer Akteur adäquat in einem demokratischen Gemeinwesen handeln zu können (vgl. Buchstein 2002).

„Assoziative Demokratie" lautet eine entsprechende Vision, in der der Vielzahl von Vereinen die Schnittstellen- bzw. Vermittlungsfunktion zwischen den als gegensätzlich gedachten Bereichen von Individuum und Staat, von privat und staatlich oder von Staat und Gesellschaft zugedacht wird. Diese Vermittlungsfunktion hat Streek (1987) als einen komplexen und institutionell zu leistenden Prozeß beschrieben, der für das Zurücklegen des langen Weges vom Individuum zur Gesellschaft von elementarer Bedeutung sei – ein Prozeß, der in einem demokratischen Gemeinwesen eine unabdingbare Voraussetzung für den erfolgreichen Übergang vom Jedermann zum Citoyen darstelle.

2. Fazit und Ausblick

Die Skizze aktueller Reformentwürfe und gesellschaftspolitischer Leitbilder verweist auf die vielfältigen Anforderungen, die gegenwärtig an Vereine gestellt werden. Diese zahlreichen Funktionszuschreibungen werden insbesondere mit der „Multifunktionalität von Vereinen" begründet (vgl. Zimmer/Priller 2001). Lange Zeit galt diese Multifunktionalität als eine maßgebliche Schwäche von Vereinen, die zumeist als antiquiert, vormodern und defizitär angesehen wurden, da sie sich der Differenzierungslogik moderner Gesellschaften entzogen und den Geleitzug der Moderne verpaßt hätten. Mittlerweile wird diese strukturelle Unbestimmtheit aber immer häufiger „als Chance und Innovationspotenzial zur Reformierung und Umgestaltung des traditionellen institutionellen Settings der Industriemoderne erachtet" (ebd.: 274) – die aktuellen Reformentwürfe und Leitbilder, in denen Vereine als Hoffnungsträger zur Linderung der angesprochenen Krisenphänomene thematisiert werden, stehen stellvertretend dafür.

Allerdings steht diesen hoffnungsfrohen Erwartungen an das Vereinswesen bislang ein gravierendes Defizit in der sozialwissenschaftlichen Forschung in Deutschland gegenüber. Dieses Defizit zeigt sich an der wenig entwickelten Theorie über die Strukturbesonderheiten von Vereinen als freiwillige Vereinigungen im Dritten Sektor ebenso exemplarisch wie am spärlichen empirischen Datenmaterial (vgl. Braun 2003b). Mit dem Versuch, das freiwillige Engagement oder die Mitgliedschaften in Vereinen differenzierter zu erfassen, wurde in letzter Zeit zwar ein deutlicher Fortschritt gemacht. Die grundlegenden methodologischen und methodischen Diskussionen, die diese Versuche ausgelöst haben, machen zugleich aber auch deutlich, daß sich die Forschung derzeit noch an ganz grundsätzlichen Fragestellungen abarbeitet. Hieran zeigt sich nicht zuletzt das Problem, daß man sich in den vergangenen Jahrzehnten vor allem aus der Perspektive der korporatismustheoretisch inspirierten Interessengruppenforschung auf die funktionale Interessenvermittlung von Verbänden zwischen Staat und Gesellschaft oder aber aus der Perspektive der Dritter–Sektor–Forschung auf *Nonprofit*-Organisationen als alternative wohlfahrtsstaatliche Dienstleister konzentrierte. Demgegenüber wurde die assoziative Lebenswelt der Menschen nur am Rande thematisiert. Dieses grundlegende Forschungsdefizit läßt sich vor dem Hintergrund der skizzierten Diskussionslinien anschaulich demonstrieren, wobei ich mich im Folgenden auf die Skizze einiger weniger Defizite beschränken werde.

Im Zuge der aktuellen Reformbestrebungen hin zu einem neuen institutionellen Arrangement der Wohlfahrtsproduktion ist zu erwarten, daß sich das Vereins- und somit auch das Verbandswesen neu definieren und positionieren muß. Denn die grundlegende Entscheidung, inwieweit soziale Dienstleistungen vom Staat, Markt oder Dritten Sektor angeboten werden, ist nicht – wie es ökonomische Theorien vermuten lassen – von individuellen Nachfragern und Anbietern auf dem Markt abhängig, sondern in erster Linie von historischen Entwicklungen und politischen Konstellationen, die auch für den Dritten Sektor zu je spezifischen Ordnungsmodellen führen. Während z.B. das Modell des Gewährleistungsstaates von einer passiven, Leistungen an Dritte kontrahierenden und kontrollierenden Rolle des Staates ausgeht, setzt das aktuelle Leitbild vom aktivierenden Staat sowohl auf die interne offensive Förderung und Nutzung von (Selbst-)Aktivierungspotenzialen als auch auf die externe offensive Förderung, Forderung und Motivierung gesellschaftlicher Akteure.

Vor diesem Hintergrund zeichnet sich derzeit bereits deutlich ab, daß die Entwicklung noch stärker als bisher in die Richtung einer Kompetenzverlagerung von der öffentlichen Verwaltung hin zu den Vereinen verläuft. Damit stellt sich allerdings die bislang ungeklärte Frage, welche neuen *intra-* und *inter*organisatorischen Arrangements sich mit der neuen Verantwortungsteilung herausbilden. Mit Blick auf die *intraorganisatorischen* Arrangements könnte man vermuten, daß die Vereine Transformationsprozesse in ihren Organisationsformen und Handlungsrationalitäten vollziehen, da sich mit den neuen externen Anforderungen mutmaßlich auch die internen Anforderungen verändern – etwa an die Organisationsstruktur, die Aufgaben und Kompetenzverteilung oder die Mitarbeiter. Horch (1996) hat diese Problematik schon vor Längerem unter dem Stichwort der „Selbstzerstörungsprozesse von Vereinen" diskutiert.

Zum anderen stellt sich die Frage nach den vermutlich neu entstehenden *interorganisatorischen* Arrangements zwischen Staat und Vereinen. Denn bislang ist unklar, ob mit einer verstärkten Einbindung von Vereinen in ein verändertes institutionelles Arrangement der Wohlfahrtsproduktion auch ein neues Kapitel staatlich-privater Kooperation aufgeschlagen wird und dabei die Autonomie der Vereine gewahrt bleibt oder ob die Tradition des funktionalen Einbaus der Vereine in den politisch-administrativen Apparat lediglich fortgesetzt wird. In dieser Perspektive stellt sich also die noch weitgehend unbeantwortete Frage, wie die Organisations-, Kommunikations- und Interaktionsmuster zwischen staatlichen Organisationen, Verbänden und lokalen Vereinen ausgestaltet werden und inwieweit die Akteure fähig sind, im Prozeß kollektiver Entscheidungsfindung klar definierte Interessen zu vertreten, strategisch zu interagieren und Kompromisse einzugehen.

Theoretische und empirische Defizite sind ebenfalls unverkennbar, wenn man die Diskussion über Vereine und die Krise der Arbeitsgesellschaft betrachtet. Dies gilt insbesondere für den Diskurs über eine grundlegende Restrukturierung der Arbeitsgesellschaft; dies betrifft aber auch die Debatte über die Beschäftigungspotenziale in Vereinen. Denn nicht nur die Frage, inwieweit und in welcher Größenordnung sich zukünftig neue Beschäftigungsverhältnisse in Vereinen auftun werden, läßt sich bislang kaum abschätzen. Auch ist unklar, inwieweit von den Mitgliedern überhaupt eine zunehmende Verberuflichung ihrer Vereine gewünscht wird. Möglicherweise sehen die Mitglieder den „besonderen Wert" ihres Vereins ja gerade darin, daß er von ihnen selbst und ohne hauptamtliches Fachpersonal organisiert wird, auch wenn dann eventuell nicht alle Vereinsziele und -aufgaben in optimaler Weise gelöst werden können. Derartige Fragestellungen, die im laufenden Diskurs über die Bürgergesellschaft eine prominente Rolle spielen, lassen sich anhand von Funktionsträgerbefragungen, die in der Vereinsforschung seit langem dominieren, nicht beantworten. Systematische Mitgliederbefragungen zu dieser Thematik stehen hingegen noch aus (vgl. Baur/Braun 2003).

Gewinnt man mitunter schon bei der Debatte über die Beschäftigungspotenziale in Vereinen den Eindruck, daß diese Debatte in erheblichem Abstand über den Köpfen der Mitglieder geführt wird, so gilt dies in besonders profilierter Weise für jene Ansätze, die auf eine Restrukturierung der Arbeitsgesellschaft und auf eine Neubewertung von Tätigkeitsformen setzen. Dies gilt vor allem für das öffentlich besonders intensiv diskutierte Konzept der „Bürgerarbeit" (Beck 1999). Zwar wird auch hier gefordert, bürgerschaftliches Engagement gegenüber Erwerbsarbeit gesellschaftlich aufzuwerten.

Bürgerarbeit soll aber in erster Linie die Nachfrage nach Erwerbsarbeit reduzieren und damit Arbeitslosigkeit abbauen. Genau dieses Resultat wird von Kritikern zu Recht bezweifelt, wenn nicht gar als vollkommen abwegig entlarvt. Vielmehr lassen neuere empirische Untersuchungen erkennen, daß die Vitalität ziviler Beschäftigungsformen eher von gut funktionierenden Arbeitsmärkten abhängt, als daß sie beschäftigungspolitische Kompensationsfunktionen übernehmen könnten (vgl. Braun 2003b).

Grundlegende Fragen stellen sich schließlich auch im Zusammenhang mit den eng miteinander verwobenen Diskussionen über Vereine und die Krise des sozialen Zusammenhalts und der Demokratie. Denn warum sollte man gerade in Vereinen bestimmte bürgerschaftliche Kompetenzen erwerben, die man nicht auch in anderen Organisationen – z.B. staatlichen oder erwerbswirtschaftlichen Organisationen – entwickeln kann? Bislang hat in der Forschung kaum jemand versucht, dieser Frage systematisch nachzugehen. Lediglich bei Offe und Fuchs (2001) findet sich ein knapper Hinweis. Sie argumentieren, daß in Vereinen weder Zielstellung noch die Mitgliedschaft selbst vorgegeben sind. „Mit diesen Ambiguitäten", sich immer wieder gemeinsamer Ziele zu vergewissern oder aber auszutreten, „müssen sich die Mitglieder bürgergesellschaftlicher Vereinigungen abfinden. Im Training der Fähigkeiten und sozialen Kompetenzen, die für den Umgang mit diesen Merkmalen sekundärer Vereinigungen notwendig sind, sehen wir ihren spezifischen Beitrag zur Bildung von Sozialkapital." (ebd.: 423 ff.) Sie gehen also davon aus, daß das Aktivsein in den spezifischen Vereinsstrukturen von den Mitgliedern bestimmte Orientierungs- und Handlungsmuster verlange, die in den entsprechenden sozialen Prozessen entweder gestützt und gestärkt oder aber erst erlernt werden und die dann als habitualisierte Orientierungs- und Handlungsmuster dauerhaft erhalten blieben.

Diese bislang eher vage und auch nicht weiter ausgearbeitete Vermutung geht zwar über das hinaus, was die Forschung bisher an Erklärungsansätzen angeboten hat. Sie würde allerdings erheblich an Substanz gewinnen, wenn man organisationssoziologische Studien über die Strukturbesonderheiten freiwilliger Vereinigungen, durch die sich letztere gegenüber staatlichen und erwerbswirtschaftlichen Organisationen auszeichnen, berücksichtigen würde (vgl. Braun 2003a). Denn dann könnten mutmaßlich auch die sehr allgemein gehaltenen und vielfach auch idealisierten Vorstellungen vom „Vereinsleben" als einem Übungsfeld demokratischen Denkens und Handelns differenzierter gefaßt, aber auch relativiert werden.

Auf einer solchen empirischen Datengrundlage könnte man dann auch die Frage detaillierter verfolgen, ob die Unterschiede in den Orientierungsmustern von Vereinsmitgliedern und den übrigen Bundesbürgern tatsächlich als Sozialisationsprozesse zu verstehen sind, die die Mitglieder in ihrem Verein durchlaufen, oder ob es sich womöglich eher um Selektionsprozesse beim Zugang zu Vereinen handelt. Anders formuliert: „Sind durch die Mitgliedschaft oder dauerhaftes Engagement gebundene Menschen von vornherein mit einer größeren Vertrauensbasis ausgestattet und organisieren sich aus diesem Grund stärker als andere, oder ist es vielmehr umgekehrt, daß sich erst über das Engagement Vertrauen formt, das weitere soziale Beziehungen und Netzwerke tragen kann?" (Heinze/ Strünck 2000: 209) Und vielleicht ließe sich ja auch zeigen, daß sich in Vereinen vor allem solche Menschen zusammenschließen, die unabhängig von ihrer Mitgliedschaft und ihrem Engagement ein höheres soziales Vertrauen und umfangreichere bürgerschaftliche Kompetenz aufweisen, deren Vertrauen und bürgerschaftliche Kompetenz aber durch die Vereinsmitgliedschaft gestützt und gestärkt werden, wobei die Eintrittsmotivation davon beeinflußt wird, welche Aufmerksamkeit der Einzelne öffentlichen Angelegenheiten gegenüber zeigt und wie stark sein soziales Vertrauen entwickelt ist. In dieser Argumentationsrichtung würden Vereine also eher Vorhandenes verstärken und festigen als Neues generieren.

Diese Problemstellung verweist bereits auf eine letzte anzusprechende Frage. Denn es ist bisher theoretisch und empirisch noch unklar, wie der Mechanismus funktionieren soll, über den die Mitglieder die in ihrem Verein ggf. erworbenen sozialen und politischen Orientierungen auf andere Lebensbereiche übertragen. So ist z.B. soziales Vertrauen per Definition spezifisch und kontextgebunden, d.h. es wird durch wiederholte *face–to–face* Interaktionen in bestimmten sozialen Kontexten generiert. Cohen (1999: 221) hat insofern argumentiert, daß *„without other mechanisms for the ‚generalization' of trust, participation in associations and membership in social networks could foster particularism, localism, intolerance, exclusion, and generalized mistrusts of outsiders, of the law, and of government"*. Zwar können unsere Ergebnisse diese Vermutung nicht erhärten, was aber auch in diesem Fall bleibt, ist das grundsätzliche Forschungsproblem, daß das Fleisch auf dem blanken Knochen der Statistik noch ausgesprochen mager ist.

Vor diesem Hintergrund bleibt es eine lohnenswerte Aufgabe, das Leistungspotenzial des Vereinswesens vor dem Hintergrund der vielfältigen Funktionszuschreibungen empirisch detailliert zu untersuchen; denn – wie Weber (1924: 447) in dem eingangs angesprochenen Vortrag salopp formulierte – „ohne solche trockene, triviale, viel Geld und viel Arbeitskraft einfach in den Boden stampfende Arbeit ist nichts zu machen".

Literatur

Baur, Jürgen/Braun, Sebastian (Hrsg.) (2003): Integrationsleistungen von Sportvereinen als Freiwilligenorganisationen, Aachen.
Beck, Ulrich (1999): Schöne neue Arbeitswelt – Vision: Weltbürgergesellschaft, Frankfurt a.M.
Braun, Sebastian (2001a): Bürgerschaftliches Engagement – Konjunktur und Ambivalenz einer gesellschaftspolitischen Debatte, in: Leviathan (29), S. 83-109.
Ders. (2001b): Putnam und Bourdieu und das soziale Kapital in Deutschland – Der rhetorische Kurswert einer sozialwissenschaftlichen Kategorie, in: Leviathan (29), S. 337-354.
Ders. (2003a): Freiwillige Vereinigungen als Produzenten von Sozialkapital?, in: Verbandsmanagement (1), S. 28-37.
Ders. (2003b): Freiwillige Vereinigungen zwischen Staat, Markt und Privatsphäre – Konzepte, Kontroversen und Perspektiven, in: Baur/Braun, S. 43-87.
Braun, Sebastian/Weiß, Christina (2005): Sozialkapital, in: Gosepath, Stefan/Hinsch Wilfried/Rössler, Beate (Hrsg.): Handbuch der politischen Philosophie und Sozialphilosophie, Berlin.
Buchstein, Hubertus (2002): Die Bürgergesellschaft – Eine Ressource der Demokratie?, in: Breit, Gotthard/Schiele, Siegfried (Hrsg.): Demokratie – Lernen als Aufgabe der politischen Bildung, Bonn, S. 198-222.
Cohen, Jean (1999): Trust, Voluntary Association and Workable Democracy – The Contemporary American Discourse of Civil Society, in: Warren, M. E. (Hrsg.): Democracy and Trust, Cambridge, S. 208-248.
Enquete-Kommission „Zukunft des Bürgerschaftlichen Engagements" Deutscher Bundestag (2002): Bürgerschaftliches Engagement: auf dem Weg in eine zukunftsfähige Bürgergesellschaft, Opladen.
Evers, Adalbert (1986): Zwischen Arbeitsamt und Ehrenamt – Unkonventionelle lokale Initiativen im Schnittpunkt von Arbeit und sozialen Diensten, in: Blanke, Bernhard/Evers, Adalbert/Wollmann, Helmut (Hrsg.): Die Zweite Stadt – Neue Formen lokaler Arbeits- und Sozialpolitik, Leviathan (Sonderheft 7), Opladen, S. 15-50.
Evers, Adalbert/Olk, Thomas (Hrsg.) (1996): Wohlfahrtspluralismus – Vom Wohlfahrtsstaat zur Wohlfahrtsgesellschaft, Opladen.
Giarini, Oriano/Liedtke, Patrick M. (1998): Wie wir arbeiten werden – Der neue Bericht an den Club of Rome, Hamburg, 2. Aufl.
Heinze, Rolf G./Strünck, Christoph (2000): Die Verzinsung des sozialen Kapitals – Freiwilliges Engagement im Strukturwandel, in: Beck, U. (Hrsg.): Die Zukunft von Arbeit und Demokratie, Frankfurt a.M., S. 171-216.

Horch, Heinz-Dieter (1996): Selbstzerstörungsprozesse freiwilliger Vereinigungen, in: Rauschenbach, Thomas/Sachße, Christoph/Olk, Thomas (Hrsg.): Von der Wertgemeinschaft zum Dienstleistungsunternehmen – Jugend- und Wohlfahrtsverbände im Umbruch, Frankfurt a.M., 2. Aufl., S. 280-296.

Münkler, Herfried (2002): Bürgerschaftliches Engagement in der Zivilgesellschaft, in: Enquete-Kommission, S. 29-36.

Mutz, Gerd (1997): Zukunft der Arbeit – Chancen für eine Tätigkeitsgesellschaft?, in: Aus Politik und Zeitgeschichte (48-49), S. 31-40.

Naschold, Frieder (1993): Modernisierung des Staates – Zur Ordnungs- und Innovationspolitik des öffentlichen Sektors, Berlin.

Offe, Claus/Fuchs, Susanne (2001): Schwund des Sozialkapitals? Der Fall Deutschland, in: Putnam, R. D. (Hrsg.): Gesellschaft und Gemeinsinn, Gütersloh, S. 417-514.

Priller, Eckhard/Zimmer, Annette (Hrsg.) (2001): Der Dritte Sektor international – Mehr Markt – weniger Staat?, Berlin.

Putnam, Robert D. (2000): Bowling Alone – The Collapse and Revival of American Community, New York.

Rifkin, Jeremy (1997): Das Ende der Arbeit und ihre Zukunft, Frankfurt a.M.

Siewert, Hans-Jörg (1984): Zur Thematisierung des Vereinswesens in der deutschen Soziologie, in: Historische Zeitschrift (Neue Folge, Beiheft 9), S. 151-180.

Streeck, Wolfgang (1987): Vielfalt und Interdependenz – Überlegungen zur Rolle von intermediären Organisationen in sich ändernden Umwelten, in: Kölner Zeitschrift für Soziologie und Sozialpsychologie (39), S. 471-495.

Weber, Max (1924): Rede auf dem Deutschen Soziologentag in Frankfurt, in: ders.: Gesammelte Aufsätze zur Soziologie und Sozialpolitik, Tübingen, S. 431-449.

Zimmer, Annette (1996): Vereine – Basiselemente der Demokratie, Opladen.

Zimmer, Annette/Priller, Eckhard (2001): Mehr als Markt oder Staat – Zur Aktualität des Dritten Sektors, in: Barlösius, Eva/Müller, Hans-Peter/Sigmund, S. (Hrsg.): Gesellschaftsbilder im Umbruch – Soziologische Perspektiven in Deutschland, Opladen, S. 269-288.

Lahouari Addi

Religion et Culture Politique dans le Monde Arabe

Le culturalisme, forme d'ethnocentrisme malgré parfois la bonne foi du chercheur, est fortement présent dans les sciences sociales, principalement dans les disciplines où le chercheur étudie des sociétés différentes de la sienne. Dans les travaux de Raphaël Pataï ou de Bernard Lewis, pour citer des exemples, « les Autres » sont analysés à travers leurs cultures, perçues le plus souvent comme cause de comportements différents mais aussi de blocage.[1] L'Arabe serait fataliste; il serait attaché au passé, soumis aux forces de la nature et invoquant Dieu à n'importe quel moment de la journée, etc.[2] A moins de faire preuve de relativisme comme outil méthodologique, un observateur étranger court toujours le risque d'exagérer l'épaisseur de la culture des groupes observés en soulignant l'importance de son rôle dans la vie quotidienne. Pour le sens commun, toute culture étrangère est exotique et bizarre. Aucun individu ne sent le poids de sa propre culture, vécue avec simplicité et transparence, comme si elle était la seule à s'articuler à la raison et à l'universel. A l'opposé, « les Autres » érigent entre eux et la nature un mur culturel qui les empêche d'être des hommes libres, rationnels et ouverts au progrès.

Ceci est le message implicite contenu dans les travaux orientalistes sur le monde arabe, travaux marqués par un regard ethnocentriste grossissant la culture des groupes observés, jugés sur le critère de la culture de l'observateur.[3] Le présupposé est que l'Occident est organisé en sociétés composées d'hommes libres, tandis que le monde arabe est un ensemble culturel où l'individu se dissout dans l'esprit collectif ou le caractère psycho-social de la collectivité. Une telle approche n'a pas pour objet la culture du groupe, mais un

---

[1] Cf. R. Pataï, 1973. Signalons du même auteur un ancien article « The Middle East as a Cultural Area », *Middle East Journal*, n° 6, 1952; Les ouvrages de B. Lewis sont nombreux et sont assez représentatifs du courant orientaliste. Cf. par exemple son ouvrage *Le langage politique de l'Islam*, Gallimard, Paris, 1987.
[2] Pour une critique des approches psychologisantes du social dans le monde arabe, cf. Barakat, 1990.
[3] Le regard ethnocentriste ne provient pas que des étrangers. Il peut aussi être reproduit par des universitaires ou des romanciers autochtones ayant reçu une formation en Occident. Ceci dit, il est à distinguer des travaux de réflexion critique qui dénoncent des pratiques sociales jugées archaïques par des groupes sociaux aspirant au progrès social.

objet particulier qu'elle construit pour montrer « un groupe social écrasé par sa propre culture ». Elle est de ce fait un discours idéologique, empruntant aux sciences sociales leur langage, et dont la finalité est de montrer, *à contrario*, l'universalité de la culture du chercheur occidental. L'orientalisme est une élaboration discursive visant à montrer le caractère particulariste des pays arabes mesuré à l'aune de l'universalisme de l'Occident.

Le défaut du culturalisme et de l'orientalisme provient de ce qu'ils supposent que les sociétés arabes et occidentales vivent la même historicité, et que par conséquent, si elles n'ont pas les mêmes institutions, c'est que les unes présentent un déficit par rapport aux autres. Ce qui est cependant oublié, c'est que le pouvoir en Occident et dans les pays musulmans n'a pas le même contenu historique. Dans le premier cas, il a perdu, avec le capitalisme et l'Etat de droit, son caractère prédateur, tandis que dans le second, les pratiques arbitraires rappellent la faiblesse des institutions et du caractère public de l'autorité. Ceci résulte des profondes transformations qui ont radicalement changé la nature du lien social. En Occident, le rapport entre l'individu et le groupe a connu un bouleversement introduit par la modernité qui a créé les bases de l'autonomie individuelle, ce que les philosophes et sociologues appellent le processus de subjectivation. Dans les sociétés arabes, les bases du travail social sont trop étroites, la division sociale du travail peu profonde, ce qui fait que l'individu n'arrive pas à s'autonomiser du groupe; ce qui n'exclut pas que, en raison de la généralisation de l'échange marchand, il utilise le groupe à son profit, manipulant les symboles et l'imaginaire dans une stratégie inconsciente de contrôle des rapports sociaux. Ceci indique que les individus ne sont pas passifs face à l'ordre symbolique hérité du passé. Ils ont suffisamment de ressources pour l'interpréter et l'utiliser comme discours de légitimation de leurs attitudes.

L'approche culturaliste nie les processus sociologiques et les évolutions historiques, et réifie deux catégories – la culture et la religion – d'où elle déduit l'ordre social et politique. C'est ainsi que les régimes politiques arabes apparaissent, en raison de leur faible institutionnalisation, comme les produits d'une dynamique culturelle qui imprimerait ses formes aux rapports d'autorité et au fonctionnement de l'Etat, affirmant ainsi que la culture est une variable indépendante ayant une forte valeur explicative. Se limitant à l'observation empirique, le culturalisme sous-estime les dynamiques sociales, tout en prenant à la lettre le discours des acteurs sur eux-mêmes. Le discours orientaliste rejoint, paradoxalement, celui de l'islamisme dont un des traits est la négation de l'histoire. Apparu récemment comme culture de contestation, l'islamisme est un produit contradictoire de la modernité et une expression d'une aspiration à la participation au champ de l'Etat privatisé par des régimes autoritaires. Il est un imaginaire social et un langage politique qui utilise la religion comme ressource à des fins de légitimation.

Cet article tentera de montrer que la culture a seulement une valeur descriptive et n'est pas externe aux processus sociaux et politiques. Les exemples de la revendication de la souveraineté divine et de la violence qui marque les rapports d'autorité montreront que le sens des catégories culturelles ne se révèle que si elles sont situées dans leur contexte historique et politique. Mais avant de développer cette approche, je rappellerai d'abord quelques éléments du débat sur la notion de culture politique et sa critique, en soulignant deux problèmes d'ordre méthodologique et en évoquant son lien avec l'imaginaire social.

I. La notion de culture politique et sa critique

Alimentant un débat incessant, le concept de *culture politique* est l'un des plus controversés en science politique depuis l'article datant de 1956 de Gabriel Almond qui l'a utilisé le premier.[4] L'acuité des controverses s'explique par le glissement méthodologique qu'un tel concept opère dans le champ de la discipline, présupposant que les formes institutionnelles du politique seraient déterminées par la culture, ce qui diluerait l'objet de la science politique dans la sociologie culturelle ou la psychologie sociale.[5] Outre cette difficulté, cette posture soulève au moins deux problèmes théoriques, l'un se posant à toutes les sciences sociales, l'autre étant relatif au comparatisme propre à la science politique.[6]

1. Deux problèmes d'ordre méthodologique

Le premier renvoie à la problématique de la culture dans le champ des sciences sociales confrontées à deux écueils : le culturalisme, réifiant la culture en en faisant une catégorie à laquelle obéiraient les hommes de manière plus ou moins passive, et l'individualisme qui présuppose que l'acteur choisit ses croyances en fonction de ses perceptions subjectives. Prises entre l'enclume du holisme (ou culturalisme) et le marteau de l'individualisme, les sciences sociales semblent condamnées à reproduire cette dichotomie entre les ap-

---

[4] G. Almond, 1956.
[5] Il faut admettre que, malgré toutes les réserves émises par de nombreux auteurs, le concept de culture politique a eu au moins le mérite d'avoir débarrassé le discours des sciences sociales des notions ambiguës comme le « caractère national » ou « l'esprit d'un peuple ».
[6] Pour une vue d'ensemble de l'usage du concept en science politique et de l'apport des autres disciplines, notamment l'anthropologie, cf. Schemeil, 1985.

proches antagoniques de l'objectivité du monde social et de la subjectivité de l'acteur. Elles se construisent en fait entre ces deux pôles méthodologiques indépassables, donnant naissance à des travaux ou des courants obéissant aux logiques du balancier. Quand un courant pousse à l'excès une méthodologie, il suscite en réaction un courant inverse. Dans un cas, l'approche cherche à expliquer à travers des causalités culturelles, ou autres; dans l'autre cas, elle essaye de comprendre le sens culturel que donne l'acteur à son action pour construire un objet cohérent où la causalité n'est pas un enjeu théorique.

Le second problème est inhérent à l'approche comparative que la science politique académique met en œuvre. C'est en comparant les niveaux de développement politique des différents pays que G. Almond, S. Verba, L. Pye et leur courant ont forgé la notion de culture empruntée au cadre conceptuel de la sociologie de T. Parsons où elle joue un rôle fondamental de contrôle et d'orientation de l'action sociale.[7] Tout système d'action posséderait un sous-système appelé « culture politique » servant à l'intégration, mais seuls les systèmes modernes produiraient une « culture civique », expression d'un développement politique s'incarnant dans l'Etat de droit et la démocratie.[8] Dans cette perspective parsonienne, les dysfonctionnements des nouveaux Etats issus de la décolonisation seraient à expliquer par une absence ou un déficit de la « culture civique ». Esquissant un structuralisme systémique totalement désincarné, David Easton poussa le raisonnement jusqu'à l'excès en construisant des systèmes à dynamique cybernétique fonctionnant avec des 'inputs' et des 'outputs', transformant le système politique en machinerie qui a besoin de fluidité - fournie entre autres par la culture politique – sans laquelle des crises apparaîtront au prix d'abaisser son rendement.[9] Pour la vogue fonctionnaliste, l'Etat moderne serait un ensemble d'institutions se cristallisant dans une *culture civique* propre à l'histoire de chaque société du monde occidental ou en voie d'occidentalisation, suggérant l'approche comparative pour expliquer les différences entre les Etats à travers les traits spécifiques à leurs histoires originale.s[10] En dehors du fait que cette démarche est porteuse de généralisations excessives et d'explication par un seul facteur, elle est en outre gênante en ce qu'elle aboutit à désigner une culture nationale comme un modèle normatif à l'aune duquel seraient

---

[7] Cf. Parsons, 1967; Parsons, 1973.
[8] Dans l'article de 1956 précédemment cité, G. Almond écrit : « Every political system is embedded in a particular pattern of orientations to political action. I have found it useful to refer to this as the political culture. »
[9] Easton, 1974.
[10] Cf. Almond/Verba, 1965; 1980.

mesurés les déficits des autres cultures, forcément en retard ou déficientes et donc génératrices de crises et d'instabilités politiques.[11]

Ces travaux ont suscité de nombreuses critiques, entre autres celle d'avoir appauvri le concept de culture provenant de l'anthropologie et la sociologie.[12] Pour ces disciplines, la culture est une vision qui construit socialement le monde en abolissant son étrangeté et en donnant du sens à l'environnement extérieur. Elle fait corps avec la société en lui fournissant ses repères, ses signifiants, son cadre légitime de compréhension de l'altérité. Dans la science politique académique, notamment chez G. Almond et S. Verba, la notion est appauvrie pour les besoins de la démonstration comparative, et est réduite à des « attitudes, des comportements et des convictions » passés en revue par des enquêtes d'opinion (*research survey*) mesurant le degré d'élaboration des cultures politiques par pays et par groupes sociaux. Elle comporte des clivages qui sont cependant surmontés par l'existence d'une culture civique commune qui protègerait le système politique des crises. Quantifiée et mesurée par des indices, la culture, dans cette perspective, perd son contenu symbolique et imaginaire pour devenir une variable dont le niveau est fixé par les besoins du système.

Cependant, malgré ces critiques, les sciences sociales en général et la science politique en particulier ne peuvent se passer du concept de culture, à condition cependant d'éviter les écueils nés d'approches systémiques qui bâtissent des logiques collectives s'autoalimentant. De ce point de vue, la science politique a beaucoup à apprendre de l'histoire où le concept est utilisé pour décrire des changements dans les processus historiques.[13] Loin de toute approche déterministe ou de causalité renvoyant à la circularité du raisonnement du type qui de « l'œuf culturel ou de la poule démocratique est le premier ».[14] Il s'agit en l'occurrence moins de trouver des causes que de décrire des évolutions politiques où les protagonistes, aux intérêts divergents, s'accusent d'être à l'origine de blocage d'une situation indésirable, l'absence de démocratie. Si la science politique se limitait à décrire et à *interpréter* l'action sociale en fonction du sens que lui donne l'acteur, peut-être que le concept de culture politique serait moins encombrant et deviendrait utile comme il l'est en anthropologie, en

---

[11] Cf. Badie, 1993. Dans une première partie intitulée « Sociologie politique de la culture », l'auteur fait la critique du culturalisme de l'école fonctionnaliste américaine, mais dans une partie ultérieure intitulée « L'analyse culturelle des systèmes politiques », il reproduit le culturalisme dénoncé précédemment, en comparant les fondements du pouvoir en Occident et en terre d'islam.
[12] Cf. Cuche, 2001.
[13] Cf. Rioux/Sirinelli, 1997.
[14] Hudson, 1995.

sociologie, en histoire... Et même dans cette limite, il n'aura de pertinence que si son contenu est défini et articulé à l'objet de la science politique (le pouvoir et les processus de sa légitimation) en relation avec les autres notions que sont la démocratie, l'autorité, l'Etat de droit, la liberté, l'égalité, etc., ce qui permettrait de faire le lien entre la culture politique et la structure des rapports d'autorité. Dans cette perspective, il serait autant arbitraire de l'isoler de l'ensemble auquel elle appartient que de lui donner un caractère déterminant.

Par ailleurs, il y a une tendance à confondre imaginaire social et culture politique dans des régimes peu institutionnalisés où précisément elle est en formation avec l'Etat. Il y a certes des liens entre institutions et culture politique mais l'idée, chez certains universitaires, est que la culture politique dans le monde arabe s'oppose à l'institutionnalisation du pouvoir et donc à la naissance de l'Etat de droit. Certains auteurs puisent dans les rapports familiaux et les liens lignagers, expliquant par l'image du père l'autoritarisme à la base d'attitudes patriarcales dans la sphère privée et de comportements patrimoniaux dans la sphère publique.[15] A ce niveau, l'objet de la science politique – le pouvoir, sa conquête, sa conservation – est égaré dans l'anthropologie de la société arabe, ou encore chez les orientalistes dans la culture, posée comme essence. Ceci crée l'illusion que les individus sont victimes de visions du monde qui leur échapperaient alors qu'ils les produisent pour expliquer et maîtriser la réalité, même si c'est dans l'imaginaire. Le monde social n'est pas un fait de nature; il n'est pas le prolongement de la vie biologique ; il est une construction imaginaire qui, certes, se cristallise, se solidifie et s'impose aux individus, mais ce monde imaginaire n'est à l'abri ni d'évolutions ni de ruptures ni aussi de stagnation.

2. Culture politique et imaginaire social

Aux prises avec les contradictions de la construction nationale et étatique, les sociétés arabes sont en train de donner naissance à des cultures politiques sur la base d'imaginaires sociaux alimentant des utopies.[16] Un imaginaire social enferme le politique en lui refusant l'autonomie, tandis que la culture politique est déjà l'expression de cette autonomie et même de la fragmentation de l'espace politique puisqu'il y aurait des cultures politiques concurrentes renvoyant à des perspectives différentes et antagoniques du lien social.[17] La

---

[15] Cf. Sharabi, 1985.
[16] J'utilise la notion d'imaginaire social dans le sens que lui donne Baczko 1984.
[17] Cf. Cefaï, 2001.

construction nationale est aussi le passage d'une conception anthropologique de la culture comme imaginaire social destiné à enlever au monde son étrangeté à une conception politique de la culture de groupes comme formulation discursive rationnelle des intérêts de ces groupes, tantôt dans la concorde nationale, tantôt en conflit pour défendre leurs membres et leurs positions dans la répartition des richesses. La culture politique serait donc un ensemble de représentations et de convictions qui légitiment un ordre politique et dans lequel la conflictualité produit des sub-cultures de groupes défendant leurs intérêts propres. Par conséquent, toute culture politique est traversée par deux dynamiques contradictoires, celle de la totalité portée à l'intégration, et celles parties, exprimées par les partis et les syndicats et portées à la conflictualité. Ce schéma serait plutôt celui de la modernité, avec ses catégories emblématiques, les partis, les associations, les élections, etc. Dans les processus où l'Etat est en construction, ce qui est le cas des sociétés arabes, l'imaginaire social connaît une réactivation et une surpolitisation conduisant chez certains groupes à la formulation d'utopies exprimant des aspirations à des changements de l'ordre politique. De ce point de vue, tout groupe social produit une culture politique dans une perspective ethnocentriste où le monde extérieur est perçu à travers des représentations produites comme des habitus.

Les crises ne sont pas dues à la rupture entre les représentations et l'ordre politique; cette explication est celle qu'avancent ceux qui contestent l'ordre politique accusé de ne pas respecter les normes et les valeurs de la société, toujours réinterprétées et réinventées par les protagonistes qui cherchent à se les approprier. Lors des crises, les représentations sont mobilisées comme ressources de contestation. *L'imaginaire social, dans ce contexte, apparaissant à l'observateur extérieur comme culture politique, serait la rationalisation discursive légitimant une action politique et une représentation du monde se transformant en volonté pour le changer.* Cet imaginaire est pertinent ou non en fonction des enjeux de la crise et de l'efficacité des autres ressources détenues par tous les protagonistes du conflit.

Un des concepts les plus cruciaux en science politique est précisément celui de *ressource politique*. Si l'on définit l'objet de la science politique comme les mécanismes de conquête et de conservation du pouvoir, ou de son institutionnalisation dans les démocraties, le concept de ressource est important dans ce sens où il permet d'identifier la nature de la compétition pour le pouvoir sur la base des ressources dont disposent les compétiteurs. Les ressources politiques sont aussi nombreuses que variées: la force, la richesse, la fidélité, le charisme, les croyances... La légitimité est une représentation construite sur la base de ressources culturelles. Un régime sans légitimité recourt à la coercition physique pour se maintenir, ce qui est le cas de tous les régimes arabes dont la légitimité a décliné. Si les régimes arabes connaissent une crise de légitimité, cela signifie que les sociétés aspirent à des changements politiques et qu'elles ne sont pas passives ou stagnantes. Il est vrai que la principale force de contestation est le mouvement islamiste, expression politico-culturelle qui a gagné en popularité dans les années 1970 et 1980, défiant le nationalisme arabe avec lequel il partage du reste un certain nombre de valeurs.

Il est à se demander cependant si l'islamisme est d'abord un mouvement religieux avec un objectif politique ou un mouvement politique utilisant la religion à des fins de mobilisation. Ce qui est sûr, c'est qu'il n'a pas une préoccupation se limitant au sacré et il n'est pas un parti tel que le définit la science politique. Il n'a pas pour objectif de préparer les croyants à la vie éternelle – et c'est la différence avec l'intégrisme – affichant l'ambition d'organiser la vie sur terre sur des bases de justice et d'égalité. Réaction politico-religieuse exprimant des attentes contradictoires qui empruntent tant à la modernité qu'à la tradition, il est un imaginaire social utilisant le passé pour reconstruire le présent à l'aide d'une utopie mobilisatrice, née dans un tissu socio-culturel en voie de sécularisation et où la religion apparaît comme hégémonique dans les activités sociales; en réalité, le mot imbrication serait plus judicieux car le politique exerce aussi des effets de domination sur le religieux. Le discours religieux est fortement présent dans toute la société avec des prétentions politiques, donnant légitimité à tout un chacun de se prononcer sur ce qui est bien ou mal, sur ce qui est juste ou ce qui ne l'est pas (*la commanderie du bien et le pourchas du mal*). Les luttes n'ont cependant pas pour enjeux des querelles religieuses, des réformes ou des schismes, mais elles sont motivées par le pouvoir ou pour peser sur l'Etat afin qu'il promulgue telle ou telle réglementation régissant la sphère publique. Ce qui est réellement en jeu en effet, ce n'est ni la religion, ni l'islamisation par « le haut » ou par « le bas », et encore moins le « *djihad* » (la conversion des incroyants par la guerre) qui n'appartient plus à la psychologie collective contemporaine, même si certains groupuscules, très minoritaires, y font référence. Le discours religieux est mobilisé pour la prise du pouvoir ou son influence, invoquant, à cet effet, la *shari'a*, la *choura*, les *salafs*, etc., autant de concepts réifiés, dont la charge symbolique véhicule des aspirations contradictoires, tantôt utopiques, tantôt démocratiques.[18] Le mouvement islamiste véhicule une idéologie politique contradictoire et la question méthodologique est de savoir s'il faut considérer son discours comme la traduction de la réalité sociale ou s'il est un langage faisant partie de cette réalité à laquelle il cherche à s'identifier.

---

[18] Cf. Addi, 1997.

II. L'islam comme langage et ressource politique

L'actualité, malheureusement violente, montre que l'islam, sur-politisé, est invoqué aussi bien par des courants conservateurs effrayés par une sécularisation balbutiante que par les couches sociales démunies qui protestent contre leur dénuement, y mêlant la condamnation de ce qui est considéré comme dégradation des mœurs.[19] Dans cette perspective, l'islam est un langage et une ressource politique utilisés par les uns et les autres pour légitimer ou contester un ordre politique, mais l'erreur à éviter est de le prendre pour un acteur politique avec une cohérence et une rationalité institutionnelles. Cette même erreur, consistant aussi à postuler qu'il a en lui-même la force de déterminer les évolutions politiques, cache la relation dynamique entre religion et société dans la double perspective holiste et individualiste. L'islam n'est donc pas un acteur politique rationnel et cohérent, mais une pratique discursive que des protagonistes de camps opposés utilisent pour défendre des positions politiques relatives à la lutte pour le pouvoir ou à son influence.

1. Islam, pluralisme et démocratie

Certains auteurs voient dans l'islamisme une résurgence de la tradition, alors que d'autres l'analysent comme la modalité contradictoire d'insertion des sociétés musulmanes dans la modernité.[20] La première tendance s'apparente à l'orientalisme et au culturalisme essentialiste et considère que l'islam véhicule dès l'origine une culture autoritaire en contradiction avec la démocratie. Ce point de vue présente la religion comme une *essence*, comme une entité dogmatique extérieure à la vie sociale des hommes, empêchés, s'agissant de l'islam, de se doter d'une organisation politique démocratique. Accablant l'islam et innocentant les musulmans, victimes malgré eux de leur religion et de leur culture, cette conception, outre qu'elle puise dans l'universalisme naïf, néglige le rôle actif qu'ont les hommes dans le vécu religieux producteur de symboles et de représentations et ignore les processus historiques. Il n'est pas en effet pertinent de savoir si le Coran permet ou non le pluralisme, sachant qu'il est toujours possible de légitimer ce dernier religieusement – ou de le condamner – du fait que le texte sacré offre plusieurs lectures et est susceptible de justifier autant l'autoritarisme que la démocratie.[21] Certes le Coran fournit un système normatif, mais du

---

[19] D'où l'impossibilité d'analyser l'islamisme en termes de classes sociales, bien que cette dimension n'y soit pas totalement absente.
[20] Cf. Burgat, 1995.
[21] Le pluralisme a existé dans l'histoire musulmane mais nous sommes préoccupés par le pluralisme politique apparu dans les démocraties

fait de l'évolution des mentalités et des aspirations, les normes sont ré-interprétées inconsciemment. Aussi, les conceptions politiques – implicites ou explicites – s'articulent à des pratiques politiques, même si celles-ci ne sont pas formalisées dans des institutions. De ce point de vue, la sociologie/anthropologie étudie la pratique (dans le sens de Bourdieu) légitimée par un système de symboles (dans le sens de Geertz), tandis que la théologie est préoccupée par la norme telle qu'elle est dans le texte sacré.[22] En fait, la force du texte sacré est qu'il obéit à l'interprétation que font les hommes pour montrer le bien fondé de leurs visions idéologiques et pour invoquer la légitimité de leurs combats. Il ne faut pas, en effet, perdre de vue que l'islam n'existe qu'à travers des hommes et des femmes qui le vivent et qui le pratiquent en lui donnant une signification provenant de leur histoire et de leur culture.

Se demander si l'islam accepte la démocratie est cependant une question anachronique car celle-ci n'est apparue qu'avec la modernité. La question pertinente renvoie en fait au pluralisme dans les sociétés musulmanes – historiquement différentes les unes des autres – dans lesquelles il convient d'analyser les formes que revêtent les luttes politiques et surtout la conception du pouvoir aussi bien chez les dirigeants que chez les administrés. Les sociétés arabes sont toutes marquées par les convulsions de la construction étatique et nationale à travers lesquelles le monopole de l'exercice de la violence cherche à s'affirmer, si tant est qu'il puisse s'imposer un jour.[23]

---

occidentales et qui est intrinsèquement lié à la sécularisation. Peter L. Berger a bien perçu le lien entre les catégories. Il écrit: « ... the phenomenon called 'pluralism' is a social-structural correlate of the secularization of consciousness. This relationship invites sociological analysis. » Berger, 1967, p. 126.

[22] Il y a deux approches du fait religieux. La première considère le sacré comme un phénomène transcendant dont l'étude relève de la théologie qui postule de l'immanence de l'ordre divin que les évolutions historiques n'affecteraient pas. C'est dans ce cadre que s'inscrivent les débats à l'intérieur de la chari'a que les fouqaha ont fixée pour l'éternité en fonction d'une essence humaine immuable. La deuxième interprète le sacré en posant le fait religieux comme une pratique exprimant l'historicité et les contradictions de la société, présupposant que ce qui est premier, c'est l'homme social appréhendé à travers sa culture historique et sa psychologie (individuelle et collective) évolutive. N'allant pas jusqu'à affirmer que l'homme crée la norme sacrée, elle postule néanmoins qu'il l'interprète, qu'il l'utilise pour justifier sa propre vision du monde confortant ses intérêts. En un mot, la théologie a pour objet le symbole contenu dans la parole divine, l'anthropologie religieuse a pour objet l'usage social du symbole.

[23] Cette réduction est aggravée par le fait que l'islam soit aujourd'hui plus l'objet de la science politique que de la sociologie ou de l'anthropologie. Bien qu'il y ait des raisons à cela, il faut être conscient des conséquences

Dans la société arabe comme ailleurs, la pluralité existe sous forme de différences sociales, économiques, idéologiques, ... mais ce sont des changements historiques qui font naître le pluralisme comme représentation et comme pratique institutionnelle qui rend politiquement compatibles les divergences qui traversent le corps social. Le pluralisme institutionnel est la traduction d'un rapport de forces, imposé comme mode de fonctionnement du champ politique, avec ses techniques électorales et d'alternance. Le rapport de forces renvoie aux ressources politiques que peuvent mobiliser les acteurs dans la lutte qui les oppose, parmi lesquelles l'économie, la religion et la violence d'Etat. Il est important de rappeler que les régimes arabes contemporains bénéficient de la modernité des techniques de répression (armée, police, justice...) beaucoup plus efficaces que par le passé, ce qui leur donne un avantage politique dans leurs rapports avec la société, sans compter le soutien des pays occidentaux plus soucieux de stabilité régionale que de changements incertains. Le rapport de force militaire qui prévalait durant la période précoloniale où les pouvoirs centraux étaient relativement fragiles devant un soulèvement d'une confédération de tribus, a fondamentalement changé en faveur de l'Etat. Les pouvoirs centraux sont sortis renforcés de l'aventure coloniale qui les a munis d'une armée disposant de chars et d'avions dissuadant désormais tout soulèvement. Le vecteur tribal étant désarmé, la contestation va prendre une forme religieuse exprimant une utopie portée par des foules urbaines.[24]

---

théoriques d'une telle posture. La science politique a pour objet un champ supposé être autonome, dans le prolongement de la différentiation sociale et de la sécularisation, se focalisant précisément sur les institutions qui forment le corps politique où se reproduit le pouvoir d'Etat. Les sociétés musulmanes présentent-elles ces caractéristiques? A l'évidence non. Si nous convenons que l'objet des sciences sociales est historique, il faut alors admettre qu'elles sont elles-mêmes traversées par cette historicité. La conséquence théorique de cette posture est que les méthodologies du fait social sont à ajuster selon que l'objet de recherche est une société sécularisée ou non. L'anthropologie, dont le spectre est assez large pour appréhender la « totalité du fait social » (M. Mauss), permet de dégager des éléments d'analyse de la religion comme système culturel (Geertz) renvoyant aux pratiques, représentations et symboles, qu'ils soient institutionnalisés ou non.

[24] Ce schéma gellnérien est cependant vrai pour les sociétés à dominance rurale et tribale et il l'est moins pour des sociétés villageoises ou à prédominance citadine.

2. L'utopie islamiste comme aspiration à contrôler l'Etat

Les changements introduits par la modernité ont brisé les anciens rapports d'autorité à la suite des déstructurations des communautés tribales et villageoises locales soumises depuis la colonisation à l'échange marchand et l'exode rural. Les systèmes d'auto-subsistance ayant été détruits, l'individu dépend de plus en plus de l'Etat dont la politique économique a des effets directs sur sa vie quotidienne et sur l'avenir de ses enfants.[25] Or, les régimes arabes ne sont pas l'expression de contradictions internes cherchant des compromis institutionnels. Ils sont plutôt nés des antagonismes avec la domination étrangère, ce qui leur donne, paradoxalement, une indépendance par rapport à la société du fait même de leur mission, sacralisée par le discours, de défendre les intérêts de la Nation. La puissance publique – l'Etat – se comporte comme une force extérieure à la société et dont les actes sont vécus comme une fatalité par des sujets sommés de participer à l'exaltation nationale sous peine d'être soupçonnés de trahison. Ce faisant, ces régimes, nés pour la plupart du combat anti-colonial, n'ont pas la volonté de mettre en place un Etat de droit et n'ont pas la capacité d'entreprendre un développement économique et social et donc de réaliser les promesses du nationalisme radical des années 1950 et 1960. Près de cinquante ans après leur naissance, les régimes arabes ont fini par s'accommoder à l'ordre colonial qui leur fournit les ressources pour se maintenir.

Sur le plan interne, l'administration d'Etat est perçue comme un phénomène hostile vécu comme un mal nécessaire et avec qui il faut composer. L'individu utilise la débrouillardise consistant à recourir au « piston » (*el ktef*) fourni par un cousin ou une connaissance; ou encore à la corruption pour obtenir le papier nécessaire. L'existence de telles pratiques conforte l'idée que l'Etat n'est pas une puissance publique puisque la fonction administrative est utilisée par le personnel comme une position stratégique dans le circuit de la prédation des richesses. L'individu utilise et manipule les solidarités lignagères pour renégocier son rapport avec l'administration omniprésente et prédatrice. C'est parce que l'administration n'est ni neutre ni au service du public que la « culture lignagère » est mobilisée comme un moyen de pression permettant d'acquérir tel ou tel papier administratif, d'où cette apparence d'anarchie dans l'espace public dominé par la loi du plus puissant. La faiblesse de la régulation juridique incite à ne compter que sur soi-même. La société arabe donne aujourd'hui l'image d'une juxtaposition d'espaces

---

[25] C'est sur cette prémisse sociologique que A. de Tocqueville fonde la participation des administrés menacés d'êtres écrasés par le totalitarisme de l'administration.

privés sans articulation entre eux, où la règle juridique n'a pas la force politique nécessaire pour être une modalité d'arbitrage. L'appareil judiciaire, suspecté de partialité, subit la pression des détenteurs de l'autorité et de ceux qui ont les moyens de corrompre les juges. L'espace public est le théâtre de la loi du plus fort dans une situation de rareté des biens, ce qui donne aux rapports sociaux une conflictualité extrême.[26] Dans ce contexte, toutes les ressources sont utilisées, notamment la privatisation de l'Etat par les agents de la puissance publique, et le recours aux solidarités lignagères pour solliciter ou arracher ses faveurs.

Précisément, l'islamisme, en se voulant universel, condamne les pratiques lignagères (*'açabiyate*), et propose d'en libérer l'Etat en le soumettant à l'éthique religieuse. Cette utopie a gagné à elle une grande partie de la population parce que dans les sociétés non sécularisées, les attentes politiques sont formulées dans un langage religieux à travers les catégories du bien et du mal et du « nous » et « eux ». Cette hypothèse a été vérifiée durant le combat anti-colonial pour l'indépendance mené par les élites nationalistes qui ont trouvé dans l'islam une puissante idéologie mobilisatrice. L'objectif n'était pourtant pas d'islamiser le colonisateur, mais plutôt de l'expulser pour affirmer l'indépendance, malgré la propagande coloniale accusant les nationalistes de prôner le *djihad* et d'être des obscurantistes et des intolérants. La même dynamique se reproduit aujourd'hui avec l'Etat national accusé par les islamistes de tourner le dos aux attentes des populations. Aussi, il faut être attentif à la nature de l'aspiration, au-delà du langage qui la véhicule. La résurgence de l'islamisme dans les années 1980 semble être une re-naissance du populisme mis à mal par les pratiques de corruption des agents de l'administration. Ayant déserté les sphères de l'Etat, le populisme, né du combat anti-colonial, a trouvé refuge dans les mosquées où il a puisé des forces nouvelles.[27] Ces considérations imposent d'être prudents dans l'analyse politique des sociétés musulmanes, car celle-ci serait tronquée si elle ne retenait que le langage des acteurs, c'est-à-dire si elle prenait leur conscience pour la réalité de leur être social.

L'expérience algérienne est, dans cette perspective, illustrative. Du point de vue idéologique, le FIS (Front Islamique du Salut) s'inscrit dans le prolongement du FLN (Front de Libération Nationale), considérant que les idéaux de ce dernier ont été trahis par la classe dirigeante. Pour mobiliser le peuple contre la France coloniale, le FLN avait donné naissance à une utopie qui devait se concrétiser dans l'Indépendance. Vécue comme un idéal collectif, celle-ci devait

---

[26] Cf. Addi, 1999, où j'ai essayé de montrer ces tensions dans le cas algérien.
[27] J'ai développé cette thèse dans: L'Algérie et la démocratie, 1995.

établir la justice et créer l'abondance, mais quelques années après, il n'y eu ni l'une , ni l'autre, d'où le rejet de la classe dirigeante et c'est de cette déception qu'est né le FIS. Ce dernier redonne vie à l'utopie nationaliste, en affirmant que celle-ci ne s'est pas concrétisée parce que les dirigeants ont perdu la foi et qu'ils se sont écartés du message coranique; d'où la popularité du FIS, d'où la violence qu'il renferme. *Mais cette violence ne provient pas de ce qu'il se réclame de l'Islam; elle provient de ce qu'il véhicule une utopie.* La violence fait irruption dès lors que l'utopie est empêchée de se réaliser. A partir de là, tuer est un devoir nationaliste. Le FIS est une seconde naissance du FLN, refusant l'échec de l'Etat national qui a dérivé vers la corruption, l'incompétence et l'arbitraire.

Promettant une communauté unie non traversée par des divergences politiques, et représentée par un leader puissant et juste, l'idéologie populiste est réfractaire au pluralisme suspecté d'affaiblir la collectivité. Les sociétés arabes semblent encore séduites par l'utopie de l'unicité, hier nationaliste, aujourd'hui islamiste. L'unicité produit deux effets: 1. la soumission à l'Etat, pour peu que l'ordre symbolique soit respecté; et 2. la privatisation de ce dernier sur la base de la force et de la violence qui découragent tout contre-pouvoir dans des sociétés où les corps intermédiaires sont faibles pour des raisons sociologiques. L'obstacle au pluralisme est donc à rechercher dans ce populisme, présentant la communauté comme un groupe naturel puisant son unité dans le biologique fondant la fraternité de sang entre ses membres. L'utopie arabe, sous sa forme nationaliste ou islamiste, consiste à *naturaliser le social* et à refouler les divergences politiques en refusant la création d'institutions représentatives qui réguleraient ces divergences.

Ce n'est donc pas un modèle culturel hérité du passé qui reproduit le champ politique comme le suppose l'approche culturaliste. Les sociétés arabes sont confrontées à des situations nouvelles et répondent par des aspirations nouvelles, même si le langage est ancien comme l'indique l'examen de deux catégories dites culturelles, la souveraineté et la violence.

III. Souveraineté et violence: deux catégories dites culturelles

Le discours culturaliste sur le monde arabe fait souvent référence aux deux catégories de souveraineté divine et de violence politique pour donner du poids à ses arguments, posant explicitement qu'elles sont des éléments constitutifs de la culture politique insensible aux changements historiques et incompatible avec les fondements de l'Etat de droit. Mais à y regarder de près, la revendication de la souveraineté divine cherche moins à créer une théocratie qu'à soumettre les dirigeants à la *vox populi* à travers la *vox dei*, et la violence politique est un moyen de protestation dans une situation où aucune institution n'assure la fonction tribunitienne de porter la voix des plus défavorisés dans le champ de l'Etat.

1. Le contenu de la revendication de la souveraineté divine

Selon le dogme islamiste, comme dans les autres religions monothéistes, le pouvoir suprême appartient à Dieu et à lui seul. Les hommes n'ont qu'à obéir aux textes qu'il a révélés pour réaliser l'ordre juste qu'il a voulu. Le droit musulman, corpus écrit essentiellement par des hommes, à l'exception de quelque quatre vingt articles provenant directement du Coran, est une construction juridique bâtie sur la morale islamique telle qu'elle existe dans le Coran et la Sunna. Le concept de souveraineté, dans le contenu sémantique que lui donne la modernité politique, est inconnu des *fouqaha* (docteurs de la loi) pour qui l'appartenance à Dieu du pouvoir suprême relève de l'évidence. La question est de savoir s'il est légitime de traduire le pouvoir suprême par souveraineté ? C'est Abou el 'Ala Mawdudi, idéologue pakistanais formé à l'occidentale, qui traduisit le mot coranique *hakimiya* par le concept moderne de souveraineté, forgé par Jean Bodin qui l'entendait comme la faculté du Prince de promulguer et d'abroger des lois. Les hommes ont toujours et partout exercé la souveraineté au nom d'un principe méta-social (Dieu, la Monarchie, la Nature, la Nation…) même s'ils n'en avaient pas conscience. En créant les règles juridiques, les *fouqaha* se sont investis une souveraineté sur la base de leur connaissance approfondie du corpus islamique, créant ainsi une science du droit avec ses différentes branches et marquée par un esprit d'érudition. Personne à l'époque, en dehors des controverses entre eux, ne leur contestait la légitimité de produire des règles juridiques. C'est ainsi que la *chari'a* est un droit humain fortement imprégné de morale islamique; c'est un droit religieux positif issu d'une activité intellectuelle humaine.

C'est dans les années 1960 et 1970 que le slogan de la « souveraineté n'appartient qu'à Dieu » apparaît dans le langage politique pour exprimer une opposition aux régimes en place édictant des règles juridiques ayant force de loi. Des universitaires et autres journalistes déduisent que les sociétés musulmanes veulent construire une théocratie où la souveraineté est entre les mains de Dieu qui la délègue à un Imam sous le contrôle d'oulémas, docteurs de la foi. Cette vision orientaliste – et islamiste! - se limite à la lettre de la revendication et ne la lie pas à son contexte politique marqué par le néo-patrimonialisme des régimes arabes.

Ce serait une erreur de croire que les foules qui manifestent en brandissant ce slogan veulent un régime théocratique. Cette revendication *el Hakimiya li Allah* est formulée pour limiter le pouvoir de régimes autoritaires et dont le personnel est corrompu. Dieu étant assimilé à la Justice et à l'Equité, la souveraineté doit être enlevée des mains de corrompus, pense-t-on, pour être exercée par ceux qui, au nom de Dieu, rétabliront l'ordre juste. Il y a évidemment une grande part d'utopie dans cette revendication, mais il ne faut pas oublier qu'elle apparaît dans une situation politique néo-patrimoniale où le pouvoir politique est privatisé par des dynasties ou des castes militaires. La revendication de la souveraineté divine exprime une volonté dont le contenu, malgré les apparences, est démocratique, dans la mesure où la démocratie est la représentation des gouvernés dans le champ de l'Etat et le contrôle des gouvernants. Elle provient de l'aspiration des larges couches de la population de se faire entendre pour bénéficier des actions de l'Etat en matière d'emploi, de logement, d'éducation, de soins, etc.

Certes ces foules qui manifestent ne sont pas conscientes du caractère humain de la souveraineté, mais cette conscience apparaîtra avec l'apprentissage et la pratique des institutions, même si le langage lui donnera un nom spécifique. Certains islamistes, ayant pris conscience que Dieu ne gère pas directement la Cité, ont introduit une distinction sémantique entre *hakimiya*, pouvoir suprême dévolu à Dieu, et *sayada*, souveraineté humaine exercée par des hommes ayant une légitimité pour le faire, trouvant un compromis dans la formule « le pouvoir suprême (*hakimiya*) à Dieu et la souveraineté (*sayada*) au peuple ».

Le champ politique dans les sociétés arabes est en train de se construire en puisant dans la culture locale pour répondre à des problèmes nouveaux, mais les enjeux demeurent les mêmes, le pouvoir et ses modalités de légitimation. Dans ces circonstances où les règles de la compétition pour le pouvoir ne sont pas institutionnalisées, c'est-à-dire ne font pas référence à une légitimité institutionnelle faisant consensus, les protagonistes – ou certains d'entre eux – se légitiment par la ressource politique disponible: la légitimité historique ou traditionnelle, la force militaire, la légitimité religieuse... Il convient de noter que cette dernière – du fait de l'enseignement généralisé de la langue arabe chez les jeunes générations – est abondante et d'un accès facile. Ceci est un des éléments explicatifs de l'instabilité des régimes arabes tous menacés par la violence. La compétition pour le pouvoir demeurera violente et anarchique tant qu'un type de légitimité – religieuse, électorale... – n'est pas acceptée par la grande majorité. Il n'y a donc pas seulement une lutte pour le pouvoir, il y a aussi une compétition entre différentes légitimités (historique, religieuse, militaire, électorale...) qui produit un autoritarisme sous des formes traditionnelle, nationaliste, islamiste…[28]

2. *Le fondement socio-politique de la violence*

Les sociétés musulmanes sont aux prises avec cette situation historique où le pouvoir est privatisé tout comme il l'était en Europe jusqu'au XIXième siècle. La déprivatisation du pouvoir se déroule toujours dans la violence, à travers des conflits sanglants et des crises aiguës, d'où dans les pays arabes les putsch, mutineries, assassinats, émeutes …[29] La différentiation sociale, l'irruption des médias, la centralisation administrative et la nécessité de politiques économiques globales imposent la tendance inéluctable de la déprivatisation du pouvoir et l'émergence d'une conscience du caractère public de l'autorité du fait même de l'acuité des problèmes sociaux qui s'expriment dans l'espace public. Le pouvoir est jugé par l'opinion, même si cette opinion n'est pas institutionnalisée à travers la liberté de la presse, les partis, l'Assemblée nationale, etc. D'un côté, il y a un pouvoir cherchant à se maintenir coûte que coûte, et de l'autre, des demandes sociales très fortes et nombreuses qui lui sont adressées et qu'il ne peut satisfaire. D'où un mécontentement incitant les adversaires du régime à le contester. Ce dernier n'hésite pas à utiliser la violence d'Etat pour les neutraliser. La violence est un moyen de gouvernement pour dissuader ceux qui cherchent à remettre en cause le régime ou à se poser en alternative. Il y a un ressentiment à l'égard de l'Etat, et la police a pour mission d'empêcher ce ressentiment de donner naissance à une opposition institutionnelle offrant une alternative crédible au régime. Les services secrets (*el moukhabarat*) ont pour tâche de protéger le pays

---

[28] Ce n'est pas succomber au développementalisme que d'affirmer que les pays arabes vivent aujourd'hui les contradictions violentes de la construction de l'Etat. Les conditions sociologiques et culturelles de la stabilité – relative – des sytèmes politiques médiévaux musulmans n'existant plus, les pays arabes seront confrontés à la violence politique aussi longtemps qu'un mode de légitimité n'est pas accepté par l'écrasante majorité de la population. Il convient de rappeler que la modernité en Occident a pacifié, pour la première fois dans l'histoire, la compétition pour le pouvoir sur la base de la légitimité électorale avec le principe de l'alternance. Dans le long terme, il n'y a aucune raison pour que la légitimité électorale ne soit pas à la base du système politique des pays arabes, même si, comme l'a dit J.M. Keynes, dans le long terme nous serons tous morts.

[29] Cet aspect semble échapper aux lecteurs de journaux européens car ils sont habitués à un pouvoir soumis à l'alternance électorale et dont les prérogatives sont institutionnellement limitées, oubliant toutefois que cela n'a pas été toujours le cas.

contre des menées subversives étrangères mais aussi – et surtout – de protéger le régime en empêchant l'émergence d'une opposition, en ayant recours à la répression légale (arrestations, procès...) et aux techniques d'infiltration, de désinformation, de corruption... Ces pratiques menées avec les moyens inépuisables de l'Etat (armée, police, médias publics...) dans des pays où les sociétés civiles sont embryonnaires sont des ressources déterminantes pour la survie du régime et sont donc un obstacle à tout changement.

Dans ces conditions, la violence est l'expression de rapports politiques inégaux, bien qu'elle apparaît de prime abord comme faisant partie de la culture politique ou de la psychologie collective. En réalité, elle est la manifestation d'un conflit qui ne trouve pas sa solution dans les institutions mais obéit plutôt au rapport de force physique: répression policière, émeutes... L'observation empirique donne à voir que cette conflictualité manifeste est le produit d'une culture locale portée à la violence. Cette observation est d'ailleurs contradictoire car elle donne à voir aussi la fidélité des gouvernés, leur soumission voire leur apathie. L'approche culturaliste souligne soit cette soumission à l'Etat, soit son rejet violent, expliquant l'une et l'autre attitude par la culture politique ou la psychologie collective. Cependant, cette posture se limite à l'observation de phénomènes sans les relier entre eux dans une explication globale. Il est vrai que les sociétés arabes sont caractérisées par ces deux catégories, fidélité et révolte, dans leurs rapports à l'Etat. Mais la fidélité se manifeste essentiellement en cas de menace extérieure et l'esprit de révolte est présent dans la vie politique interne.

La révolte n'est pas contradictoire avec la fidélité car elle est alimentée par le désir des populations de trouver un « Prince juste » auquel elles seraient fidèles, entendant par là un régime politique qui traiterait équitablement les administrés dans le respect de l'ordre symbolique.[30] Elle est une protestation désespérée dénonçant l'incapacité de l'administration locale à satisfaire les demandes sociales les plus urgentes. Elle éclate le plus souvent quand les équilibres de la répartition des biens rares sont rompus. Ne visant pas à créer un nouvel ordre, elle cherche uniquement à rétablir les mécanismes de l'ancien ou à attirer l'attention du pouvoir central.[31] Par le passé, au Maghreb, les révoltes avaient pour théâtre les campagnes (le *bled siba*); aujourd'hui, elles éclatent dans les villes populeuses et frondeuses, hostiles aux plans d'ajustement structurel du FMI (Fonds monétaire international) incitant à la suppression des subventions

---

[30] Mounia Bennani a perçu cette contradiction lors d'une enquête menée auprès de jeunes marocains reproduite dans un livre au titre significatif: Bennani, 1994.
[31] Dès les premières années de l'indépendance de l'Algérie, Jeanne Favret avait perçu la signification politique de la révolte. Cf. Favret, 1963.

des biens de consommation courante (pain, huile, sucre, café…)[32], ce qui pousse « la rue » à manifester son hostilité à sa manière: l'apathie, les rumeurs, la raillerie, l'émeute[33]…, catégories constituant une culture politique où l'analyse sociologique montre qu'elle est un produit de l'autoritarisme plutôt que sa cause.

Caractéristiques des sociétés arabes, ces deux catégories – fidélité et révolte - structurent la relation à l'Etat, considéré comme un corps extérieur auquel les membres de la communauté nationale ne s'identifient qu'en cas de menace étrangère.[34] Aux yeux des administrés, l'Etat aurait deux fonctions: protéger la collectivité des menaces extérieures et distribuer équitablement biens et services. Les populations lui sont fidèles tant qu'il remplit la première, et elles se révoltent sporadiquement quand il faillit à la deuxième. Fidélité et révolte renvoient à deux attitudes différentes face à l'Etat, soutenu et rejeté en même temps par des populations simultanément loyales et frondeuses. Les castes militaires qui ont pris le pouvoir dans les années 1950 et 1960 (Egypte, Irak, Syrie, Algérie…) se sont inscrites dans ces deux tendances en désignant l'impérialisme occidental comme une menace à l'indépendance nationale, et en choisissant le socialisme comme modalité de distribution étatique des biens et services. L'anti-impérialisme et le socialisme ont été acceptés comme langage, pourtant d'origine marxiste, parce qu'ils correspondaient à des attentes populaires.[35]

---

[32] La révolte populaire (appelée communément « la rue » par les technocrates) constitue un moyen de pression qu'exercent les gouvernements sur le FMI effarouché par les changements de régime.

[33] Depuis avril 2001, les émeutes en Kabylie se sont données un cadre organisé (la coordination des *'arch*) pour s'inscrire dans la durée jusqu'à la satisfaction de la plate-forme d'El-Kseur, dont l'objectif est la rupture avec le régime. Deux des revendications (n° 2 et 11) contenues dans le document provoqueraient, si elles étaient satisfaites, une transition démocratique similaire à celle des anciennes dictatures communistes de l'Europe de l'Est, en ce qu'elles exigent la comparution devant des tribunaux des responsables militaires qui ont donné l'ordre de tirer sur la foule, et que toutes les fonctions d'autorité politique soient électives. Le problème est que cette révolte ne s'est pas étendue au reste de la population.

[34] La légitimité des régimes arabes nationalistes dits radicaux provient de leur discours anti-israëlien. L'existence d'Israël dans la région a favorisé la domination de castes militaires et a caché les contradictions entre les régimes et les populations flattées d'avoir des dirigeants qui rehaussent l'honneur national blessé par l'Occident. La popularité de Nasser dans les années 1950 a été bâtie sur son intransigeance verbale à l'égard d'Israël, comme les menaces américaines contre l'Irak ont rehaussé le prestige de Saddam Hussein avant sa chute.

[35] D'où le profond malentendu entretenu par le contenu idéologique de ces notions originaires de la critique philosophique du capitalisme et

Les régimes en question tirent en grande partie leur légitimité de la menace extérieure (l'Occident, Israël...) qu'ils exagèrent parce qu'elle sert leurs intérêts.[36] Les dirigeants insistent sur la première mission par des discours proclamant leur intention de défendre la nation, « menacée de l'intérieur par ceux qui exploitent les difficultés internes en critiquant l'Etat confronté à des dysfonctionnements de croissance ». L'équation à laquelle les dirigeants arabes sont confrontés est la suivante: comment continuer à s'identifier à la Nation pour s'approprier l'Etat dans un contexte où la menace intérieure est plus dangereuse que la menace extérieure? Pour s'approprier l'Etat, les dirigeants ont besoin de s'identifier à la nation dont ils se posent comme les seuls défenseurs. Par le passé, l'opposition était soupçonnée de critiquer la nation et non la politique économique et sociale du régime, d'où les violations quotidiennes des droits de l'homme à l'encontre de personnes inculpées et jugées devant des tribunaux pour « trahison, atteinte à l'unité nationale et collaboration avec des puissances étrangères »[37]. Qu'en sera-t-il dans une situation où ce discours n'est plus crédible?

Les sociétés arabes de la deuxième moitié du vingtième siècle ont produit un schéma politique où l'élite dirigeante, s'identifiant à la communauté, prétend représenter son unité. La privatisation du pouvoir procède de ce que nul n'a le droit de parler au nom de la communauté en dehors du leader. Toute autre alternative mettrait en danger l'existence de la nation; d'où la promotion d'élites dociles et de partis d'opposition – démocratisation oblige – loyaux à qui il est demandé de renoncer à conquérir le pouvoir et de se contenter de faire de la figuration afin de renforcer l'image du régime. En l'absence de débats libres pour clarifier les enjeux, l'attachement des populations à la collectivité nationale est transformé en soumission au régime.[38] Mais pour unitaire qu'il soit, ce schéma ne

---

de la propriété privée formalisée par Marx et Lénine. De ce point de vue, le socialisme arabe n'a jamais été un projet post-capitaliste; d'où la reconversion facile à l'économie de marché (*el infitah*) prônée désormais par ceux qui, hier, chantaient les vertus du secteur public.

[36] Même s'il en a tiré des aides financières substantielles, le régime égyptien a été fragilisé par la paix conclue avec Israël. Le régime de Bashar el Assad est confronté à ce même problème de perte de légitimité s'il change de politique avec Israël. Obtiendra-t-il comme l'Egypte des aides pour compenser ce qu'il aura perdu en terme de légitimité?

[37] C'est sous ce motif d'inculpation que l'universitaire égyptien Sa'd Eddine Ibrahim a été condamné à sept années de prison sans susciter un vaste mouvement de protestation dans le pays.

[38] En 1963, en Algérie, la dissidence armée du FFS en Kabylie a pris fin avec le début du conflit avec le Maroc. Les dissidents ont proclamé la fin des opérations militaires contre le régime pour rejoindre la frontière ouest du pays menacé.

prévoit aucune institution servant de canal légal à la protestation des différentes catégories de la population. Sans institutions la véhiculant (les partis légaux ne sont pas représentatifs et les élections sont truquées), la contestation prend dès lors la forme violente du coup d'Etat militaire et des émeutes.

Bibliographie

Addi, Lahouari (1995): L'Algérie et la démocratie, La Découverte.
Addi, Lahouari (1997): Political Islam and Democracy, dans: Adenius, H. (ed.): Democracy's Victory and Crisis, Cambridge University Press.
Addi, Lahouari (1999): Les mutations de la société algérienne, La Découverte.
Almond, Gabriel (1956): Comparative Political Systems, dans: The Journal of Politics 18.
Almond, Gabriel/Verba, Sidney (1965): The Civic Culture, Princeton University Press.
Almond, Gabriel (1980): The Civic Culture Revisited, Princeton University Press.
Baczko, Bronislaw (1984): Les imaginaires sociaux, Payot.
Badie, Bertrand (1993): Culture et politique, Economica.
Barakat, Halim (1990): Beyond the Always and the Never – A Critique of Social Psychological Interpretations of Arab Society and Culture, dans: Sharabi, Hisham (ed.): Theory, Politics and the Arab World – Critical Responses, London/New York, Routledge.
Bennani, Mounia (1994): Soumis et rebelles – Les jeunes au Maroc, Paris, Editions du CNRS.
Berger, Peter L. (1967): The Sacred Canopy. Elements of a Sociological Theory of Religion, Doubleday.
Burgat, François (1995): L'islamisme en face, La Découverte.
Cefaï, Daniel, (ed.) (2001): Cultures politiques, PUF.
Cuche, Denys (2001): La notion de culture dans les sciences sociales, La Découverte.
Easton, David (1974): Analyse du système politique, Paris, A. Colin.
Favret, Jeanne (1963): La tradition par excès de modernité, Revue française de sociologie.
Hudson, M. Michael C. (1995): The Political Cultural Approach to Arab Democratisation – The Case for Bringing It Back In, Carefully, dans: Brynen, R./Korany, B. /Noble, P. (eds.): Political Liberalization and Democratisation in the Arab World, vol. 1, Lynne Rienner Publishers.
Lewis, Bernard (1987): Le langage politique de l'Islam, Paris, Gallimard.

Parsons, Talcott (1967): Sociological Theory and Modern Society, New York, The Free Press.
Parsons, Talcott (1973): Societés! Essai sur leur évolution comparée, Paris, Dunod.
Pataï, Raphael (1973): The Arab Mind, New York, Charles' Scribner's Sons.
Rioux, Jean-Pierre/Sirinelli, Jean-François (1997): Pour une histoire culturelle, Seuil.
Schemeil, Yves (1985): Les cultures politiques, dans: Grawitz, M./Leca, J.: Traité de Science Politique, PUF, vol. 2.
Sharabi, Hisham (1985): Le néo-patriarcat, Gallimard.

Themenhefte

- 53 Rotes China Global
- 52 Deutsche Ostpolitik
- 51 Geheime Dienste
- 50 Kerniges Europa
- 49 Militär in Lateinamerika
- 48 Internet Macht Politik
- 47 Europäische Arbeitspolitik
- 46 Globale Finanzmärkte
- 45 Von Dynastien und Demokratien
- 44 Modernisierung und Islam
- 43 Großmächtiges Deutschland
- 42 Europäische Außenpolitik
- 41 Transatlantische Perspektiven II
- 40 Transatlantische Perspektiven
- 39 Wohlfahrt und Demokratie
- 38 Politisierung von Ethnizität
- 37 Vergelten, vergeben oder vergessen?
- 36 Gender und IB
- 35 Krieg im 21. Jahrhundert
- 34 EU-Osterweiterung im Endspurt?
- 33 Entwicklungspolitik
- 32 Balkan - Pulverfaß oder ... ?
- 31 Recht in der Transformation
- 30 Fundamentalismus
- 29 Die autoritäre Herausforderung
- 28 Deutsche Eliten und Außenpolitik
- 27 10 Jahre Transformation in Polen
- 26 (Ab-)Rüstung 2000
- 25 Dezentralisierung & Entwicklung
- 24 Wohlfahrtsstaaten im Vergleich
- 23 Kooperation im Ostseeraum
- 22 Die Ostgrenze der EU
- 21 Neue deutsche Außenpolitik?
- 20 Demokratie in China?
- 19 Deutsche und Tschechen
- 18 Technokratie
- 17 Die Stadt als Raum und Akteur
- 16 Naher Osten
- 15 Identitäten in Europa
- 14 Afrika - Jenseits des Staates
- 13 Deutschland und Polen
- 12 Globaler Kulturkampf?
- 11 Europa der Regionen
- 10 NATO-Osterweiterung
- 9 Gewalt und Politik
- 8 Reform der UNO
- 7 Integration im Pazifik
- 6 Zerfall von Imperien
- 5 Migration
- 4 Geopolitik
- 3 Realer Post-Sozialismus
- 2 Chaos Europa
- 1 Neue Weltordnung

http://www.welttrends.de
E-Mail: bestellung@welttrends.de

*Benjamin Stachursky**

Globale Normen, lokaler Aktivismus
Advocacy NGOs und die Sozialisierung der Menschenrechte von Frauen am Beispiel Ägyptens

Im Laufe der 1990er Jahre hat sich auf der internationalen Ebene ein Verständnis von Frauenrechten als Menschenrechten als zentraler Bezugsrahmen für Bemühungen zur Ermächtigung von Frauen durchgesetzt und gefestigt. Einen wesentlichen Beitrag zu dieser Entwicklung haben NGOs und Aktivistinnen aus allen Regionen der Welt in ihrer Rolle als '*norm-entrepreneurs*' (Finnemore/Sikkink 1998) auf der internationalen Ebene gespielt. Durch einen Prozess der transnationalen Vernetzung und Professionalisierung dieser Organisationen im Zusammenhang mit den UN-Weltkonferenzen der 1990er Jahre konnte mit Blick auf die Normsetzung im Bereich der Menschenrechte von Frauen auf internationaler Ebene eine beeindruckende Erfolgsgeschichte geschrieben werden (Neuhold 1995). Keine vergleichbaren Erfolge für die Frauenrechtsbewegung lassen sich jedoch bis heute bei der nationalen Umsetzung dieser Normen erkennen. So muss man weiterhin eine extreme Diskrepanz zwischen ihrer Verankerung auf zwischenstaatlicher Ebene einerseits und der tatsächlichen Verbesserung der konkreten Lebensbedingungen von Frauen auf der nationalen Ebene andererseits feststellen (*Human Rights Watch* 1995; UNIFEM 2002; Khagram/Riker/Sikkink 2002).

Der Internalisierung und Umsetzung internationaler Normen auf nationaler Ebene ist in den vergangenen Jahren im Bereich der Internationalen Beziehungen (IB) zunehmend Aufmerksamkeit gewidmet worden. Hierbei wurden insbesondere konstruktivistische Erklärungsansätze genutzt, um die zentrale Rolle von NGOs und ihrer transnationalen Netzwerke bei solchen Sozialisierungsprozessen, die zu einer Veränderung des Verhaltens normverletzender Akteure beitragen, zu beleuchten und zu problematisieren. Im Bereich der Menschenrechte sind diese Ansätze vorrangig anhand empirischer Fallstudien zur Sozialisierung internationaler Normen durch staatliche Akteure geprüft worden. Wenig Aufmerksamkeit wurde jedoch einer weiteren zentralen Dimension der Arbeit dieser Organisationen gewidmet – nämlich solche Aktivitäten, bei denen die Zivil-

---

* Für wertvolle Anmerkungen zu diesem Beitrag danke ich Dr. Armin Triebel und Dr. Anna Holzscheiter.

gesellschaft nicht nur das ‚Terrain', sondern auch das ‚Ziel' der Arbeit von NGOs darstellt (Uvin 2000). Angesichts der ‚privaten Natur' eines bedeutenden Teils der Verstöße gegen die Menschenrechte der Frauen stellt gerade die auf gesellschaftlichen Wandel abzielende Arbeit einen zentralen Aspekt von Bemühungen zur Verbesserung des Status' der Frauen dar. Dieser Beitrag richtet daher seine Aufmerksamkeit primär auf die Rolle von NGOs auf diesem Gebiet.

Während Frauen in allen Regionen der Welt geschlechtsspezifischen Formen der Diskriminierung ausgesetzt sind, stellt dieses Phänomen in den Ländern des Nahen und Mittleren Ostens (MENA) ein besonders akutes Problem dar (UNDP 2002).[1] Dies lässt sich zum einen an einem besonders hohen Grad der rechtlichen und sozialen Diskriminierung von Frauen, zum andern an einer breiten politischen und sozialen Resistenz gegenüber Bemühungen zur Verbesserung des Status' von Frauen aufweisen (Nazir 2005). Ägypten, welches in vieler Hinsicht als „Trendsetter" (Perthes 2002) in der Region gilt, stellt hier keine Ausnahme dar. Zwar konnten im Verlauf der letzten Jahre einige Fortschritte beim ‚*Empowerment*' von Frauen registriert werden, doch bleiben sie in vielen Bereichen des öffentlichen Lebens und in besonderem Maße in der privaten Sphäre weitreichenden Formen der Diskriminierung ausgesetzt.

Ägypten kann auf eine langjährige Tradition von zivilgesellschaftlichem Aktivismus zur Verbesserung des Status' der Frauen zurückblicken. Bereits im Verlauf der 1920er Jahre entstanden erste unabhängige Frauenorganisationen. In engem Zusammenhang mit den eingangs genannten Entwicklungen auf der internationalen Ebene ist in Ägypten (wie auch in der gesamten MENA-Region) insbesondere während der 1990er Jahre ein quantitativer und qualitativer Umbruch zu beobachten, der u.a. zur Herausbildung von „*advocacy* NGOs" als neuen Formen von organisiertem Aktivismus beigetragen hat. Viele dieser Organisationen sehen in einem spezifischen, menschenrechtszentrierten Diskurs den Bezugsrahmen ihrer Arbeit, die stark auf verschiedenen Formen der transnationalen Interaktion aufbaut. Hierdurch haben sich, wie im Folgenden beschrieben wird, einerseits wichtige neue Handlungsmöglichkeiten, andererseits aber auch neue Herausforderungen für die beteiligten Akteure ergeben (Würth 2003).

---

[1] Die Verfasser des von UNDP 2002 erstmals herausgegebenen *Arab Human Development Report* zählen tiefgreifende Defizite in der Ermächtigung der Frauen zu den zentralen Problemen in den Ländern der MENA-Region.

Unter Berücksichtigung solcher Entwicklungen, soll dieser Beitrag auf die mögliche Rolle ägyptischer *advocacy* NGOs und ihrer transnationalen Netzwerke bei der Sozialisierung internationaler Frauenrechtsnormen auf einer breiten gesellschaftlichen Ebene eingehen. Gefragt wird hierbei, ob diese NGOs, besonders durch ihre auf die Zivilgesellschaft abzielenden Tätigkeiten, auf diesem Gebiet als Vermittler zwischen internationalen Normen einerseits und den lokalen Werten und Normen andererseits fungieren, ob und in welchem Ausmaß sie hierdurch sozialen Wandel auf einer breiten gesellschaftlichen Ebene beeinflussen können und ob sich Prozesse der Transnationalisierung, wie sie bei den hier besprochenen Organisationen zu beobachten sind, eher fördernd oder eher hemmend auf ihre Arbeit im Bereich der Menschenrechte von Frauen vor Ort auswirken.

Zur Beantwortung dieser Fragen werden im folgenden Abschnitt zunächst einige zentrale Merkmale internationaler Frauenrechtsstandards hervorgehoben. Darauf aufbauend befasst sich Kapitel 2 anhand einiger Bereiche exemplarisch mit dem rechtlichen und sozialen Staus von Frauen in Ägypten. Kapitel 3 leitet über zu den Aktivitäten von *advocacy* NGOs im Bereich der Frauenrechte. Es werden zunächst (4.) die Strukturen dieser NGOs und die zentralen Debatten über ihren gesellschaftlichen und politischen Status beleuchtet sowie (5.) die rechtlichen und sozialen Rahmenbedingungen für deren Arbeit diskutiert. Anschließend werden sowohl Probleme und Erfolge ihrer lokalen Arbeit (6.) als auch ihrer Aktivitäten zur transnationalen Vernetzung (7.) eingehend erörtert. Abschließend werden zentrale Schlussfolgerungen zu Möglichkeiten und Grenzen der NGO-Arbeit in Ägypten gezogen, und es wird auf weiterführende Fragestellungen hingewiesen.

1. Menschenrechte von Frauen: Internationale Normen und lokaler Kontext

Die Etablierung des Verständnisses von Frauenrechten als Menschenrechtsnormen auf der internationalen Ebene gilt als tiefgreifender Prozess der Transformation des vorherrschenden Menschenrechtsverständnisses und ist eng mit einer zentralen normativen Innovation verbunden – der Aufhebung der strikten analytischen Trennung zwischen öffentlicher und privater Sphäre (Holthaus 1996). In der Tat handelt es sich bei einem bedeutenden Teil der Verletzungen der Menschenrechte von Frauen um sogenannte ‚*private wrongs*', also solche Verletzungen, die nicht auf Handlungen staatlicher, sondern privater Akteure zurückzuführen sind. Die Anerkennung solcher geschlechtsspezifischer Verletzungen hat daher maßgeblich dazu beigetragen, dass die Agenda der Menschenrechte, welche traditionell auf die vertikale Ebene des Verhältnisses zwischen Staat und Individuum begrenzt war, auf die horizontale Ebene des Verhältnisses zwischen Individuen, der Gemeinschaft und der Familie ausgeweitet wurde. Somit konnte solchen Verletzungen auf der horizontalen Ebene ‚Sichtbarkeit' auf der internationalen Ebene verschafft werden (Tomasevski 1998).

Während die Diskriminierung von Frauen mit einer Vielzahl politischer, ökonomischer und sozialer Faktoren im Zusammenhang steht, wird dem Faktor Kultur in der Literatur häufig eine übergeordnete Rolle zugeschrieben und hierbei auf vielfältige Formen kultureller Resistenz gegenüber Veränderungen des Status' der Frauen hingewiesen (Friedrich-Ebert-Stiftung 2002). Das Verhältnis zwischen internationalen Normen einerseits und nationalen kulturellen/religiösen Normen und Werten andererseits ist somit von Relevanz. In der Tat dient nicht selten die Behauptung, die Beziehung zwischen Frauenrechten und traditionellen und/oder religiösen Normen sei ein Problem, dazu, die Begründung, Akzeptanz und somit die Realisierbarkeit internationaler Standards auf einer breiten gesellschaftlichen Ebene infrage zu stellen. Entsprechend werden Veränderungen der Stellung der Frau oft als gesellschaftlicher Verfallsprozess oder als Prozess der ‚Verwestlichung' dargestellt (Rao 1995). So sehen sich moderne Kampagnen für Frauenrechte immer wieder mit Vorwürfen des kulturellen Imperialismus konfrontiert – hierbei vor allem mit dem Vorwurf, dass es sich bei diesen Bemühungen um unangemessene Versuche handele, westliche Werte und Kultur Gesellschaften aufzuzwingen, die hierzu weder einen Bezug haben, noch davon profitieren (Sikkink 2001). Angesichts der starken Formen politischer, aber gerade auch sozialer Widerstände gegenüber Maßnahmen des *Empowerment* von Frauen weisen viele Experten darauf hin, dass neben der gesetzlichen Verankerung von Reformschritten der Veränderung gesellschaftlichen Bewusstseins zentrale Relevanz zukommt. Solch ein tiefgreifender Wandel im Geschlechterverständnis in der politischen, gesellschaftlichen und familiären Sphäre scheint insbesondere dann notwendig, wenn eine weitreichende und dauerhafte Verbesserung des Status' der Frauen in der öffentlichen wie in der privaten Sphäre erlangt werden soll:

„Regardless of all the international standards and accompanying national legislation, unless there is resonance in national civil society, there is little scope for real transformation. Although international civil society has been active in the field of women's rights, at the national level, when it comes to family and community in many countries, civil society is much more conservative." (Coomaraswamy 1997)

Auch in Ägypten gehören bis heute Debatten über die ‚Frauenfrage' zu den politischen und sozialen Themen, die am stärksten kontrovers sind. Hierbei handelt es sich keineswegs nur um juristische oder philosophische Debatten zwischen Eliten, sondern in der ganzen Gesellschaft um sehr emotional geführte Auseinandersetzungen über grundsätzliche Werte, das Verständnis von Moralität oder gesellschaftlicher Ordnung (Katulis 2005).

Nachdem im folgenden Abschnitt anhand einiger Bereiche exemplarisch auf den rechtlichen und sozialen Staus von Frauen in Ägypten eingegangen wird, wendet sich der restliche Teil des Beitrags der Arbeit ägyptischer Frauen- und Menschenrechts-NGOs zu, die in diesem Kontext mit verschiedenen Strategien und unter Rückgriff auf internationale Menschenrechtsstandards zur Verbesserung der Stellung der Frauen beizutragen versuchen.

2. Rechtlicher und sozialer Status von Frauen in Ägypten

Die ägyptische Verfassung aus dem Jahr 1971 legt die Gleichheit zwischen Männern und Frauen fest: „*Citizens are equal before the law. They have equal rights and duties regardless of sex, origin, language, religion or belief.*"[2] Die Garantie der Gleichberechtigung, wie sie auch in Artikel 11 für den politischen, ökonomischen, sozialen und kulturellen Bereich festgelegt ist, wird jedoch mit Hinweis auf das Sharia-Recht aufgeweicht.[3] Auf internationaler Ebene hat Ägypten 1981 als erstes arabisches Land die UN-Frauenrechtskonvention CEDAW ratifiziert, diesen Schritt jedoch mit substantiellen Vorbehalten (‚*reservations*') zu den Artikeln 2, 9/2, 16 und 29/1 verknüpft (*Egyptian NGO Coalition on CEDAW* 2000).[4]

---

[2] Art. 40, *Constitution of the Arab Republic of Egypt*. Siehe: http://www.egypt.gov.eg/english/laws/Constitution

[3] Unter Sadat wurde 1980 Artikel 2 der Verfassung geändert und Sharia-Recht von ‚*einer*' zu ‚*der*' Quelle der Verfassung zu gemacht. Würth weist jedoch darauf hin, dass der Verfassungsrang des islamischen Rechts per se nicht die Diskriminierung der Frau nach sich ziehe. Vielmehr sei die Auslegung dieser Artikel durch die entsprechenden Gerichte ausschlaggebend und müsse daher im Einzelfall untersucht werden (Würth 2003: 53f.).

[4] Der Gleichheitsgrundsatz in Art. 2 ist mit Hinweis auf die Inhalte des Sharia-Gesetzes mit einem generellen Vorbehalt belegt; der Vorbehalt gegen Art. 9/2 richtet sich gegen die Verleihung der Staatsbürgerschaft an Kinder mit ägyptischer Mutter und nicht-ägyptischem Vater (das entsprechende ägyptische Gesetz 26/1975 wurde jedoch 2004 geändert (Leila 2004)); Art. 16 befasst sich mit dem Personenstandsrecht und wird ebenfalls mit Hinweis auf Sharia-Recht eingeschränkt; durch den Vorbehalt zu Art. 29/1 lehnt die

Trotz des in der Verfassung verankerten Gleichheitsgebots, der internationalen Verpflichtungen der ägyptischen Regierung durch den Beitritt zu CEDAW sowie mancher Fortschritte während der letzten Jahre lassen sich in der Praxis weiterhin deutliche Elemente der Benachteiligung von Frauen im rechtlichen, politischen und sozio-ökonomischen Bereich aufweisen: „Überspitzt könnte man formulieren, dass Verfassungsartikel, die die Gleichheit von Männern und Frauen formulieren, sich im Prinzip auf die ‚öffentliche' Sphäre beschränken, vor allem auf die Gleichheit in Ausübung des Wahlrechts, im Recht auf Gesundheit und Ausbildung usw." (Würth 2003: 53) Während somit formal im öffentlichen Bereich Frauen und Männer gleichgestellt sind, weisen Gesetze, welche die private Sphäre betreffen, vor allem das Personenstandsrecht, eine deutliche Benachteiligung von Frauen auf. Über den gesetzlichen Rahmen hinaus wirken sich – sowohl in der öffentlichen wie in der privaten Sphäre – eine Reihe an Faktoren im Alltag erschwerend auf die Umsetzung der Rechte von Frauen aus (Zaki 1995).

Die fortdauernd schlechte ökonomische Lage gehört zu den zentralen Problembereichen des Landes und wirkt sich auf die Lebenssituation breiter Bevölkerungsschichten aus.[5] Hinzu kommen die Auswirkungen des bereits in den 1970er Jahren begonnenen wirtschaftlichen Liberalisierungskurses und der ab 1991 in Zusammenarbeit mit Weltbank (WB) und Internationalem Währungsfond (IWF) durchgeführten *Economic Reform and Structural Adjustment Programmes* (ERSAPs), die beide maßgeblich zu einem Rückzug des Staates aus zentralen wirtschaftlichen und sozialen Bereichen geführt haben. Wie unten näher ausgeführt wird, ist der Status von Frauen hiervon in besonderem Maße betroffen (El-Baz 1997).[6] Als weiterer Faktor werden gemeinhin die im gesamten politischen und

---

ägyptische Regierung die Regelung zur Beilegung von Streitigkeiten über die Auslegung des Vertragswerks durch ein Schiedsverfahren ab, da dies als Beeinträchtigung der eigenen Souveränität gewertet wird (Zum Ratifikationsstatus von CEDAW siehe: www.ohchr.org/english/countries/ratification/8_1.htm [10.12.2005]). Besonders kritisch werden von Experten die Vorbehalte zu den Artikeln 2 und 16 gewertet: „*Such reservations are inconsistent with the object and purpose of the treaties, and as such, with Egypt's international obligation to work to modify and eliminate religious and cultural norms that foster inequality.*" (Human Rights Watch 2004: 3)

[5] Nach UN-Schätzungen leben heute 16,7% der Bevölkerung unter der Armutsgrenze (El-Azhary Sonbol 2005: 70).

[6] Es ist anzumerken, dass die ERSAPs maßgeblich zur Vertiefung der Kluft zwischen Stadt- und Landbevölkerung, Arm und Reich beigetragen haben. Je nach Klassenzugehörigkeit hat sich somit die wirtschaftliche Liberalisierungspolitik unterschiedlich auf den Status von Frauen ausgewirkt.

gesellschaftlichen System stark ausgeprägten patriarchalen Strukturen gesehen (Seif El Dawla/Abdel Hadi/Abdel Wahab 1998: 75-77). Die Auswirkungen dieser Strukturen stehen heute im engen Zusammenhang mit einer zunehmenden Erstarkung religiös-konservativer Kräfte, die maßgeblich zu einer ‚Islamisierung' des öffentlichen Diskurses und der Verbreitung eines konservativen Frauenbildes beitragen (Karam 1998; Raouf Ezzat 2001; Seif El Dawla 1996).

Im Folgenden soll anhand einiger Beispiele gezeigt werden, inwiefern die oben genannten Umstände sich auf die gegenwärtige Situation von Frauen in Ägypten auswirken und de facto zu ihrer Stellung als Bürgerinnen zweiter Klasse beitragen.

Obwohl Frauen bereits seit 1956 über das aktive und passive Wahlrecht verfügen und schon in der ersten Hälfte des 20. Jahrhunderts aktiv am ägyptischen Unabhängigkeitskampf beteiligt waren, ist der Grad politischer Partizipation und Repräsentanz von Frauen heute sehr niedrig: „*The gender gap in illiteracy, education and employment, in addition to the predominant local culture, which discourages women's participation in politics, play an important role in maintaining quite a significant gender gap in political participation.*" (Zulficar 2003) So waren im Jahr 2000 nur 35% der Frauen in die Wahllisten eingetragen (*National Council for Women* 2002: 61) und der Prozentsatz weiblicher Parlamentarierinnen beläuft sich für das Erste Haus (*People's Assembly*) auf 2,4% und auf 5,7% für das Zweite Haus (*Shura Council*) (CAPMAS 2000, zit. in: Zulficar 2003). Auf lokaler und kommunaler Ebene liegt die Quote von weiblichen Abgeordneten mit durchschnittlich 1,2% noch niedriger.[7]

Obwohl Verfassung und bestehende Gesetze im Arbeitsrecht die Gleichheit der Geschlechter bei Einstellung, Kündigung und Gehaltszahlung garantieren, bestehen in der Praxis starke Diskrepanzen. Trotz einer steigenden Partizipation haben Frauen bis heute nur einen begrenzten Zugang zum Arbeitsmarkt – der Frauenanteil am Arbeitsmarkt beträgt 30%[8] – und ein bedeutender Anteil der Frauen arbeitet im informellen Sektor und verfügt somit über keine Form der sozialen Absicherung (*World Bank* 2003). Die weibliche Arbeitslosenquote liegt bei 22,7%, die männliche beträgt 5,1%.[9] Mit

---

[7] *Ministry of Local Administration, Councils and Legal Affairs*, 1997 (Zit. in: *National Council for Women* 2002: 63).
[8] Von diesen Frauen arbeiten 39% im landwirtschaftlichen, 7% im industriellen und 54% im Dienstleistungsbereich. Siehe: http://devdata.worldbank.org/genderstats/genderRpt.asp?rpt=profile&cty=EGY,Egypt,%20Arab%2Rep.&hm=ome [10.12.2005].
[9] Siehe: http://devdata.worldbank.org/genderstats/genderRpt.asp?rpt=profile&cty=EGY,Egypt,%20Arab%2Rep.&hm=ome [10.12.2005].

Recht wird von einem Trend hin zu einer *„feminization of unemployment"* gesprochen (El-Azhary Sonbol 2005: 77). Auch bei der Bezahlung bestehen in der Praxis starke Formen der Diskriminierung.[10] Darüber hinaus sehen sich viele Frauen mit einem wachsenden gesellschaftlichen Druck zu einer Rückkehr in die häusliche Sphäre konfrontiert. Ein verbreitetes Argument hierbei ist, dass angesichts der angespannten Arbeitsmarktlage Männern, den eigentlichen Ernährern der Familien, Vorrang gegeben werden müsse. Auch fördert die starke Islamisierung des öffentlichen Diskurses zunehmend eine Rückkehr zu einem konservativen Verständnis der Geschlechterrollen, das Frauen primär eine Rolle als Mütter und Hausfrauen zuschreibt. Gleichzeitig aber drängt weiterhin eine hohe Anzahl an Frauen auf den Arbeitsmarkt, da viele Familien vor der Notwendigkeit stehen, über zwei Einkommen zu verfügen, um im Alltag die finanziellen Nöte zu meistern (Jürgensen 2004).

Artikel 18 der Verfassung garantiert die gleiche Behandlung von Jungen und Mädchen in der Bildung und schreibt die Grundschulpflicht vor. Im Verlauf der letzten Jahre konnten auf diesem Gebiet, dem sowohl von Entwicklungs- und Gender-Experten als auch von der breiten Öffentlichkeit eine zentrale Rolle bei der Verbesserung des Status' der Frauen beigemessen wird (UNDP 2002), wichtige Fortschritte erzielt werden. Trotzdem bleibt weiterhin eine deutliche Kluft zwischen den Geschlechtern zu erkennen. Die Analphabetenrate in der weiblichen Bevölkerung konnte beispielsweise zwischen 1980 und 2000 von 75.3% auf 56,2% reduziert werden, ist aber immer noch deutlich höher als die der männlichen Population (33,4% im Jahr 2000). Ähnlich verhält es sich bei der Rate der Grundschulabschlüsse unter den ägyptischen Frauen, die von 70% im Jahr 1990 auf 88% im Jahr 2000 verbessert werden konnte, aber ebenfalls hinter der männlichen Rate von 93% im Jahr 2000 zurückbleibt.[11] Mit 48% sind fast die Hälfte der eingeschriebenen Studierenden an ägyptischen Universitäten heute Frauen[12], was als gute Ausgangsposition für zukünftige Fortschritte im Bereich der Bildung gewertet wird.

Das Personenstandsrecht (Ehe, Scheidung, Sorgerecht und Erbschaft) gehört hinsichtlich der Diskriminierung von Frauen zu den

---

[10] Nach Schätzungen von UNDP betrug im Jahr 2000 das Durchschnittseinkommen von Frauen 2003 US$ verglichen mit 5227 US$ bei Männern (Zit. in: El-Azhary Sonbol 2005: 77).
[11] Siehe: http://devdata.worldbank.org/genderstats/genderRpt.asp?rpt= profile&cty=EGY,Egypt,%20Arab%2Rep.&hm=ome [10.12.2005].
[12] University *Supreme Council, University Education Development Center, Statistical Administration* 2000/2001(Zit. in: *National Council for Women* 2002: 18).

problematischsten Bereichen des ägyptischen Rechtssystems. Im Gegensatz zu anderen Teilen des ägyptischen Rechts beruht das für den muslimischen Bevölkerungsteil[13] gültige Personenstandsrecht vorrangig auf dem islamischen Sharia-Recht. Die zum Teil noch aus Gesetz 25 aus dem Jahr 1920 stammenden Bestimmungen haben sich als besonders resistent gegenüber Reformversuchen erwiesen und stehen in starkem Kontrast zu der Realität der heutigen ägyptischen Gesellschaft (*Human Rights Watch* 2004).[14] Als positives Element in diesem Rechtsgebiet kann das im Januar 2000 verabschiedete sogenannte *Khul'*-Gesetz gewertet werden, welches Frauen die Scheidung ohne Zustimmung des Ehemannes ermöglicht, sofern sie auf materielle Ansprüche gegenüber ihrem Mann verzichten (*Human Rights Watch* 2004).[15] Als Fortschritt kann auch die Einrichtung von Familiengerichten im Oktober 2004 betrachtet werden, welche zu einer Beschleunigung und Vereinfachung gerichtlicher Verfahren in diesem Bereich beitragen sollen (*Human Rights Watch* 2004). Die ungleiche Behandlung von Frauen in Gesetz und Praxis im Personenstandsrecht bleibt jedoch bestehen. Gerade das Scheidungsrecht beinhaltet bis heute deutliche Elemente der Diskriminierung von Frauen und wirkt sich auf vielfältige Bereiche ihres Lebens aus. Ebenso bleiben die Auslegung und Anwendung bestehender Gesetze – auch weit über den Bereich des Scheidungsrechtes hinaus – durch (männliche) Richter stark von patriarchalen Strukturen geprägt (*Human Rights Watch* 2004). Obwohl Ende 2002 die erste Frau zur Richterin (des Obersten Verfassungsgerichts) berufen wurde, bleibt in der Tat das gesamte Rechtssystem bislang Frauen weitgehend verschlossen (*Human Rights Watch* 2004).

Als letztes Gebiet, auf dem die Menschenrechte von Frauen als besonders gefährdet angesehen werden müssen, soll hier auf Gewalt gegen Frauen eingegangen werden. Gewalt gegen Frauen stellt ein ernstes und weit verbreitetes Problem in der ägyptischen Gesell-

---

[13] Das Personenstandsrecht für nicht-muslimische Bürgerinnen und Bürger wie beispielsweise koptische Christen, die ca. 10% der Bevölkerung ausmachen, wird von Bestimmungen der eigenen Glaubensrichtung geregelt.
[14] Vor den Reformschritten der letzten Jahre wurde Gesetz 25/1920 bereits durch das Gesetz 25/1929 und das Gesetz 100/1985 verändert. Gesetz 44/1979, ein weiterer unter Sadat unternommener Reformversuch, wurde 1985 durch das Oberste Verfassungsgericht aufgrund formaler Mängel außer Kraft gesetzt.
[15] Kritiker des Gesetzes weisen jedoch darauf hin, dass diese Form der Scheidung nur wohlhabenden Frauen zugute komme, da es sich der größte Anteil der Frauen nicht leisten könne, auf diese materiellen Ansprüche zu verzichten (*Human Rights Watch* 2004).

schaft dar. Zwar liegen nur sehr wenige offizielle Statistiken in diesem Bereich vor, doch gehen Frauenrechtsorganisationen davon aus, dass Frauen in der häuslichen wie in der öffentlichen Sphäre vielfachen Formen der Gewalt, von verbaler Belästigung bis hin zu Vergewaltigung und ‚Ehrenmorden', ausgesetzt sind.[16] Ein wichtiger rechtlicher Fortschritt wurde hier mit der Aufhebung des Artikels 291 des Strafrechts durch das Parlament im Jahr 1999 erzielt. Artikel 291 ermöglichte es einem Vergewaltiger, der Strafe für sein Verbrechen zu entgehen, sofern er sein Opfer heiratete (Zulficar 2003). Vergewaltigung in der Ehe stellt hingegen bis heute keine Straftat dar (Benninger-Budel 2001). Gewalt gegen Frauen wird weiterhin von staatlichen Institutionen wie der Polizei und Gerichten nur selten verfolgt. Auch neigen breite Teile der Gesellschaft – darunter nicht selten die Familien der Opfer sowie viele Opfer selbst – dazu, insbesondere häusliche Gewalt gegen Frauen zu verharmlosen und zu rechtfertigen (*National Council for Women* 2002). Obwohl das Ministerium für soziale Angelegenheiten inzwischen 150 Familienberatungszentren eingerichtet hat, haben die meisten Opfer von Gewalt gegen Frauen bis heute nur sehr begrenzten Zugang zu rechtlicher, psychologischer und sozialer Unterstützung (*Human Rights Watch* 2004).

Eine der wohl verbreitetsten Formen der Gewalt gegen Frauen stellt die weibliche Genitalverstümmelung (*female genital mutilation*, FGM) dar. Laut offizieller Statistiken sind heute über 95% der ägyptischen Frauen beschnitten, 75% der Frauen sprechen sich für die Weiterführung der Praxis aus, 61% der Frauen gehen davon aus, dass Männer FGM beibehalten wollen und 11% der Frauen sprechen sich gegen die Weiterführung der Praxis aus (*National Council for Women* 2002). Politisch und gesellschaftlich ist das Thema besonders seit 1994 in die öffentliche Debatte vorgedrungen, nachdem CNN während der UN-Weltbevölkerungskonferenz (ICPD) in Kairo eine Dokumentation über FGM in Ägypten mit Filmaufnahmen einer Beschneidung gesendet hatte. Das Thema wird seitdem vehement und kontrovers auf allen gesellschaftlichen Ebenen diskutiert (Katulis 2004). Nachdem das Kassationsgericht im Dezember 1997 die Rechtmäßigkeit eines Dekrets des Gesundheitsministers aus dem Jahr 1996 bestätigt hat, ist die Durchführung von FGM für ärztliches und nicht-ärztliches Personal offiziell verboten.[17]

---

[16] Aus einer Umfrage der NGO *Center for Egyptian Women's Legal Assistance* (CEWLA) geht hervor, dass 67% der Frauen im städtischen und 30% der Frauen im ländlichen Bereich im Zeitraum 2002-2003 mindestens einmal von Formen häuslicher Gewalt betroffen waren (Zit. in: El-Azhary Sonbol 2005: 74).

[17] Nach der ICPD wurde durch ein Dekret des Gesundheitsministers die Durchführung von FGM allein Ärzten erlaubt. Aufgrund des großen nationalen und internationalen Protests gegen die „Verärztlichung" des

Trotz landesweiter Initiativen zur Bekämpfung von FGM durch staatliche wie nicht-staatliche Akteure bleibt die Praxis bis heute jedoch weit verbreitet.[18]

3. Die ‚Frauenfrage' und organisierte Formen des Aktivismus in Ägypten

Bemühungen einzelner Persönlichkeiten, Frauen den Zugang zur öffentlichen Sphäre zu ermöglichen, lassen sich in Ägypten bis weit ins 19. Jahrhundert zurückverfolgen. 1923 wurde die erste ägyptische, unabhängige Frauenorganisation, die *Egyptian Feminist Union* (EFU), gegründet, die sich im Rahmen des nationalen Unabhängigkeitskampfes für die politische, soziale und rechtliche Gleichheit ägyptischer Frauen einsetzte. Im Laufe der folgenden drei Jahrzehnte entstanden mehrere Frauenorganisationen, die ebenfalls ihre Anstrengungen für die Befreiung der Frauen im Rahmen eines breiteren politischen anti-kolonialen Kampfes führten (*New Woman Research & Study Center* 1996).

Mit der Revolution von 1952 und der Machtübernahme Nassers setzte eine Politik der strikten Kontrolle politischer und sozialer Oppositionskräfte ein, von der alle Parteien und unabhängigen Organisationen betroffen waren. Im Zuge dieser Politik wurden bereits 1956 die meisten politisch aktiven Frauenorganisationen aufgelöst. Während der folgenden zwei Jahrzehnte beschränkte sich die Arbeit von Frauenorganisationen weitgehend auf den Bereich der sozialen Fürsorge und Wohltätigkeit. Erst im Verlauf der 1980er Jahre entwickelten sich wieder Strukturen unabhängiger Organisationen. Unter Präsident Mubarak wurde in diesen Jahren die bereits von seinem Vorgänger Sadat begonnene Liberalisierungspolitik fortgesetzt, ab 1991 auch im Rahmen der ERSAPs. Der hierdurch bewirkte zunehmende Rückzug des Staates aus vielen Bereichen der Wohlfahrt und sozialen Sicherung hat zu einer verstärkten Übernahme sozialer Aufgaben durch zivilgesellschaftliche Organisationen beigetragen, die besonders bei Gesundheit und Erziehung das entstehende Vakuum gefüllt haben (Zubaida 1992).[19]

Phänomens wurde das Dekret zurückgezogen (Seif El Dawla 1996; *U.S. Department of State* 2001).

[18] Obwohl bisher keine eindeutigen Daten über die Wirksamkeit der laufenden Kampagnen zur Bekämpfung von FGM vorliegen, lassen einige Untersuchungen annehmen, dass bei der jüngsten Generation von Mädchen ein leichter Rückgang der Praxis registriert werden könnte (*U.S. Department of State* 2001).

[19] Nach offiziellen Angaben der ägyptischen Regierung gab es im Jahr 1997 330 Organisationen, die spezifische Leistungen für Frauen und weitere 14.748, die soziale Dienste im weiteren Sinne angeboten ha-

Der oben skizzierte Trend hat zu einer starken Zunahme serviceorientierter NGOs sowie ‚traditioneller' islamischer wohlfahrtsorientierter Organisationen beigetragen. So sind von den inzwischen über 18.000 registrierten Nichtregierungsorganisationen verschiedener Art heute ca. 31% karitative Organisationen und 25% Entwicklungs-NGOs (Zulficar 2003). Im Zuge dieser Entwicklung bedienten sich besonders islamische Organisationen zunehmend ihrer karitativen Rolle, um effektiv ihren gesellschaftlichen Einfluss zu stärken: *„These welfare activities constitute a solid material base from which to establish ties of patronage and networks of loyality and influence."* (Kandiyoti 1996: 8) Heute zählen diese Organisationen daher zu den wichtigsten und in der Gesellschaft am stärksten verwurzelten zivilgesellschaftlichen Akteuren (Bayat 2002).

Neben dem quantitativen Zuwachs service- und wohlfahrtsorientierter NGOs ist seit Anfang der 1980er Jahre auch ein qualitativer Umbruch zu beobachten, der zur Entstehung eines neuen Typus unabhängiger Organisationen geführt hat. Hierbei handelt es sich um Organisationen, die sich nicht mehr ausschließlich in den traditionellen Bereichen der sozialen Fürsorge und Wohltätigkeit betätigen, sondern ebenso daran interessiert sind,

„[...] soziale Veränderungen in Gang zu bringen, eine öffentliche Meinung herzustellen, Einfluss und Macht ihrer Anhängerschaft zu vergrößern und eine Bewegung zu schaffen. Frauenrechte standen bei diesen Organisationen hoch oben auf der Tagesordnung. Vor allem die Frauenorganisationen erfuhren diesen Wandel im Selbstverständnis und der Zielsetzung." (Seif El Dawla/Ibrahim 1995: 114)

Eine der ersten dieser neuen, in der englischsprachigen Literatur als *advocacy* NGOs[20] bezeichneten Organisationen, war die 1982 von Nawal El-Saadawi und anderen Aktivistinnen gegründete *Arab Women's Solidarity Association* (AWSA).[21] Viele der zunächst informellen Gruppen im Bereich der Frauen- und Menschenrechte,

---

ben (*Committee on the Elimination of All Forms of Discrimination Against Women* 2000: 49).

[20] Sofern nicht weiter spezifiziert, wird die Bezeichnung ‚NGO' im weiteren Verlauf dieses Beitrages für solche *advocacy* Organisationen verwendet, die internationale Menschenrechtsnormen als zentralen Bezugsrahmen ihrer Arbeit werten und um ‚*Empowerment*' und sozialen Wandel bemüht sind.

[21] Im Juni 1991 wurde die Organisation wegen angeblicher finanzieller Unregelmäßigkeiten aufgelöst und Lizenz und Besitz der AWSA einer islamischen Frauenorganisation zugesprochen. Die Auflösung der AWSA wird von vielen Beobachtern mit der kritischen Position der Organisation gegenüber dem Irak-Krieg in Verbindung gebracht.

die in diesen Jahren entstanden und sich später zu NGOs entwickelten, wurden (wenn auch nicht ausschließlich) von Mitgliedern der Studentenbewegung der 1970er Jahre gegründet. Diese NGOs waren somit Ausdruck der politischen und sozialen Bestrebungen einer gebildeten städtischen Elite, die nicht zuletzt von den Inhalten sich herausbildender globaler Bewegungen in Bereichen wie Menschen- und Frauenrechte oder Umwelt inspiriert waren (Carapico 2000). NGOs haben sich hierbei gewissermaßen als Auffangbecken für viele Aktivisten entwickelt, die in den Parteien, in den Gewerkschaften und den Berufsverbänden aufgrund starker staatlicher Kontrolle sowie eines hohen Grades an Kooptation keine Möglichkeit für politische und soziale Arbeit mehr sahen (Masonis El-Gawhary 2000). Gerade im Frauenrechtsbereich bildeten sich auch viele dieser Gruppierungen als Reaktion auf den zunehmenden Einfluss islamistischer Kräfte auf den öffentlichen Diskurs und die damit verbundenen Rückschritte für den Status der Frauen (Pratt 2004).

Die Verbreiterung des NGO-Spektrums hat sich im Verlauf der 1990er Jahre verstärkt und ist neben den bereits angedeuteten nationalen Faktoren auch eng mit einer Reihe internationaler Entwicklungen verknüpft. So hatte sich bereits seit Ende der 1980er Jahre auf der internationalen Ebene im breiteren Kontext von Demokratisierungsbemühungen ein Trend zu Fördermaßnahmen für zivilgesellschaftliche Akteure etabliert (Carothers 1999). Gerade NGOs wurden hierbei als zentrale Akteure bei Prozessen des politischen und sozialen Wandels gesehen, was sich nicht zuletzt in der gezielten finanziellen und organisatorischen Förderung dieser Organisationen durch internationale Geldgeber ausdrückte (Bayat 2002). Dieser Trend hat insbesondere für die MENA-Region nach den Ereignissen des 11. Septembers 2001 durch die neu ausgerichtete Nahost-Politik mit einem zusätzlichen Schwerpunkt auf zivilgesellschaftliche Fördermaßnahmen durch die USA sowie weitere westliche Länder zugenommen (Hawthorne 2005).

Weitere prägende Impulse sind von den UN-Weltkonferenzen der 1990er Jahre ausgegangen, die durch die Öffnung für und die Einbeziehung von NGOs auch zur Weiterentwicklung und Ausrichtung lokaler Organisationen beigetragen haben. Für ägyptische Frauen- und Menschenrechts-NGOs waren insbesondere die UN-Weltbevölkerungskonferenz (ICPD) im September 1994 in Kairo und die UN-Weltfrauenkonferenz 1995 in Beijing von zentraler Bedeutung.[22] Unter starkem

---

[22] Einzelne ägyptische Organisationen haben bereits an den vorherigen drei UN-Weltfrauenkonferenzen in Mexiko (1975), Kopenhagen (1980) und Nairobi (1985) teilgenommen, erst ab der ICPD kam es jedoch zu einer massiven Partizipation (*New Woman Research & Study Center* 1996).

internationalem Druck sah sich die ägyptische Regierung in der Vorbereitungsphase der ICPD genötigt, lokale NGOs einzubinden. Diese hatten selber anfangs wenig Interesse gezeigt, sich an der Organisation und Durchführung der Konferenz zu beteiligen (Seif El Dawla/Ibrahim 1995). Unter der Leitung der Feministin und Frauenrechtsaktivistin Aziza Hussein wurde daraufhin im Juli 1993 ein NGO-Forum einberufen, welches die Aktivitäten der NGOs vor und während der ICPD unterstützte und koordinierte. Den über 400 teilnehmenden ägyptischen NGOs wurde dadurch ein Handlungsspielraum verschafft, „über den sie vier Jahrzehnte nicht verfügt hatten" (Seif El Dawla/Ibrahim 1995). Dies bot den bis dahin weitgehend isoliert arbeitenden NGOs mit sehr unterschiedlichem Hintergrund die Möglichkeit, sich näher zu kommen, Ideen auszutauschen, über Formen der Kooperation zu diskutieren und der Öffentlichkeit eigene Forderungen zu präsentieren. Auch ermutigte der Austausch mit Organisationen aus anderen Regionen der Welt einige ägyptische NGOs, bis dahin tabuisierte Themengebiete der ‚privaten Sphäre' wie häusliche Gewalt und Beschneidung von Frauen zu thematisieren. Nach Ansicht vieler Beobachter war die ICPD somit ein zentrales Moment, das sich belebend und stärkend auf die lokale NGO-Szene ausgewirkt hat: „*This conference has proven, that once local associations and NGOs are given freedom of interaction, they become positively productive.*" (Hussein 1994: 5).

Im Gegensatz zur ICPD wird Konferenz in Beijing 1995 von den meisten Beobachtern weniger positiv hinsichtlich der Auswirkungen auf die lokale NGO-Gemeinschaft gesehen. Dies liegt einerseits an der restriktiveren Politik der ägyptischen Regierung, die nach der Öffnung von Freiräumen für NGOs im Rahmen der ICPD bemüht war, „das Haus wieder aufzuräumen" (Seif El Dawla/Ibrahim 1995: 118). Gleichzeitig hinderten – im Gegensatz zur vorherigen Konferenz in Kairo – die geografische Entfernung und die daraus resultierenden finanziellen und organisatorischen Hürden viele NGOs, an der Konferenz teilzunehmen. Trotzdem konnten mehrere ägyptische NGOs nicht zuletzt durch die finanzielle Unterstützung internationaler Geldgeberinstitutionen nach Beijing reisen, was aber auch zu starken Auseinandersetzungen und Verteilungskämpfen zwischen NGOs geführt hat (Al-Ali 2000).

Die hier beschriebenen Entwicklungen auf der nationalen wie auf der internationalen Ebene haben somit im Verlauf der 1990er Jahre zu einer Diversifizierung der ägyptischen NGO-Landschaft beigetragen und die transnationale Vernetzung und diskursive Einbindung lokaler *advocacy* NGOs in ein internationales Menschenrechtsregime gefördert. Neben den neuen Handlungsmöglichkeiten, die hierdurch für diese Organisationen entstanden, führte dies auch zu zusätzlichen Reibungspunkten sowohl zwischen Staat und *advocacy* NGOs als auch zwischen diesen Organisationen und anderen zivilgesellschaftlichen Akteuren.

4. *Advocacy* NGOs: Einige grundsätzliche Debatten

Mit nur wenigen Ausnahmen sind NGOs heute zur Durchführung ihrer Arbeit auf die Finanzierung durch ausländische Geberinstitutionen angewiesen.[23] Ein bedeutender Teil der Menschen- und Frauenrechts-NGOs haben sich bereits während der frühen 1990er Jahre und besonders im Verlauf der Vorbereitungen für die ICPD und die Beijing-Konferenz für die Annahme dieser transnationalen Form der Unterstützung entschlossen.[24] Die Debatte über ‚*foreign funding*' bleibt bis heute umstritten, da das Entgegennehmen ausländischer, meist westlicher Finanzmittel angesichts des politischen und sozialen Klimas im Land auch immer wieder heikle Fragen über die inhaltliche Ausrichtung der Arbeit von NGOs aufwirft. Einerseits wird das Thema oft von NGO-Gegnern instrumentalisiert[25],

---

[23] Genaue Angaben zur Finanzierung der Arbeit einzelner NGOs und/oder Projekte sind nur schwer auszumachen. Dies hängt zu einem bedeutenden Teil mit den schweren politischen und gesellschaftlichen Rahmenbedingungen, unter denen NGOs operieren, und dem besonders heiklen Status ausländischer Finanzierung zusammen. Nur wenige NGOs stellen angesichts dieser Situation der Öffentlichkeit Informationen zu ihrem jährlichen Budget und ihren Geldgebern zur Verfügung, was nicht selten zu Vorwürfen mangelnder Transparenz führt. Zu den größten Geberinstitutionen, die in Ägypten und der MENA-Region insbesondere Menschen- und Frauenrechtsarbeit fördern, gehören u.a. die Europäische Union, internationale Organisationen wie UNDP, nationale Entwicklungsorganisationen wie die kanadische CIDA (für einen Überblick der in Ägypten unterstützten Projekte siehe: http://les.acdicida.gc.ca/servelet/JKMSearchController), die dänische DANIDA, die US-amerikanische USAID sowie große Stiftungen wie die US-amerikanische *Ford Foundation* und die holländische NOVIB. Ebenfalls finanzieren die Botschaften einiger westlicher Länder wie auch deutsche politische Stiftungen einzelne Projekte.

[24] Die Frage der Annahme ausländischer Finanzmittel hat bei mehreren NGOs zu heftigen internen Debatten bis hin zu Spaltungen einzelner Gruppen geführt. Besonders prominent sind hier der Fall des *New Woman Research Center* (NWRC) (Al-Ali 2000) und der *Egyptian Organization for Human Rights* (EOHR) (El Sayed Said 1994).

[25] Der Vorwurf, durch die Annahme ausländischer Finanzmittel auch eine westliche Agenda zu verfolgen, wird häufig sowohl von Vertretern des regierungs- als auch des islamistischen Lagers verwendet. Hierbei wird häufig darüber hinweggesehen, dass die ägyptische Regierung wie auch islamistische NGOs stark durch ausländische Mittel unterstützt werden. Das *Ibn Khaldun Center for Development Studies* (ICDS) hebt folgende Zahlen hervor: „*The entire annual amount of foreign fund received by all 20,000 Egyptian NGOs does not exceed $40 million, which amounts to 1% of the foreign funds that Mubarak's regime collected.*" (*Ibn Khaldun Center for Development Studies* 2005). Eben-

um die Arbeit von NGOs zu delegitimieren. Andererseits weisen viele Untersuchungen auf die Gefahr hin, dass NGOs durch ihre finanzielle Abhängigkeit von ausländischen Finanzmitteln ihre Arbeit möglicherweise weniger an den Bedürfnissen ihrer lokalen Basis als an der Agenda internationaler Geberinstitutionen ausrichten (Pitner 2000). Auch selbstkritische Aktivisten räumen in diesem Punkt durchaus ein, dass eine unreflektierte transnationale Ausrichtung der Aktivitäten von NGOs zum Zweck zu werden droht, anstatt als Mittel zur Bekämpfung lokaler Probleme zu dienen, und sich somit meist negativ auf das Verhältnis zwischen NGOs und der breiteren Bevölkerung auswirkt (Jad 2004).[26]

Die stetig wachsende Zahl von *advocacy* NGOs sowie ihre kontinuierlich zunehmenden Aufgabengebiete und Aktivitäten werden von Jad als ein Prozess der ‚NGOisierung' beschrieben, der die Struktur und Ausrichtung der Frauenbewegungen in der MENA-Region grundlegend verändert hat: *„The formation of women's NGOs with particular social aims marks a very different form and structure for Arab women's activism from those that predominated in earlier periods."* (Jad 2004) Im Gegensatz zu traditionellen Organisationen, die eine breitere Mitgliedschaft aufweisen und weitgehend auf wohltätiger und freiwilliger Basis arbeiten, zeichnen sich die neuen NGOs im Menschen- und Frauenrechtsbereich durch eine stark professionalisierte Struktur aus. Die meisten dieser Organisationen haben sich im Verlauf der Jahre auf bestimmte Arbeitsgebiete wie Forschung, Rechtsberatung oder Aufklärungskampagnen spezialisiert und bestehen aus hoch qualifiziertem Personal, das die inhaltliche und administrative Arbeit ausführt. Im Hinblick auf Frauenorganisationen bemerkt Al-Ali (2000: 81) dementsprechend: *„Being a women activist can be a 'career' in contemporary Egypt, where a new field for jobs has been created within the wider NGO movement."*. Ein Großteil dieser Organisationen hat ihren Sitz in den zentralen Stadtvierteln Kairos. Gute Englischkenntnisse, die Beherrschung des internationalen Menschenrechts- und Zivilgesellschafts-Jargons sowie gute Kontakte zu Geberorganisationen gehören zu den zentralen Qualifikationen von NGO-Personal. NGO-Aktivisten gehören somit zu der kleinen Gruppe gut verdienender ‚*urban professionals*'. Die Entscheidungskompetenzen sind meist stark in den Händen einer oder weniger zentraler Figuren konzentriert, und nur

---

falls werden die Aktivitäten islamistischer NGOs seit den 1970er Jahren fast ausschließlich durch Geber aus den Golfstaaten finanziert (Würth 2003).

[26] Ein weiterer Teilaspekt der Debatte über die (ausländische) Finanzierung von NGOs betrifft das Problem mangelnder Transparenz bei der Verwaltung der Finanzen bei vielen Organisationen (Bayat 2002).

wenige Organisationen pflegen einen partizipatorischen Ansatz (Carothers 1999). Dementsprechend sehen sich viele NGOs mit dem Vorwurf des Elitismus und dem Problem der geringen sozialen Verwurzelung konfrontiert.

Die meisten NGOs geben an, direkt oder indirekt internationale Menschen- und Frauenrechtsstandards als Bezugsrahmen ihrer Arbeit zu sehen. Diese Orientierung an einem internationalen, oft als ‚westlich' wahrgenommenen Diskurs führt immer wieder zu öffentlichen Debatten über die Legitimität der Arbeit von NGOs. Frauenrechtsorganisationen sind angesichts der Sensibilität der Frauenfrage hiervon in besonderem Maße betroffen:

„The question of identity is as central to their activism as concrete struggles over women's rights and aspirations. For secular women activists even more is at stake as their rejection of Islam as the only possible framework for political struggle and nationbuilding evokes suspicion and doubt about their place within the indigenous landscape of ‚traditions' and ‚authenticity'." (Al-Ali 2000: 2)

Der richtige Umgang mit lokalen kulturellen und religiösen Werten und Normen wird von Aktivistin zu Aktivistin unterschiedlich eingeschätzt und reicht von einer strikten Ablehnung der Einbeziehung bis zu einer bewussten Aneignung und Verwendung kultureller und religiöser Argumente (*Harvard Law School Human Rights Program* 2000).

5. NGOs und der Staat: Rechtliche und politische Rahmenbedingungen

Das Verhältnis zwischen Staat und Nichtregierungsorganisationen (sowie weiteren zivilgesellschaftlichen Akteuren) kann als angespannt und von wechselseitigem Misstrauen geprägt bezeichnet werden. Wie auch für alle anderen ägyptischen NGOs ergeben sich die gesetzlichen Rahmenbedingungen für die Arbeit von Frauenrechtsorganisationen insbesondere aus den Bestimmungen des Vereinsgesetzes. Bis 1999 bzw. 2003 galten hier die noch aus der Zeit Nassers stammenden, sehr restriktiven Regelungen des Gesetzes 32 aus dem Jahr 1964. Nach einer intensiven Lobbykampagne nationaler zivilgesellschaftlicher Akteure und internationaler Geldgeber kündigte die ägyptische Regierung 1998 an, das Vereinsgesetz reformieren zu wollen. Im darauf folgenden Jahr wurde es durch das Gesetz 153/1999, das sogenannte ‚NGO-Gesetz', ersetzt, welches jedoch national und international aufgrund der weiterhin bestehenden Einschränkungen für Nichtregierungsorganisationen großen

Protest auslöste. Im Mai 2000 wurde das Gesetz vom Verfassungsgericht aufgrund von Verfahrensfehlern kassiert und zunächst wieder Gesetz 32/1964 angewendet. Schließlich wurde 2002 das in nur geringfügigen Punkten überarbeitete NGO-Gesetz als Gesetz 84/2002 erneut eingebracht und verabschiedet. Dies ist seit Juni 2003 in Kraft (*Human Rights Watch* 2005).

Obwohl das neue NGO-Gesetz von Beobachtern und Aktivisten in mancher Hinsicht als Fortschritt gegenüber dem noch aus den 1960er Jahren stammenden Vorgängergesetz gewertet wird, bleibt es nach wie vor hinter international anerkannten Standards zurück: „*Its provisions – and even more strikingly, the broad and arbitrary way in which it is applied – violate Egypt's international legal obligations to uphold freedom of association.*" (*Human Rights Watch* 2005: 1). Gesetz 84/2002 räumt der ägyptischen Regierung weitgehende Kontrollrechte über die Selbstorganisation von NGOs ein. So müssen sich diese Organisationen u.a. zur offiziellen Registrierung beim Ministerium für soziale Angelegenheiten bewerben. Die Zuteilung des legalen Status' kann einer Organisation verweigert werden, wenn sie sich politischer Arbeit widmet oder die ‚öffentliche Ordnung' und die ‚öffentliche Moral' bedroht. Im Falle einer Fortsetzung der Arbeit nach Ablehnung der Registrierung droht den Organisationen die strafrechtliche Verfolgung.[27] Ein weiterer kritischer Aspekt des NGO-Gesetzes betrifft die Annahme ausländischer Finanzmittel, die einer Autorisierung des Ministeriums für soziale Angelegenheiten bedarf und somit die Möglichkeit eröffnet, die Finanzen einer Organisation zu blockieren. Auch kann das Ministerium in die interne Verwaltung der Organisationen eingreifen, u.a. indem es Kandidaten für Vorstandswahlen zurückweisen kann, bis hin zu der Möglichkeit, Organisationen per Dekret aufzulösen. Das Gesetz ermöglicht es der Regierung somit, rechtlich, administrativ und finanziell die Arbeit ägyptischer NGOs zu kontrollieren und gegebenenfalls zu behindern.

---

[27] Dem *New Woman Research Center* (NWRC) – einer NGO, die sich seit Anfang 1984 hauptsächlich der Aufgabe widmet, die Öffentlichkeit für Frauenrechtsfragen zu sensibilisieren – wurde beispielsweise vom Ministerium aus „Sicherheitsgründen" die Registrierung verweigert. Das NWRC ist gerichtlich gegen diese Entscheidung des Ministeriums vorgegangen und bekam im Herbst 2003 auf diesem Wege Recht. (Human Rights Watch 2003) Eine Anzahl weiterer Organisationen setzen bis heute die rechtlichen Auseinandersetzungen fort, um die Entscheidung des Ministeriums für soziale Angelegenheiten, ihnen keine Zulassung zu erteilen, anzufechten. So beispielsweise die *Egyptian Initiative for Personal Rights* und die *Egyptian Association Against Torture* (*Egyptian Organization for Human Rights* 2005).

Die Erfahrungen mehrerer Organisationen seit 2003 haben gezeigt, dass die Sicherheitsdienste, obwohl dies nicht gesetzlich verankert ist, einen besonders großen Einfluss auf die Erteilung der Registrierung ausüben und auch darüber hinaus die Aktivitäten, Mitglieder und Finanzierung einzelner Organisationen strikt kontrollieren. Während diese Umstände für die Arbeit der vielen wohlfahrtsorientierten Organisationen, die als *„active partner to the sustainable development"*[28] vom Staat mit Wohlwollen gesehen und gefördert werden, meist kein Problem darstellen, kann die Arbeit der auf sozialen und politischen Wandel ausgerichteten und oft regierungskritischen NGOs hierdurch stark behindert werden. Zu diesem Typus von NGOs gehören die meisten hier angesprochenen Frauen- und Menschenrechtsorganisationen: *„The problem is, if an organization is not in favor with the government, there remain many levers against them in the new law."* (Schemm 2002)

Über die Bestimmungen des NGO-Gesetzes hinaus wird der Handlungsspielraum von NGOs durch weitere Gesetze und Verordnungen, besonders die seit 1981 geltenden Notstandsgesetze, eingeschränkt. Die Militärverordnung Nr. 4 aus dem Jahr 1992 sieht beispielsweise die Verhängung einer Haftstrafe von mindestens sieben Jahren für die unautorisierte Annahme von Finanzierungsmitteln vor. Die Verordnung ist bereits verwendet worden, um die Arbeit von Menschenrechtsaktivisten zu kriminalisieren.[29] Über den gesetzlichen Rahmen hinaus werden staatlich kontrollierte Medien und religiöse Einrichtungen immer wieder eingesetzt, um das Ansehen und die Legitimität von NGOs oder einzelner Aktivisten durch gezielte Kampagnen in der Bevölkerung zu beschädigen. (Pitner 2000)

Einen etwas anderen, aber gerade im Frauenrechtsbereich sehr zentralen Aspekt des Verhältnisses zwischen Staat und NGOs stellt die Einrichtung nationaler Institutionen zur Förderung von Menschenrechten und/oder Geschlechtergleichheit dar, die unter unmittelbarem Einfluss der politischen Führung stehen. Im Februar 2000 wurde durch einen Erlass des Präsidenten die Bildung des *National Council for Women* (NCW) angeordnet, dem Suzanne Mubarak, die

---

[28] *President Mubarak's Address to a Joint Session of the People's Assembly and the Shura Council*, November 19, 2003. Siehe: www.sis.gov.eg/online/html110/o191123v.htm (Zit. in: Hawthorne 2005: 94).

[29] Besonderes Aufsehen erregte im Jahr 2000 die Verhaftung des Universitätsprofessors und Menschenrechtsaktivisten Saad Eddin Ibrahim und seiner Mitarbeiter des *Ibn Khaldun Center for Development Studies*, u.a. wegen unautorisierter Annahme ausländischer Finanzmittel. Erst im Rahmen eines Kassationsverfahrens wurde im März 2003 die in den vorherigen zwei Instanzen (2001 und 2002) verhängte siebenjährige Haftstrafe aufgehoben (*Human Rights Watch* 2005).

ägyptische *First Lady*, als Präsidentin vorsitzt.[30] Die Rolle des NCW wird von Frauenrechtsaktivistinnen durchaus kontrovers beurteilt. Während die einen die Aktivitäten des NCW und das persönliche Engagement von Frau Mubarak als Zeichen eines erfolgreichen ‚*Mainstreaming*' der Frauenrechtsproblematik werten, welche auch der Arbeit von NGOs Legitimität verleihen, weisen andere auf die Gefahr der Kontrolle durch Kooptation hin und fürchten, dass die Ziele unabhängiger Frauenrechtsorganisationen verwässert werden könnten. Tatsächlich haben NGOs schon seit langer Zeit zu vielen der Themenbereiche, die vom NCW aufgegriffen worden sind, gearbeitet, wobei der Ansatz des NCW in den entsprechenden Bereichen meistens hinter den progressiven Elementen der NGO-Ansätze zurück bleibt (Jürgensen 2004)[31].

Ausgehend von der oben beschriebenen Entwicklung der Aktivitäten, Struktur, Rahmenbedingungen und Debatten über die Arbeit von *advocacy* NGOs, soll im folgenden Abschnitt darauf eingegangen werden, inwiefern es diesen Akteuren in Ägypten gelingt, einen Prozess des gesellschaftlichen Wertewandels und letztlich eine Verbesserung der Stellung der Frau zu erwirken.

6. *Advocacy* NGOs und ihre Bemühungen um einen gesellschaftlichen Wertewandel

Im Verlauf der 1990er Jahre haben NGOs durch ihre Bemühungen wesentlich zur Popularisierung eines breiteren Menschenrechtsdiskurses in Ägypten beigetragen und gerade auch die Frauenfrage zu einem wichtigen Bestandteil politischer und sozialer Debatten gemacht. Zwar sind die Positionen von Menschen- und Frauenrechtsaktivisten nicht repräsentativ für den gesellschaftlichen *Mainstream*, doch, so Jürgensen, „kommt ihnen als Motoren der Diskussion eine zentrale Rolle hinsichtlich der Auswahl und Prioritätensetzung von Themen zu" (Jürgensen 2004: 295). So haben Frauen(rechts)-NGOs neben der traditionellen Thematisierung der benachteiligten Stellung von Frauen in der öffentlichen Sphäre zunehmend auch darauf hingearbeitet, die strikte Trennung zwischen privater und öffentlicher Sphäre aufzuheben und lange Zeit tabuisierte ‚private' Themen wie FGM, Gewalt gegen Frauen und die Ungleichheiten im Personenstandsrecht zum Gegenstand öffentlicher Debatten zu

---
[30] Siehe: www.ncw.org.eg.
[31] Eine ähnlich kontroverse Debatte über die Gefahren der Kooptation ist über den im Juni 2003 ins Leben gerufenen *National Council for Human Rights* (NCHR) geführt worden, dem auch Vertreter zivilgesellschaftlicher Organisationen angehören. Der NCHR soll die menschenrechtliche Situation im Lande evaluieren und dafür Reformvorschläge vorlegen.

machen. Inwiefern sich solche Diskussionen auch in einer tatsächlichen Veränderung der alltäglichen Praxis auf der breiten gesellschaftlichen Ebene auf diesen Gebieten widerspiegeln, lässt sich angesichts der Komplexität solcher Veränderungsprozesse sowie der langen Zeiträume, die hierfür nötig sind, allerdings nur bedingt feststellen.

Gerade bei den genannten sensiblen Themen, die eng mit nationalen Traditionen und Religion verbunden sind, sind Frauen- und Menschenrechts-NGOs, die sich in ihrer Arbeit an internationalen Normen orientieren, immer wieder auf heftige Widerstände gestoßen sowie auf Vorwürfe, eine westliche Agenda zu verfolgen (Pratt 2004). Hierbei sehen sich *advocacy* NGOs mit einer besonders heiklen politischen und sozialen Lage konfrontiert, da gerade die ‚Frauenfrage' häufig als zentraler ‚Austragungsort' eines breiteren Machtkampfes zwischen dem ägyptischen Staat und der islamistischen Bewegung, der stärksten oppositionellen Gruppierung im Land, fungiert (*Human Rights Watch* 2004). Die hier angesprochenen NGOs stehen somit bei ihren Bemühungen, die Wahrnehmung der Stellung der Frau auf einer breiten gesellschaftlichen Ebene zu beeinflussen und zu verbessern, zwei Akteursgruppen mit weitgehenden Ressourcen gegenüber. Während der Staat über das Bildungswesen und die zum großen Teil kontrollierten Medien vielfältige Möglichkeiten der Beeinflussung der öffentlichen Meinung hat, bilden die Moscheen und die große Anzahl religiöser wohltätiger Einrichtungen ein dichtes soziales Netz, über welches islamistische Gruppierungen weite Teile der Bevölkerung erreichen können. Angesichts ihrer geringen sozialen Verwurzelung und den begrenzten materiellen und infrastrukturellen Möglichkeiten, müssen *advocacy* NGOs daher immer wieder nach Strategien suchen, um ihre Anliegen, welche sich an internationalen Frauenrechtsstandards orientieren, an den lokalen Kontext anzupassen und Möglichkeiten der Kooperation mit anderen Akteuren zu schaffen. Die folgenden Beispiele sollen einen Einblick in unterschiedliche Ansätze von NGOs, mit dieser Problematik umzugehen, ermöglichen.

Bereits Mitte der 1980er kamen eine Gruppe von NGOs und einzelne Aktivistinnen zusammen, um gegen Rückschritte im Personenstandsrecht anzukämpfen, die als deutliches Anzeichen des wachsenden Einflusses religiös-konservativer Elemente in der ägyptischen Gesellschaft gewertet wurden.[32] Die Bemühungen dieser

---

[32] 1985 wurden angesichts wachsender Opposition aus religiös-konservativen Kreisen die im Jahr 1979 unter Sadat per Erlass eingeführten Reformen des Personenstandrechts außer Kraft gesetzt. Nach einer heftigen Protestreaktion säkularer Gruppierungen wurden binnen zwei Monaten durch ein neues Gesetz die meisten, wenn auch nicht alle, im Erlass von 1979 festgelegten Rechte für Frauen wieder hergestellt (Al-Ali 2000).

Organisationen haben im Rahmen diverser Kampagnen über die Jahre maßgeblich zu Reformschritten auf diesem Gebiet beigetragen. Hierbei haben sich Frauenrechts-NGOs angesichts der starken religiösen Konnotation dieses spezifischen Problembereichs für eine Diversifizierung der eigenen (an internationalen Menschenrechtsstandards orientierten) Strategien entschieden: „*a strategy of engagement in the religious discourse, based on women's reading of their rights under the principles of Shari'a*" (Zulficar 2003: 11). Die Kampagne, die zur Verabschiedung des *Khul*-Gesetzes im Jahr 2000 führte, kann als erfolgreiches Beispiel dieser Strategie gewertet werden: „*It was therefore essential for the women's movement to diversify its strategies and adopt a credible strategy that could reach out and win the support of simple, ordinary religious men and women.*" (Zulficar 2003: 11). So wird auch von Heba Raouf Ezzat, einer dem islamistischen Lager nahestehenden Aktivistin und Universitätsdozentin, betont, dass das Gesetz von den höchsten religiösen Instanzen geprüft und für Sharia-konform erklärt wurde (2001). Ebenfalls ist es im Fall des *Khul*-Gesetzes gelungen, in den Medien eine offene Debatte über das Gesetz zu führen und somit eine breite Öffentlichkeit über verschiedene Aspekte der Reform zu informieren, was trotz einer organisierten Opposition zu einer hohen Akzeptanz des neuen Gesetzes beigetragen hat (El-Azhary Sonbol 2005).

Angestoßen und bestärkt durch die internationalen UN-Konferenzen wurden ab den frühen 1990er Jahren dann auch Themen wie FGM und häusliche Gewalt verstärkt von *advocacy* NGOs aufgegriffen. Auf Berichte von lokalen NGOs über das hohe Ausmaß häuslicher Gewalt hatte die offizielle ägyptische Delegation auf der ICPD und in Beijing 1995 noch mit Leugnen reagiert (Pratt 2004). Inzwischen haben die fortgesetzten Bemühungen ägyptischer Frauenrechts-NGOs zu ersten ermutigenden Entwicklungen geführt. Bereits seit 1993 bietet die in Kairo ansässige NGO *El Nadim Center for the Psychological Rehabilitation of Victims of Violence* Opfern von Folter und häuslicher Gewalt medizinische und psychologische Unterstützung an.[33] Die *Association for the Development and Enhancement of Women* (ADEW) führt das erste Frauenhaus in Ägypten (und der MENA-Region), in dem Frauen und Kindern, die häuslicher Gewalt zum Opfer fallen, Schutz und umfangreiche Un-

---

[33] Im Sommer 2004 wurde dem *El Nadem Center*, das als ärztliche Einrichtung registriert ist, nach einer Kontrolle durch das Gesundheitsministeriums mit der Schließung gedroht. Nach Angaben des Ministeriums hätten die Aktivitäten des Centers außerhalb des für eine ärztliche Einrichtung Erlaubten gelegen. Menschenrechtsorganisationen werteten dies als Versuch, die Aktivitäten des *El Nadem Centers* im Bereich der Bekämpfung von Folter und häuslicher Gewalt zu behindern (*Amnesty International* 2004).

terstützung angeboten werden.³⁴ Der Erfolg bei der Kampagne zur bereits erwähnten Gesetzesänderung (Artikel 291) aus dem Jahr 1999 kann als Anzeichen eines einsetzenden Wandels gewertet werden. Auch suchen Menschen- und Frauenrechtsorganisationen in der gesamten MENA-Region zusammen mit internationalen Organisationen und NGOs weiterhin nach Ursachen und möglichen Strategien zur Bekämpfung dieses Missstandes (*Alliance for Arab Women* 2003). Trotzdem bleibt Gewalt gegen Frauen in allen gesellschaftlichen Schichten weit verbreitet und toleriert und wird weiterhin nicht als breiteres soziales Problem betrachtet. Die Rolle der Medien ist in dieser Hinsicht besonders kritisch zu bewerten. So ist beispielsweise bei der Behandlung des Themas der häuslichen Gewalt eine Tendenz zur Darstellung von Männern als Opfern zu beobachten (UNIFEM *Western Asia Regional Office* 1999). Auch verbreiten mehrere Programme weiterhin ein stereotypes Bild von Frauen: „*Programs emphasiszing polygamy, the roles of dominant men and submissive women, and the virgin/whore dichotomy dominate public television and perpetuate societal patriarchy.*" (El-Azhary Sonbol 2005: 82) NGOs wie das NWRC sowie der NCW führen entsprechend Programme zur Überwachung der Medien durch.

Einzelne NGOs arbeiteten bereits seit den 1970er Jahren für die Bekämpfung von FGM, haben aber, besonders ab Mitte der 1990er, durch die Formierung einer *National FGM Task Force* maßgeblich zu einer starken Intensivierung der Arbeit auf diesem Gebiet und der Entstehung einer breiten gesellschaftlichen Debatte über das Phänomen beigetragen. Nachdem in der Vergangenheit religiöse und politische Führungspersönlichkeiten eine ambivalente Haltung zur Bekämpfung von FGM eingenommen hatten (Karam 1998), sind auf höheren politischen und religiösen Ebenen Anzeichen eines Sinneswandels unverkennbar. So sprachen sich auf einer internationalen Konferenz zur Bekämpfung von FGM in Kairo im Juni 2003 schon hohe religiöse (islamische wie koptische) Repräsentanten sowie Suzanne Mubarak selber deutlich gegen FGM aus (Ezzat/ Hammouda 2003).³⁵ Trotz dieser Fortschritte auf der hohen politischen und religiösen Ebene sowie des bereits erwähnten erwirkten Verbots der Durchführung von FGM, welches 1997 durch das Kassationsgericht bekräftig wurde, bleibt die Praxis auf der breiten gesellschaftlichen Ebene weiterhin tief verwurzelt. Auf dieser Ebene einen Gesinnungswandel herbeizuführen, erweist sich als erheblich schwerer: „*In cases of cultural tradition, accountability by the state*

---

34 Siehe: http://www.adew.org/adew/?pg=pro
35 Vergleiche auch: *Cairo Declaration for the Elimination of FGM*. Siehe: www.crlp.org/pdf/pdf_fgm_cairo2003_eng.pdf [10.12.2005].

is rarely sufficient. Harmful practices may continue even when governments try to force compliance." (Cerna/Wallace 1999: 647)

In Zusammenarbeit mit lokalen NGOs wurde 2003 von der Regierung über den *National Council for Childhood and Motherhood* (NCCM)[36] eine national angelegte Kampagne zur Bekämpfung von FGM gestartet.[37] Eine weitere, 2004 im Fernsehen durchgeführte Kampagne zur Sensibilisierung der öffentlichen Meinung hinsichtlich der Abkehr von dieser Praxis hat zu einer Intensivierung der gesellschaftlichen Debatte über dieses Thema geführt, bisher aber noch keine messbare Wirkung gezeigt (Katulis 2004). Die Erfahrungen ägyptischer NGOs haben darüber hinaus gezeigt, dass in diesem sehr sensiblen Bereich ein direkter Rückgriff auf internationale Frauenrechtsstandards häufig wenig Wirkung zeigt, da die angesprochenen Menschen hiermit nicht vertraut sind und somit nur eine geringe Resonanz erzeugt werden kann:

„Human rights declarations, treaties, and languages aside, an appeal informed by an understanding of human rights but which draws upon local cultural and religious notions of common sense, justice, and dignity is often the best way to promote human rights and change the cultural norms that violate them." (Wassef 2000)

Trotz der beachtlichen Probleme auf diesem Gebiet haben positive Entwicklungen in einigen Teilen des Landes gezeigt, dass auch auf gesellschaftlicher Ebene ein Prozess des Wandels möglich ist. Hierbei handelt es sich jedoch um sehr langfristige Prozesse, bei denen eine enge Zusammenarbeit und Vertrautheit mit einzelnen Gemeinden und Familien notwendig ist, um im Einzelnen die Gründe für das Fortbestehen der Praxis zu verstehen und einen Wandel der Überzeugungen herbeizuführen (Abdel Hadi 2003; Abdel Hadi 1998).

Neben den bereits angesprochenen Formen der Zusammenarbeit mit regierungsnahen Einrichtungen und den Medien soll an dieser Stelle noch kurz das Verhältnis zwischen *advocacy* NGOs und Akteuren aus dem islamistischen Lager, der stärksten politischen und sozialen Oppositionskraft im Land, thematisiert werden. Wie bereits erwähnt wurde, wirkt sich der zunehmende Einfluss religiös-konservativer Kräfte in Ägypten sowie in der gesamten MENA-Region erschwerend auf die Umsetzung internationaler

---

[36] Das NCCM wurde 1988 durch Dekret 54 des Präsidenten ins Leben gerufen und befasst sich als höchste Regierungsorganisation mit der Planung und Umsetzung der Arbeit der Regierung im Bereich des Schutzes und der Entwicklung von Kindern. Siehe: www.nccm.org.eg.

[37] Siehe: http://www.undp.org.eg/news/press/2005%20press/ FGM%20meniya.htm [10.12.2005].

Frauenrechtsnormen aus. Gleichzeitig ist jedoch auf die Existenz islamistischer Frauenorganisationen zu verweisen, die sich mit eigenen Forderungen für eine Verbesserung der Situation von Frauen einsetzen und somit eine alternative Form von *Gender*-Aktivismus verkörpern. Trotz einer starken Polarisierung zwischen säkularen und islamistisch orientierten NGOs (Raouf Ezzat 2001) finden sich so auch immer wieder Belege für eine Kongruenz der Ziele zwischen Organisationen beider Lager. So hebt Duval de Dampierre hervor, dass beispielsweise im Rahmen von ICPD und der Beijing-Konferenz progressive NGOs beider Lager durchaus in Bereichen wie der Förderung der Frauen im öffentlichen Leben, der Bekämpfung häuslicher Gewalt und der Praxis der Beschneidung von Frauen (FGM) sowie der Reform des Scheidungsrechtes sehr ähnliche politische Sichtweisen teilten, auch wenn sie jeweils „verschiedene Strategien und unterschiedliches Vokabular in der Verfolgung ihrer gemeinsamen Ziele" (Duval de Dampierre 1995: 43) verwendeten. In der alltäglichen Arbeit scheinen jedoch die ideologischen Barrieren zwischen den Lagern weiterhin hoch zu sein, so dass wechselseitiges Misstrauen und gegenseitige Anschuldigungen bisher eine stetige Zusammenarbeit verhindern (Würth 2003).

7. Die zunehmende Transnationalisierung der Aktivitäten von NGOs – Ein zweischneidiges Schwert

Die vorangegangenen Kapitel haben bereits an verschiedenen Stellen darauf hingewiesen, inwiefern sich Prozesse der Transnationalisierung von Menschenrechtsaktivitäten auf die Arbeit ägyptischer *advocacy* NGOs auswirken. Da dieser Entwicklung allgemein in jüngster Zeit in der Fachliteratur – insbesondere in der Theorie der Internationalen Beziehungen – große Relevanz beigemessen wird, sollen hierzu im folgenden Abschnitt einige zusammenfassende Betrachtungen angestellt werden.

Allgemein wird insbesondere in sogenannten konstruktivistischen Analysen der Schaffung und Wirkung internationaler Menschenrechtsnormen die zunehmende Transnationalisierung der Menschenrechtsarbeit als ein Prozess wahrgenommen, der vorwiegend positive Effekte auf die Handlungsmöglichkeiten von NGOs auf der nationalen Ebene hat (Risse/Ropp/Sikkink 1999). Dabei werden insbesondere die Chancen betont, die sich transnational agierenden NGOs bieten, innenpolitische Schranken zu umgehen und trotz einer Einschränkung ihres innergesellschaftlichen Aktionsradius' am internationalen Menschenrechtsdiskurs teilzunehmen. Gleichzeitig wird bei der Sozialisierung von Menschenrechtsstandards auf staatlicher Ebene darauf hingewiesen, dass lokal operierende NGOs diese internationalen Normen instrumentalisieren können, um Druck „von unten" (nationale Zivilgesellschaft) und „von oben" (internationale Gemeinschaft) auf nationale politische Entscheidungsträger auszuüben (Brysk 1993).

Wie sich allerdings in der hier dargestellten Bestandsaufnahme der Rolle und Arbeit von *advocacy* NGOs im Bereich der Menschenrechte von Frauen in Ägypten gezeigt hat, wirken sich die Tendenzen der Transnationalisierung nicht nur förderlich auf die Aktivitäten dieser Akteure aus. Gerade wenn es darum geht, die auf die Zivilgesellschaft ausgerichteten Dimensionen des NGO-Aktivismus zu thematisieren, zeigt sich, dass eine transnationale Einfärbung durchaus auch problematische Aspekte im Hinblick auf die Akzeptanz und Glaubwürdigkeit von NGOs mit sich bringt. Nicht selten stehen transnational orientierte NGOs unter Verdacht, westliche, ‚fremde' Wertvorstellungen zu propagieren und damit dem Kultur-Imperialismus des Westens Vorschub zu leisten. Dies umso mehr in Fällen, in denen sich ihre Menschenrechtsaktivitäten durch externe Geldgeberinstitutionen aus den westlichen Industrienationen finanzieren – sind diese doch vielfach an Vorgaben gebunden, was Programmatik, Inhalt und Jargon von Menschenrechtsarbeit betrifft. Die Konkurrenz um ausländische Finanzierung innerhalb der NGO-Gemeinschaft wirkt ihrerseits in Richtung einer Zersplitterung der NGO-Landschaft. Während sich demnach die Teilnahme an internationalen Foren einerseits ‚ermächtigend' auf die Aktivitäten von *advocacy* NGOs auswirkt, weisen Elemente wie das ‚*foreign funding*' und die damit verbundenen Auflagen durchaus auch auf mehr einseitige, asymmetrische Aspekte der Transnationalisierung hin. Der sudanische Universitätsprofessor und Menschenrechtsaktivist An-Na'im (2000) sieht diese Strategien der transnationalen Vernetzung für *advocacy* NGOs in der MENA-Region zwar als pragmatische Notwendigkeit, weist in diesem Kontext jedoch auch auf die Gefahren einer „*human rights dependency*" hin. Hier scheinen in Zukunft sowohl internationale Akteure als auch lokale NGOs daher wesentlich stärker darüber reflektieren zu müssen, in welcher Form sich Transnationalisierung vollziehen soll, wenn die Entstehung einer starken und selbstständigen lokalen Menschen- und Frauenrechtsgemeinschaft gefördert werden soll. Neben der Notwendigkeit von Lernprozessen auf der Ebene lokaler Akteure, auf die in den abschließenden Bemerkungen eingegangen wird, bedeutet dies auch für die ausländischen Geberinstitutionen, dass sie verstärkt auf lokale Realitäten und Agenden eingehen müssten, um das Spannungsfeld ‚lokal-global', in dem viele NGOs agieren, zu berücksichtigen (Hawthorne 2005).

8. Abschließende Bemerkungen

In Ägypten hat sich im Verlauf der 1990er Jahre mit der Entstehung von *advocacy* NGOs eine Form von Aktivismus[38] entwickelt, der sich zur Verbesserung der Lage der Frauen am internationalen Diskurs der Menschenrechte von Frauen orientiert und auf verschiedenen Formen transnationaler Vernetzung aufbaut. Angesichts der starken politischen und gesellschaftlichen Widerstände gegen Veränderungen im Status der Frauen wurde eingangs darauf hingewiesen, dass einem Wandel gesellschaftlicher Wertvorstellungen und Praktiken eine zentrale Rolle bei Anstrengungen zur Verbesserung des Status' der Frauen in ihrem alltäglichen Leben zukommt. Diese Beobachtung wurde mit der Frage nach der Rolle von *advocacy* NGOs und ihren transnationalen Netzwerken bei solchen Prozessen der Sozialisierung internationaler Frauenrechtsstandards auf einer breiten gesellschaftlichen Ebene verknüpft. Wie gezeigt wurde, stehen die hier diskutierten NGOs vor einer Reihe interner sowie externer Herausforderungen, die sich erschwerend auf ihre Versuche der Vermittlung zwischen globalen Normen und lokalen Realitäten auswirken: ihre Abhängigkeit von ausländischen Finanzierungsmitteln, der Drahtseilakt zwischen transnationaler Vernetzung und Verantwortlichkeiten gegenüber ihrer lokalen Basis sowie die restriktiven politischen und sozialen Rahmenbedingungen ihrer Arbeit.

Die benannten Probleme werden von NGO-Aktivisten durchaus realistisch und selbstkritisch anerkannt, jedoch scheint die lokale NGO-Gemeinschaft hierfür bisher noch keine übergreifenden Lösungsansätze gefunden zu haben. Oft wird auf die politischen und sozialen Rahmenbedingungen verwiesen, die keine anderen Handlungsmöglichkeiten zuließen (Jürgensen 2004).[39] Durchaus kann

---

[38] Wie in diesem Beitrag gezeigt wurde, beinhaltet der Begriff ‚Aktivismus' unterschiedliche Facetten. Einerseits wird hierbei eine Form von (gutgemeintem) Aktionismus bezeichnet, der jedoch auf starke materielle, rechtliche sowie mentale Hindernisse stößt. So kann Aktivismus auch als notwendiger Aktivitätsüberschuss verstanden werden, der nötig ist, um sich widerständigen Verhältnissen selbst um den Preis der eigenen Gefährdung zu stellen. Ferner bezeichnet der Begriff auch eine ambivalente soziologische Kategorie, wie die Konkurrenz zwischen unterschiedlichen zivilgesellschaftlichen Formen von *Gender*-Aktivismus (an internationalen Normen oder islamistisch orientiert) belegt. Für den wertvollen Hinweis auf die Mehrdeutigkeit dieses Begriffs danke ich Herrn Dr. A. Triebel.

[39] Bereits gegen Ende der 1990er Jahre haben Aktivistinnen und Aktivisten aus der MENA-Region in unterschiedlichen Foren mit einer Bestandsaufnahme der Arbeit lokaler Menschenrechts-NGOs begonnen und die hier angeführten Problembereiche extensiv diskutiert (Siehe: *Harvard Law School Human Rights Program* 2000).

aber auch auf Fortschritte auf einzelnen Gebieten verwiesen werden. So versuchen größere NGOs mit langjähriger Erfahrung zunehmend, die Voraussetzungen für einen Umgang auf gleicher Augenhöhe mit internationalen Geldgebern zu schaffen, indem sie zunächst eine eigene Agenda setzen und erst dann um ausländische Gelder werben (Pitner 2000). Auch lassen sich verstärkt Bemühungen erkennen, dem Vorwurf entgegenzutreten, die an einer internationalen Agenda ausgerichteten Anliegen von *advocacy* NGOs spiegelten nicht die wahren Probleme der breiten Bevölkerung wider (Masonis El-Gawhary 2000). Gerade Frauenrechtsorganisationen sind besonders bemüht, den Eindruck einer strikten Trennung zwischen „Basisgruppen, die sich die Schuhe dreckig machen, und Gruppen, die die öffentliche Meinung beeinflussen wollen" (El-Gawahry 1995) zu widerlegen. So bieten angesichts der besonders schweren Folgen der wirtschaftlichen Lage für Frauen viele dieser NGOs auch Dienstleistungen für Frauen an, verknüpfen diese aber, im Gegensatz zu traditionellen Organisationen, mit *Empowerment*-Maßnahmen (Masonis El-Gawhary 2000). Entsprechend werden auch die Tätigkeiten von Frauen-NGOs im Kontext der breiteren NGO-Gemeinschaft von Beobachtern besonders positiv bewertet:

„Women's NGOs are often the most impressive sector of the advocacy NGO world. [...] Women NGOs often seem better able to connect to an extensive constituency than most other NGOs and to bridge the urban-rural gap so common in the NGO world. They take up issues of immediate interest to their constituents, and their agenda naturally synthesizes economic, political, and social concerns." (Carothers 1999: 217)

Obwohl der Einfluss internationaler bzw. transnationaler Faktoren auf die Entwicklung der ägyptischen NGO-Gemeinschaft sehr groß ist, sollten *advocacy* NGOs daher nicht allein als ‚Produkt' externer, westlicher Einflüsse gesehen werden: „*Rather, civic activism through NGOs is a way of responding to contemporary socioeconomic circumstances.*" (Carapico 2000: 15) Die Erfahrungen der hier behandelten *advocacy* NGOs, welche internationale Frauenrechtsstandards als Bezugsrahmen ihrer Arbeit wählen, zeigen aber, dass diese Organisationen immer wieder vor der Herausforderung stehen, die Inhalte internationaler Normen auf die Gegebenheiten des Kontextes, in dem sie arbeiten, herunterzubrechen. Viele dieser NGOs sind daher bemüht, durch Workshops, Konferenzen und Trainings Frauen (und Männer) über ihre Rechte auf der nationalen sowie auf der internationalen Ebene aufzuklären und hierfür Bewusstsein zu schaffen. Doch ist die Reichweite dieser Aktivitäten durch den zeitlich und finanziell begrenzten Rahmen solcher Projekte meist auf kleinere Zielgruppen beschränkt, so dass diese Aktivitäten nur

Lokaler Aktivismus – *Advocacy* NGOs

bedingt Einfluss auf breitere gesellschaftliche Diskurse ausüben können (Jad 2004). Um weite Teile der Bevölkerung zu erreichen und einen dauerhaften Sinneswandel einzuleiten, der sich auch in einer Veränderung alltäglichen Verhaltens widerspiegelt, nimmt daher die Zusammenarbeit von *advocacy* NGOs mit weiteren zivilgesellschaftlichen und politischen Akteuren eine wichtige Rolle ein. Jedoch ist es bisher NGOs nur in einzelnen Fällen gelungen, durch eine fortdauernde Zusammenarbeit mit anderen Akteuren (z.B. Presse, islamistischen Frauenorganisationen, aber auch staatlichen Einrichtungen) über die begrenzte Reichweite der eigenen Aktivitäten hinaus breitere Teile der Bevölkerung zu erreichen:

„The Arab women's NGOs in their actual forms and structures might be able to play a role in advocating Arab women's rights in the international arena, provide services for certain needy groups, propose new policies and visions, generate and disseminate information. But, in order to affect comprehensive, sustainable development and democratisation, a different form of organisation is needed with a different, locally grounded vision and a more sustainable power basis for change." (Jad 2004; siehe auch: Hawthorne 2005: 105)

Angesichts der Schwierigkeiten, die sich für *advocacy* NGOs in Ägypten bei der lokalen sowie internationalen Koordination ihrer Aktivitäten ergeben, können diese auf gesellschaftlicher Ebene bislang ihre Rolle als ‚*norm entrepreneurs*' im Bereich der Menschenrechte von Frauen nur begrenzt wahrnehmen. So ist es diesen Organisationen bisher auf einigen Gebieten gelungen, eine Rolle als Motoren der Debatte einzunehmen und Dikussionen zu schwierigen und lange Zeit tabuisierten Themen anzustoßen. Hierdurch konnte in manchen Fällen auch ein entsprechender Wertewandel eingeleitet werden, wie die veränderte Haltung hoher politische und religiöser Persönlichkeiten zu bestimmten Fagen oder die Reformen einzelner diskriminierender Gesetze gezeigt haben. Wie jedoch dargestellt wurde, haben diese positiven Veränderungen bisher in vielen Fällen leider noch nicht zu einer tatsächlichen und tief greifenden Verbesserung der alltäglichen Lebenssituation einer großen Mehrheit der ägyptischen Frauen geführt. Es bleibt daher abzuwarten, ob *advocacy* NGOs in Zukunft auch bei der Internalisierung und Umsetzung internationaler Normen auf einer breiten gesellschaftlichen Ebene zu einer treibenden Kraft heranwachsen können.

Literaturverzeichnis

Abdel Hadi, Amal (1998): We Are Decided – The Struggle of an Egyptian Village to Eradicate Female Circumcision, Cairo Institute for Human Rights Studies, Cairo.

Abdel Hadi, Amal (2003): Empowerment – From Theory into Practice – CEOSS Experience in the Area of the Eradication of Female Genital Cutting, Cairo, CEOSS.

Al-Ali, Nadje (2000): Secularism, Gender and the State in the Middle East – The Egyptian Women's Movement, Cambridge, Cambridge University Press.

Alliance for Arab Women (2003): Violence Against Women: Dimensions and Consequences, Cairo.

Amnesty International (2004): Egypt: Medical Center Harassed and Intimidated by Authorities, Faces Imminent Closure, 12.06.2004. Http://web.amnesty.org/library/Index/ENGMDE120062004?open&of=ENG-EGY [10.12.2005].

An-Na'im, Abdullahi A. (Interview 2000): Problems of Dependency – Human Rights Organizations in the Arab World, in: Middle East Report 214, S. 20-23/46-47.

Bayat, Asef (2002): Activism and Social Development in the Middle East, in: International Journal of Middle East Studies 34(1), S. 1-28.

Benninger-Budel, Carin (2001): Violence Against Women in Egypt. Report prepared for the Committee on the Elimination of Discrimination Against Women, Geneva, OMCT. Http://www.omct.org/pdf/vaw/EgyptEng2001.pdf [30.03.2006].

Brysk, Alison (1993): From Above and Below – Social Movements, the International System, and Human Rights in Argentina, in: Comparative Political Studies 26(3), S. 259-85.

Carapico, Sheila (2000): NGOs, INGOs, GO-NGOs and DO-NGOs – Making Sense of Non-Governmental Organizations, in: Middle East Report 214, S. 12-15.

Carothers, Thomas (1999): Aiding Democracy Abroad – The Learning Curve, Washington, D.C., Carnegie Endowment for International Peace.

Cerna, Christina M./Wallace, Jennifer C. (1999): Women and Culture, in: Askin, Kelly D./Koenig, Dorean M. (eds.): Women and International Human Rights Law, vol. 1, New York, Transnational Publishers, S. 623-50.

Committee on the Elimination of All Forms of Discrimination Against Women (2000): Consideration of reports submitted by States parties under article 18 of the Convention on the Elimination of All Forms of Discrimination against Women, combined fourth and fifth periodic reports of States parties, Egypt, U.N. Doc. CEDAW/C/EGY/4-5, 30 March 2000. Http://www.un.org/womenwatch/daw/cedaw/cedaw24/cedawcegy45.pdf. [16.11.2006].

Coomaraswamy, Radhika (1997): Reinventing International Law – Women's Rights as Human Rights in the International Community, The Edward A. Smith Visiting Lecturer, Harvard Law School Human Rights Program. Http://www.law.havard.edu/programs/HRP [26.06.2002].

Duval de Dampierre, Soraya (1995): „Westliche" versus „islamische" Frauenrechte? Beobachtungen von der Internationalen Konferenz für Bevölkerung und Entwicklung", in: INAMO, 1 (2), S. 41-44.

Egyptian NGO Coalition on CEDAW (2000): The Shadow Report, Cairo.

Egyptian Organization for Human Rights (2005): Critical Analysis of the New Associations' Law. EOHR Report. Http://www.eohr.org/report/2005/re0704.htm [14.10.2005].

El Sayed Said, Mohamed (1994): The Roots of Turnmoil in the Egyptian Organization for Human Rights – Dynamics of Civil Institution-Building in Egypt", in: Cairo Papers in Social Science 17(3), S. 65-87.

El-Azhary Sonbol, Amira (2005): Egypt, Freedom House, 28.04.2005. Http://www.freedomhouse.org.

El-Baz, Shahida (1997): The Impact of Social and Economic Factors on Women's Group Formation in Egypt, in: Chatty, Dawn/ Rabo, Annika (Hrsg.): Organizing Women – Formal and Informal Women's Groups in the Midlle East, Oxford, Berg, S. 147-71.

El-Gawahry, Karim (1995): NGOs zwischen Basisarbeit und Regierungsgeschäft, in: INAMO, 1(1), S. 45-46.

Ezzat, Dina/Hammouda, Dahila (2003): Putting Down the Scalpell, in: Al Ahram Weekly Online, 26 June-2 July 2003, 644, Http://weekly.ahram.org.eg/2003/644/eg7.htm [10.12.2005].

Finnemore, Martha/Sikkink, Kathryn (1998): International Norm Dynamics and Political Change, in: International Organization 52(4), S. 887-913.

Friedrich-Ebert-Stiftung (2002): Frauenrechte in islamischen Ländern im Spannungsfeld von nationaler Kultur und universellen Menschenrechten, Bonn, Friedrich-Ebert-Stiftung.

Harvard Law School Human Rights Program (2000): International Aspects of the Arab Human Rights Movement. An Interdisciplinary Discussion Held in Cairo March 1998. Organized by the Human Rights Program Harvard Law School and the Center for the Study of Developing Countries at Cairo University, Harvard Law School Human Rights Program.

Hawthorne, Amy (2005): Is Civil Society the Answer?, in: Carothers, Thomas/ Ottaway, Marina (Hrsg.): Uncharted Journey: Promoting Democracy in the Middle East, Wahington D.C., Carnegie Council for International Peace), S. 81-113.

Holthaus, Ines (1996): Frauenmenschenrechtsbewegungen und die Universalisierung der Menschenrechte, in: Peripherie, 16(61), S. 6-23.

Human Rights Watch (1995): The Human Rights Watch Global Report on Human Rights, New York u.a., Human Rights Watch.

Human Rights Watch (2003): Egypt's New Chill on Rights Groups, 21.06.2003. Http:// www.hrw.org/press/2003/06/egypt062103.htm [10.12.2005].

Human Rights Watch (2004a): Divorced From Justice – Women's Unequal Access to Divorce in Egypt. Http://www.hrw.org/reports/2004/egypt1204/ [10.12.2005].

Human Rights Watch (2004b): Egypt: Torture Victims Clinic Threatened with Closure, 13.07.2004. Http://hrw.org/english/docs/2004/07/13/egypt9059.htm [10.12.2005].

Human Rights Watch (2005): Egypt: Margins of Repression. State Limits on Nongovernmental Organization Activism. Http://www.hrw.org/reports/2005/egypt0705/ [08.07.2005].

Hussein, Aziza (1994): Egypt Country Report (Interview), in: Civil Society, 3(10), S. 4-5.

Ibn Khaldun Center for Development Studies (2005): Presse Release – Demagogues and rabble-rousers conduct a media campaign against ICDS for receiving foreign funds. Http://www.eicds.org/english/activities/pressreleases/05/march28.htm [10.12.2005].

Jad, Islah (2004): The NGOisation of Arab Women's Movements, 14.05.2005. Available: http://www.kit.nl/specials/assets/images/NGOisation-IslahJad-2004.pdf.

Jürgensen, Carsten (2004a): Die Frauengleichstellungsdebatte, in: Faath, Sigrid (Hrsg.): Politische und gesellschaftliche Debatten in Nordafrika, Nah- und Mittelost – Inhalte, Träger, Perspektiven, Hamburg, Deutsches Orient-Institut, S. 319-39.

Jürgensen, Carsten (2004b): Die Menschenrechtsdebatte, in: Faath, Sigrid (Hrsg.): Politische und gesellschaftliche Debatten in Nordafrika, Nah- und Mittelost. Inhalte, Träger, Perspektiven, Hamburg, Deutsches Orient-Institut, S. 295-318.

Karam, Azza M. (1998): Women, Islamism and the State. Contemporary Feminism in Egypt, Houndmills, Macmillan.

Katulis, Brian (2005): The Impact of Public Attitudes, Freedom House. Http://www.freedomhouse.org/template.cfm?page=169 [28.05.2005].

Katulis, Brian (2004): Women's Rights in Focus: Egypt – Findings from May-June 2004 Focus Groups with Egyptian Citizens on Women's Freedom, Freedom House, 10.05.2005. Http://www.freedomhouse.org.

Khagram, Sanjeev/Riker, James V./Sikkink, Kathryn (2002): From Santiago to Seattle – Transnational Advocacy Groups Restructuring World Politics, in: Khagram, Sanjeev/Riker, James V./Sikkink, Kathryn (Hrsg.): Reconstructing World Politics. Transnational Social Movements, Networks and Norms, Minneapolis, University of Minnesota Press, S. 3-23.

Khan, Salma (2002): Customary Practices, Culture and Human Rights of Women – The Role of the Convention on the Elimination of all Forms of Discrimination Against Women, in: Human Rights Advisory Council (Hrsg.): Vth International Workshop of National Institutions for the Promotion and Protection of Human Rights. Rabat-Morocco, April, 13-15, 2000, Rabat, Human Rights Advisory Council, S. 285-306.

Khan, Salma (2003): Die Konvention über die Beseitigung jeder Form von Diskriminierung der Frau und der politische Charakter ‚religiöser' Vorbehalte", in: Riumpf, Mechthild/Gerhard, Ute/Jansen, Mechthild M. (Hrsg.): Facetten islamischer Welten. Geschlechterordnungen, Frauen- und Menschenrechte in der Diskussion, Bielefeld, transcript, S. 103-22.

National Council for Women (2002a): Egypt – Gender Indicators, Cairo.

National Council for Women (2002b), Egyptian Women in Figures 2002, Cairo.

Nazir, Sameena (2005): Challenging Inequality – Obstacles and Opportunities towards Women's Rights in the Middle East and North Africa, Freedom House, 28.05.2005. Http://www.freedomhouse.org/template.cfm?page=163. [16.11.2006].

Neuhold, Britta (1995): Von „Equal Rights" zu „Gender Justice" – Der mühsame Weg der Vereinten Nationen zum „Empowerment" von Frauen, in: Österreichische Zeitschrift für Politikwissenschaft 24(4), S. 377-97.

New Woman Research & Study Center (1996): The Feminist Movement in the Arab World, Cairo, Dar El-Mostaqbal Al Arabi.

Perthes, Volker (2002): Geheime Gärten. Die neue arabische Welt, Berlin, Siedler Verlag.

Petersohn, Alexandra, (1999): Islamisches Menschenrechtsverständnis unter Berücksichtigung der Vorbehalte muslimischer Staaten zu den UN-Menschenrechtsverträgen, Dissertation, Bonn, Rheinische-Friedrich-Wilhelms-Universität.

Pitner, Julia (2000): NGOs' Dilemmas, in: Middle East Report 214, S. 34-37.

Pratt, Nicola (2000): Egypt Harasses Human Rights Activists, in: Middle East Report Online, 20.04.2005. Http://www.merip.org/mero/mero081700.html.

Pratt, Nicola (2004): Understanding Political Transformation in Egypt – Advocacy NGOs, Civil Society and the State, in: Journal of Mediterranean Studies, 14(1/2), S. 237-62.

Rao, Arati (1995): The Politics of Gender and Culture in International Human Rights Discourse, in: Peters, Julie/Wolper, Andrea (Hrsg.): Women's Rights, Human Rights – International Feminist Perspectives, New York, London, Routledge, S. 167-75.

Raouf Ezzat, Heba (2001): The Silent Ayesha – An Egyptian Narrative, in: Bayes, Jane H./Tohidi, Nayereh (Hrsg.): Globalization, Gender, and Religion, New York u.a.,Palgrave, S. 231-58.

Risse, Thomas/C. Ropp, Stephen/Sikkink, Kathryn (Hrsg.) (1999): The Power of Human Rights. International Norms and Domestic Change, Cambridge, Cambridge University Press.

Schemm, Paul (2002): The NGO law is back, and few are left to stop it this time, in: Cairo Times, 16-22 May, 6:11.

Seif El Dawla, Aida (1996): Women's Rights in Egypt, 20.09.2005. Http://waf.gn.apc.org/journal8p25.htm.

Seif El Dawla, Aida/Ibrahim, Somaya (1995): Ägyptsche Frauenorganisationen auf dem Weg von Kairo nach Peking, in: Feministische Studien 13(1), S. 113-18.

Seif El Dawla, Aida/Hadi, Amal Abdel/ Abdel Wahab, Nadia (1998): Trade-offs and Strategic Accomodations in Egyptian Women's Reproductive Lives, in: Petchesky, Rosalind P./Judd, Karen (Hrsg.): Negotiating Reproductive Rights – Women's Perspectives Across Countries and Cultures, London, New York, Zed Books, S. 69-107.

Sikkink, Kathryn (2001): Historical Precursors to Modern Campaigns for Women's Human Rights – Campaigns Against Footbinding and Female Circumcision, in: Askin, Kelly D./Koenig, Dorean M. (Hrsg.): Women and International Human Rights Law, vol. 3, Ardsley, Transnational Publishers, S. 797-818.

Tomasevski, Katarina (1998): Rights of Women: From Prohibition to Elimination of Discrimination, in: International Social Science Journal 158, S. 545-58.

U.S. Department of State (2001): Egypt: Report on Female Genital Mutilation (FGM) or Female Genital Cutting (FGC), 10.11.2005. Http://www.state.gov/g/wi/rls/rep/crfgm/10096.htm. [16.11.2006].

UNDP (2002): Arab Human Development Report – Creating Opportunities for Future Generations, New York, United Nations.

UNIFEM (2002): Progress of the World's Women 2002, New York, United Nations.

UNIFEM Western Asia Regional Office (1999): Violence Against Women Campaign: Campaign Report, Amman, Http://www.arabwomenconnect.org/docs/ASRO_HR_violence.pdf.

Uvin, Peter (2000): The Role of NGOs in International Relations, in: Stiles, Kendall (Hrsg.): Global institutions and local empowerment – Competing theoretical perspectives, Houndmills, Macmillan Press, S. 9-29.

Wassef, Nadia (2000): Ending Female Genital Mutilation Without Human Rights.

World Bank (2003): Arab Republic of Egypt – Gender Assessment.

Würth, Anna (2003): Dialog mit dem Islam als Konfliktprävention? Zur Menschenrechtspolitik gegenüber islamisch geprägten Staaten, Berlin, Deutsches Institut für Menschenrechte.

Zaki, Moheb (1995): Civil Society & Democratization in Egypt, Cairo, Ibn Khaldoun Center for Development Studies.

Zubaida, Sami (1992): Islam, the State & Democracy – Contrasting Conceptions of Society in Egypt, in: Middle East Report 22(6), S. 2-10.

Zulficar, Mona (2003a): The Egyptian Women in a Changing World, Shalakany Law Office Publications. Http://www.ecwregypt/ English/researches/2004/changingworld.htm [10.11.2005].

Zulficar, Mona (2003b): The Islamic Marriage Contract in Egypt – An Instrument of Social Change, Cairo, Shalakany Law Office Publications.

Zulficar, Mona (2003c): The Political Rights of Women in Egypt, Shalakany Law Office Publications. Http://www.ecwregypt.org/ English/researches/2004/politicalrights.htm [10.11.2005].

 Für Studenten und Dozenten!

1 | Nachdenken über Europa

2 | Autoritäre Regime

3 | Grenzen der EU

4 | Wissenschaftliches Schreiben

5 | Politische Herrschaft in Süd- und Mittelamerika

6 | Internationale Beziehungen: Konzepte

7 | Politische Regime im Nahen und Mittleren Osten

8 | Kommunale Politik und Verwaltung

Anregend für die Debatte, unverzichtbar für's Seminar,
kostengünstig für das studentische Budget (nur 8 € pro Lehrtext)

 Bestellungen:
Universitätsverlag Potsdam: ubpub@uni-potsdam.de

Heidi Wedel

The Role of Civil Society Organisations for Democratisation
Lessons from Turkey

From the late 1980s, fed by developments in Eastern Europe in the wake of the collapse of the Iron Curtain, great hopes were pinned on civil society as a means of liberation from authoritarian regimes. These developments triggered a debate on whether or not the Eastern European case could be a model for liberalisation and democratisation in the Middle East. In Germany, this discourse was further developed by a group of political scientists in the Institute of Middle Eastern Politics at Free University of Berlin. The group pointed at the role of political Islam as a major factor distinguishing Middle Eastern societies from Eastern European societies.[1] As part of the attempts to analyse the nuclei of civil society in the Middle East and the role they could assume in democratisation, my focus within this group was on civil society in Turkey. Turkey is the most secular country in the Middle East and in spite of all deficiencies in the legal framework and actual practice Turkey is more advanced in the process of transition from authoritarian rule than most other countries in the region. I concluded that civil society was developing in Turkey, but that the then ongoing armed conflict and the escalating violence and polarisation made civil society in the Kurdish East impossible and obstructed the nuclei of civil society in the West of the country.[2]

Ten years on and six years after the end of the armed conflict, in this synoptic review I will try to assess the contribution of civil society to a deepening of democratisation in Turkey. Having set out my definition of civil society, I will discuss the different forms civil society assumed in Turkey and their potential contribution to democratisation and peace within society.

1. Definition of Civil Society

The concept of civil society is problematic as it is used in a variety of meanings. These range from liberal concepts of civil society as a pluralistic society which includes the governmental institutions of a liberal-democratic state to Gramsci's socialist concept of a coalition

---
[1] Ibrahim/Wedel 1995: 16-17.
[2] Wedel 1995.

of societal organisations against the cultural hegemony of the state. Yet, civil society is also an intriguing concept, as it allows discussing forms of democratisation that go beyond liberal institutional definitions of democracy that focus on characteristics such as representation and parliamentarianism, separation of power and rule of law. In addition, the concept of civil society is helpful for the analysis of political participation in non-democratic/non-liberal states, as it looks at political participation outside the official institutions of liberal democracies in the above cited liberal sense.

For the purpose of this article, I will work with a narrow definition of civil society developed from the collaboration with colleagues from Free University of Berlin such as Ferhad Ibrahim and Ali Schirazi in the middle of the 1990s.[3] My definition of civil society is based on three constituting elements:

i) Normative element: Civil society supports and embodies values of "civility" such as plurality, tolerance and non-violence.[4]
ii) Institutional element: civil society is constituted by the voluntary, inter-mediate organisations of citizens such as associations, foundations, interest groups, platforms, circles and other more or less structured forms of organisation which have gained a relative autonomy from the state. Such organisations are often called NGOs (non-governmental organisations).
iii) Regime/contextual element: Civil society is constituted between state and society, outside state structures and with a relative autonomy from the state. It does not aim at overthrowing or taking over state power or becoming part of the state. Civil society rather acts as a watchdog over state power, making its faults and weaknesses known to the public, calling for state accountability and presenting alternative policy approaches. Civil society organisations may cooperate with state structures or rather act in opposition to the state. According to our definition political parties may or may not be part of civil society, depending on the political context and the role of each single party within this context.

This definition naturally excludes some forms of political participation which might be included in broader definitions of civil society.

The first element excludes for example armed opposition groups or some identity based organisations which are not ready to deal peacefully and on the basis of tolerance with people and communities

---

[3] Compare Ibrahim/Wedel 1995: 10-11.
[4] Norton (1995: 11-12) also refers to the values of civility in his discussion of civil society which is similar to our independently developed definition.

of different identity (the Others), such as some fundamentalist/Islamist or ultra-nationalist associations.

The second element excludes unstructured forms of political participation such as the ad-hoc activities of urban poor which I studied in my research on local political participation and gender.[5] However, it is interesting to ask whether in authoritarian regimes unorganised forms of participation e.g. cultural counter-voices can constitute an element contributing to the development of civil society.[6]

The third element excludes political parties competing for state power as well as trade unions or professional unions which have been co-opted by the state (corporatist organisations and structures).[7]

Working with a narrow definition of civil society enables us to differentiate between civil society and other expressions of political participation or democracy. From my point of view this differentiation is crucial for the assessment of the potential of civil society to contribute to democracy and peace within societies. This is especially helpful in the analysis of modernising nation states such as Turkey. Turkey's democracy still suffers from the lasting effects of its modernisation ideology Kemalism, which quite typically relied on a strong modernising state elite. While the military and the civil bureaucracy were striving to develop and "westernise" the country, they not only "postponed" democracy and pluralism, but also excluded many groups from active participation in the reform process. Claiming to work "for the people in spite of the people", the elite suppressed any articulation of separate interests and identities. In such a context it is interesting to analyse, how after decades of top down modernisation, segments of society begin to develop alternative visions and to participate in the making of society.

My thesis is that civil society defined by the above three elements strives at broadening and deepening political participation with the inclusion of new societal groups and can be a new vision of societal transformation, which develops and possibly implements political, social, ecological and/or economic alternatives. Civil society can create "democratic, ecological and just pockets" within a less democratic, ecological and just political system and society.

I would like to discuss this thesis on the basis my observations of civil society in Turkey. I had the opportunity to gain a deeper insight into Turkish civil society both through academic field re-

---

[5] Wedel 1999.
[6] See Schirazi 1995 on Iran.
[7] In my view, liberal definitions such as Shils (1991) that include all political parties or even state bodies such as the judiciary and the executive are so broad that they blur the difference between civil society and a democratic political system.

search as a political scientist and by active cooperation as a women's rights activist and a human rights defender. I have had contacts, observed and actively cooperated with many civil society organisations in Turkey over years – with some of them from their very beginning. In addition, I conducted interviews with a number of representatives. Still, my inside knowledge will always be limited and in addition filtered by my own cultural background. On the other hand, as an outsider and academic not affiliated with any one group, I was in the fortunate position to have contacts with divergent groups. At least, my analysis will hopefully add another view indicating what is noteworthy for a foreign researcher.

2. Forms of Civil Society in Turkey

2.1 New Social Movements

According to Jean Cohen and Andrew Arato "social movements constitute the dynamic element in processes that might realise the positive potentials of modern civil societies".[8] We differentiate between "new" and "old" social movements as ideal types in the following way: "New social movements are inclined towards affective concerns, expressive relations, and horizontal organisations. Old social movements are inclined towards material concerns, instrumental relations, orientation towards the state, and vertical organisation."[9]

In Turkey, new social movements came into being a few years after the military coup in the 1980s with the emerging women's movement, human rights movement, and ecological movement. They gave way to a new political culture which questioned the concept of the patrimonial state and asserted that citizens have rights which they can claim from the state. They mobilised a huge number of supporters. An increase of the number of members and supporters and the self-organisation of the affected people are their deliberate goals.

Compared to other forms of political organisation new social movements demonstrate a bigger heterogeneity in political and social terms, bringing professional experts and affected people (e.g. lawyers and victims of human rights violations and their families or battered women) together in the same association. If heterogeneity is dealt with in a constructive way it fosters internal pluralism. In the Turkish new social movements, internal pluralism is indeed amazing when compared to other forms of political organisation in Turkey. Yet this pluralism does not go beyond certain political camps. For

---

[8] Cohen/Arato 1992: 492.
[9] Mainwaring/Viola 1984: 19-20.

example, most of the people involved in the biggest human rights organisation *IHD* come from a leftist background or belong to the Kurdish movement, whereas Islamic oriented people founded another human rights organisation called *Mazlum Der* in 1991.[10] The issues taken up by these two organisations and the people who turn to them for help are mainly related to the respective political camps. But the leading activists of these organisations believe in the universality of human rights and expressively state that they are open to everybody. After initial hesitation both human rights organisations put their reservations aside and started a certain degree of networking and cooperation with each other.

Especially for the women's movement in Turkey, internal democracy is an expressed goal. Women's groups have tried new forms of organisation without hierarchical organisation, although this is very difficult in a society in which status and hierarchies still play a major role and under a Law on Associations that prescribes strict forms of organisations.

In conclusion, new social movements have managed to a certain extent to establish democratic pockets with a new political culture within the still hierarchical political and social system.

2.2 Old Social Movements

Although to a much lesser extent than new social movements, old social movements can also form a part of civil society. It was only after the adoption of a more liberal constitution in Turkey that a trade union and leftist movement could develop in Turkey from the 1960s onwards. Their attempts to organise and mobilise workers and the urban poor and to topple the political regime involved major parts of this movement in an armed struggle against the regime and armed clashes with the far-right.

The leftist movement never fully recovered from the military coup in 1980. The small armed leftist groups which re-established in the 1980s certainly do not fall under our definition of civil society. Yet, with the political reorganisation since the 1980s many old leftists or former leftists have joined new forms of political organisations, including the new social movements, or have formed their own associations. Whereas the leftist associations have less impact on society nowadays, leftists within social movement organisations are contributing to a major extent to general political opinion building and activities.

The trade union movement has never regained its previous vigour. It is mainly the public service trade unions which mobilise mass membership actions (demonstrations, civil obedience acts). They

---

[10] Compare Plagemann 2000.

also participate in platforms with other organisations and in discussions on general political issues such as economic policies, the Kurdish question or high security prisons. In this respect, trade unions in Turkey fall under our definition of civil society.

Another social movement, the urban social movement and especially the neighbourhood organisations of the urban poor, exhibits more elements of old than of new social movements.[11] While in Turkey's squatter areas we can discern a political consciousness that comes close to the one of urban social movements as well as collective action on behalf of related concerns, these actions lack the institutional element of civil society organisations. Thus in Turkey, we cannot speak of urban social movements as networks of neighbourhood organisations, or part of civil society.[12]

In general terms, since by their very nature old social movements mainly pursue material goals (often for a specific societal segment) they contribute less to the values of civility than the new social movements which strive for ideal goals such as human rights, women's rights, peace and ecology.

2.3 Identity Movements

In Turkey, like in many parts of the world, identity movements have widely replaced the old social movements. The Islamist movement has been successful in recruiting masses and organising on the grass roots level, thus opening spaces of political participation to marginalised groups such as the urban poor. The Kurdish movement has succeeded in mass mobilisation from the early 1990s. However, such movements only partly comply with the criteria for civil society. Since they organise the interests of a specific ethnic or religious group, they are less inclined to pluralism and tolerance. They have problems acknowledging gender differences and rights, which they perceive as a threat to the unity of their group. Last but not least, their armed wings certainly do not meet the criterion of non-violence. Human rights abuses by these armed groups reinforced the polarisation of society and were another obstacle for cooperation or tolerance between groups. Militarist culture and thinking had a huge impact even on NGOs within these movements. In addition, the Islamist movement is widely dominated by political parties. Where possible, they have used their own local or state power to bar the access of secular NGOs to state resources and limit their room for manoeuvre. It is mainly when they themselves encounter repression that identity movements seem to meet the three criteria for civil

---

[11] Mainwaring/Viola 1984: 19-20 and 28.
[12] Wedel 1999: 297.

society: civility, voluntary organisation and relative autonomy from the state.

2.4 Academics and Civil Rights Organisations

Academics and civil rights organisations (such as *Helsinki Citizens Assembly*) largely contributed to the development of the concept and discourse of civil society in Turkey. Since the early 1980s feminists and other critics of Kemalism have raised the political awareness for the rights of individuals and the respect for difference. Through the media they had the chance to promulgate calls for tolerance to a wider audience. Thus they laid the theoretical foundations for civil society, although the associations formed by these intellectuals are often pretty elitist and non-inclusive.

2.5 Interest Groups and Professional Organisations

Organisations of the professional middle classes such as *Bar Associations*, *Medical Chambers*, the chamber of architects and engineers *TMMOB* or the association of businessmen *TÜSIAD* increasingly raised their voices promulgating alternative solutions for policies related to their work areas: human rights, the rule of law, environmental issues, urban planning or the Kurdish issue. In some instances they pledged for integration into state policy planning, asserting the capacities of civil society and the state's need to benefit from their specialised knowledge. In other instances they rather acted as a mouthpiece of oppositional views which due to their respected status was less prone to persecution. However, even these established organisations may be at risk of prosecution as soon as they go beyond the narrow areas of pure professional interest formulation.

Since every professional has to be a registered member of these organisations in order to be allowed to practice, professional associations are not truly "voluntary" associations. However, active involvement is a voluntary and deliberate act. These associations actively play an intermediate role between state and society, challenging and controlling state policies. Due to their very nature in terms of membership, but also in their interaction – or rather lack of interaction – with organisations of non-middle-class citizens, professional organisations are non-inclusive. Some professional organisations and middle-class interest groups have openly disdained "populism" and concessions to the "masses". Their attitude towards the lower classes and their political associations sometimes resemble those of the Turkish state elites asserting to know what is good for the people ("For the people in spite of the people"). This attitude can lead to support for the state against the lower strata of society and the belief that the state should protect the achievements of modernisation against backward masses[13] and indeed protect the material assets of the middle-class.

2.6 Charities

Charities can be regarded as part of civil society in so far as they not only fill gaps left by governmental social services, but also try and support groups such as internally displaced or street children neglected by state agencies for political reasons. Furthermore, some charities develop and implement new approaches to social problems allowing or encouraging the active participation of the target group with its specific knowledge. Although generally run by middle-class people they can contribute to extending participation to lower classes. Islamic charities seem to be more successful in bridging the cultural gap between the classes in Turkey. In some cases, charities are directly involved in political work at the grassroots level, using charitable work as a means to get access to their target groups, win confidence and then discuss broader political issues. In repressive political regimes charities can also be a disguise for political work otherwise banned or threatened with fierce political persecution.

3. Contribution of Civil Society to Democratisation and Peace

All these different forms of civil society organisations have invited and enabled new segments of society to actively participate in politics and thus contributed to broaden democratisation of Turkey. Some of them have also deepened democracy by contributing new forms of pluralism. Since civil organisations are often theme-oriented they bring together members of different political/ideological backgrounds who share the same concerns. Thus the membership of some of the civil organisations is quite heterogeneous. This especially applies to new social movements which – by their very nature – strive for idealistic rather than material concerns. Dealing constructively with internal heterogeneity develops internal pluralism. And fostering an internal democratic culture, associations can also contribute to a culture of pluralism and peace in the wider society.

For example, in the 1990s the IHD Istanbul branch benefited from the diversity of backgrounds and interests of its membership by establishing commissions specialised on certain issues such as workers' rights, minority rights or children's rights. Discussions within the association not only contributed to the development of a broad, encompassing understanding of human rights, but also to the development of a new democratic culture of tolerance and plurality

---
[13] Wedel 1995: 125-126, compare Yerasimos 2000: 17-18.

within the association. Eren Keskin told me in an interview in 1994 that within IHD people who might have previously fought each other have learnt to listen to each other and discuss their different positions peacefully. Unfortunately, it has been extremely difficult to uphold this democratic culture.

The local groups of Amnesty International (AI) in Turkey probably constitute the best example of how people of diverse backgrounds can work together in one civil society organisation. Whereas most of the IHD members have their political roots either in the Turkish left or in the Kurdish movement (that is the two groups most affected by human rights violations in the 1980s and 1990s) the AI membership includes people from diverse ethnic, religious and political backgrounds. Within AI Turkey, strongly Islamic oriented members peacefully cooperate with secularist Kemalists for their shared concerns.

Prevalent ideologies in Turkey had rather focused on group rights such as the nation, the religious group or class. To the contrary, the concept of human rights is based on the belief that each individual independent of their class, nation, ethnicity, sex, or religion has rights in their own that need to be protected. This concept has developed and spread in Turkey only from the late 1980s. Within this relatively short period it has gained quite some ground in Turkish society. It is a major achievement of the human rights and women's movements to have raised awareness for such rights and to call for the protection of the rights of the Other.

Whereas some IHD branches reflect prevalent prejudices against people of diverging sexual orientation, other branches have e.g. protested against police violence against transvestites. And while for example, some wings of the Turkish left did not show tolerance towards any expression of Kurdish identity, parts of the Turkish feminist movement repeatedly demonstrated solidarity with Kurds as a group exposed to repression.[14] Demonstrating respect for the Other or even actively showing support for their rights to live differently is an important contribution for a peaceful dealing with Otherness.

The early 1990s were also the beginning of a series of dialogues between groups of different ideologies or ethnic backgrounds. The international conference of Helsinki Citizens Assembly housed first dialogues between Islamists and secularists, Kurdish and Turkish women. The Kurdish-Turkish women's dialogue developed into a women's peace initiative which held regular meetings before and during the Habitat Conference in 1996. They discussed the role of

---

[14] In 1993/94 feminists even collectively joint the DEP in an act of solidarity although in principle they rejected the idea of political party membership.

women in armed conflict not only as victims, but also as a group with potentials for conflict resolution.

Turkish recent history saw an armed conflict between state security forces and the armed wing of the Kurdish movement as well as armed clashes between groups who exploited ethnic or religious differences for their ideologies. At the peak of the armed conflict, business organisations understood that the ongoing conflict was harmful to investment and thus to their own interests. Although probably not out of an altruistic motivation, these organisations such as *TÜSIAD* and *TOBB* prepared important papers in which they suggested a variety of measures for conflict resolution. Other professional organisations have submitted proposals to ease the socio-economic plight of the displaced such as *TMMOB* with a booklet on the problems of urban infrastructure in Diyarbakir. Although professional associations by definition organise around the rights of their specific membership and often act in competition with other social classes, their socio-economic projects or policy proposals had the potential to reduce tensions that might have otherwise lead to unrest and an escalation of violence, thus contributing to peaceful development. Socio-economic improvements can also free the energies of the poor from a mere struggle for survival and allow them to engage in more constructive activities. Thus it can contribute to a broadening and deepening of political participation.

After the end of the armed conflict in 1999, the Kurdish movement has diverted their energies from armed struggle to the development of civil society, propagating peace and democratisation. Pro-Kurdish parties (*HADEP*, and later *DEHAP*) have won local elections in many Kurdish cities and started to initiate not only infrastructure projects easing the situation of the displaced people, but also giving rooms and facilities to NGOs. During the conflict, nearly all associations, including local branches of the Human Rights Association had been closed. Since the end of the conflict these branches have been reopened and new branches have been established. They still suffer from a number of restrictions, state interference and even persecution, but have already achieved progress in awareness raising and building of a new, peaceful culture. Professional organisations, trade unions and other local organisations have challenged the taboo regarding the Kurdish language and culture. Local NGOs have been visited by NGOs from the west of the country and established first dialogues, for example between women's organisations. Only recently, more than 60 Kurdish civil society organisations (trade unions, professional organisations and associations) called upon the wing of PKK that has resumed armed struggle to lay down their arms forever.[15]

---

[15] Berliner Zeitung, August 22, 2005, quoted in the DTF press bulletin 050828.

The end of the armed conflict has facilitated the development of civil society in the Kurdish region. In addition, contacts between Turkish and Kurdish NGOs can foster the development of peace in society if they avoid paternalism and are based on an understanding of equality. But the conflict which has cost the lives of more than 30,000 people has also cut deep wounds in peoples' brains and feelings. It will probably take time to overcome the polarisation and segregation of society, the resentments and grieves. The values of civility, tolerance, pluralism and non-violence can contribute a lot to overcoming the polarisation and militarisation of society. Whether peace will go beyond mere silence of weapons will depend to a large extent on whether civil society will be allowed to develop and whether civil society will be successful in spreading the values of civility and to demonstrate solidarity which trespasses the borders of gender, social class, ethnicity, political, and religious orientation.

References

Berliner Zeitung, August 22, 2005.
Cohen Jean L./Arato, Andrew (1992): Civil Society and Political Theory, Cambridge (MA).
Ibrahim, Ferhad/Wedel, Heidi (1995): Einleitung, in: Ibrahim, Ferhad/Wedel, Heidi (eds.): Probleme der Zivilgesellschaft im Vorderen Orient, Opladen, pp. 9-22.
Mainwaring, Scott/Viola, Eduardo (1994): New Social Movemets, Political Culture, and Democracy – Brazil and Argentina in the 1980s, in: Telos (61), pp. 17-52.
Norton, Augustus Richard (ed.) (1995): Civil Society in the Middle East, Leiden.
Plagemann, Gottfried (2000): Human Rights Organisations – Defending the Particular or the Universal?, in: Yerasimos, pp. 433-473.
Schirazi, Asghar (1995): Gegenkultur als Ausdruck der Zivilgesellschaft in der Islamischen Republik Iran, in: Ibrahim/Wedel, pp. 135-163.
Shils, Edward (1991): Was ist eine Civil Society?, in: Michalski, Krzysztof (ed.): Europa und die Civil Society. Stuttgart, pp. 13-51.
Wedel, Heidi (1995): Ansätze einer Zivilgesellschaft in der Türkischen Republik – Träger der Demokratisierung oder neue Eliteorganisation?, in: Ibrahim/Wedel, pp. 113-134.
Wedel, Heidi (1999): Lokale Politik und Geschlechterrollen – Stadtmigrantinnen in türkischen Metropolen, Hamburg.
Yerasimos, Stefanos (2000): Civil Society, Europe and Turkey, in: Yerasimos, Stefanos et al. (eds.): Civil Society in the Grip of Nationalism. Istanbul, pp. 11-23.

Leonardo Secchi

Agenda-Building in Brazilian Municipalities: When and How Citizens Participate

Brazil is a Federative Republic divided in three autonomous political-administrative levels: federal, state and municipal. Brazilian Federal Constitution, promulgated in 1988, has passed several responsibilities and competences to the municipal level, among others attributions such as health policies, economic development, urbanization. The role of municipal executive power includes elaboration, implementation and control of public policies in these areas.

A considerable number of research has been carried out in Brazil about the effects of administrative reforms at the federal level of the public administration. However, the production and publication of scientific studies about paradigmatic changes in the public management and its impact on the policy-making in Brazilian municipalities is still scarce and disconnected (Almeida and Carneiro 2003). Furthermore, studies using an analytical approach of the policy-making process are considered rare in the Brazilian bibliography (Frey 2000). Aware of these gaps in the scientific literature, two research projects were elaborated and executed by researchers of the *Grupo de Pesquisa em Gestão e Desenvolvimento* (Research Group on Management and Development) of University of Chapecó (Unochapecó – Brazil) between August 2003 and July 2004. The first research focused on identifying the predominant administrative model in the municipal level in Santa Catarina state. The second one focused on analysing the policy-making process of different policy areas in municipalities located in that region. This paper presents the results of this second research, specifically in what refers the first stage of the policy-making process: identification of public demand and agenda-building.

It is important to stress out that Santa Catarina is a state located in the Southern region and one of the main states of the Brazilian federation in terms of economic development (GDP and GDP *per*

---

* The author would like to thank Unochapecó and CAPES (Brazilian government) for the financial support.
** Paper adapted from a previous work presented at the IX International Research Symposium on Public Management (Milan, Italy - 2005) and at the Annual Conference of the European Group of Public Administration (Bern, Switzerland - 2005).

capita) and exports. Several indicators of human and economic development of Santa Catarina, such as Human Development Index, literacy rate, infant mortality rate, sanitary structures, appear among the best-classified positions in Brazilian federation. Santa Catarina has relatively small territorial dimensions (95,443 km^2), a population of approximately 5.5 million people, predominantly formed by immigrants from Germany, Italy, Portugal (Azores islands), and with African, Ukrainian, Polish and Japanese minorities.

This research had an exploratory-descriptive type and a theoretical-empirical design, based on a collective case study (Stake 1994) in six different municipalities of the west region of Santa Catarina. The following are the selected cases:

1. *Chapecó*, which is the main economical and political city of the west region of Santa Catarina. Chapecó has approximately 160,000 inhabitants, and its economy is based on agribusiness, one of the most developed in Brazil.
2. *Pinhalzinho*, which is one of the cities in the west region of Santa Catarina that had expressive development rates over the last ten years. Pinhalzinho has consolidated its position as an important industrial pole, especially in the furniture sector. The commercial activity of Pinhalzinho is also considerable.
3. *São Miguel do Oeste,* which is one of the main cities of that region with 33,000 inhabitants and an economy based on industry and agriculture, mainly cultivation of tobacco.
4. *Cordilheira Alta*. Since 1992 the municipality emancipated from Chapecó, it is a small municipality with 3,000 inhabitants. The main economic activities of Cordilheira Alta are agriculture and cattle raising.
5. *Cunhataí*, the smallest municipality of the research, colonised predominantly by Germans and with an economy based on agriculture.
6. *Ponte Serrada*, which has approximately 10,000 inhabitants and an economy based on agriculture.

The selection criterion of cases was a random sampling (six cases among the cities of the west of Santa Catarina), distributed in two cities considered regional poles, two medium-sized cities (between 5,000 and 30,000 inhabitants) and two small cities (up to 5,000 inhabitants).

The data were collected through semi-structured interviews, qualitative document analysis and personal observation. Semi-structured interviews were applied to 20 people: among them municipal mayors, department managers, members of the city councils and civil servants.

The data analysis was qualitative and used the triangulation technique (Triviños 1987). The data analysis process was divided in three phases: pre-analysis (during the interviews and first contact with documents), analytical description (classifying information in analytical categories) and referential interpretation (treatment and reflection, interrelating the empirical data with the literature).

This paper does not have the ambition to propose inference of its results to a wider population or to generalise its conclusions for other municipalities or other Brazilian regions. Nevertheless, the findings that we report here contribute to shed some light on the policy-making process that happens away from the large urban centers, trying to capture some relevant aspects of the Brazilian mosaic regarding patterns of political relationship between politicians and population in the agenda-building process.

Policy-Making Process

In each level public administrations try to respond to public demands through policies, programs and public actions. Policies can be considered priorities and guidelines, while programs and actions are concrete activities in order to implement public policies.

Accordingly to the „traditional" political science approach, public policies are considered one of the products of power competition (*politics*) within a political, ideological and cultural system (Easton 1973). On the other hand, public policies receive a much broader concept from policy studies' scholars. In this approach, public policies are considered a wide variety of interactions, decisions and non-decisions held by a plurality of actors to solve a collective problem (Regonini 2001).

Starting from 1950s, many theoretical contributions started to see policies as a continuous and sequential process (Jones 1984). Thus, from an analytical point of view, elaboration of public policies is nothing but a sequence (the policy cycle) of different and interdependent stages, beginning from problem perception and finishing with policy termination.

Several interpretations of the policy-making process and its framework for analysis can be found in literature of political sciences and policy studies (Jones 1984; Dye 1987; Regonini 2001). Nevertheless, all academic interpretations about policy-making take into account some basic stages: agenda-building (problem recognition, problem definition and agenda setting), formulation of proposals (and the following decision), policy implementation (with their programs and specific actions), evaluation (in terms of outcome, impact, equity, etc), and concluding the cycle, policy termination (in the cases of resolution of the problem or obsolescence of the policy). Figure 1 illustrates the process and its sub-phases:

Figure 1: policy-making process

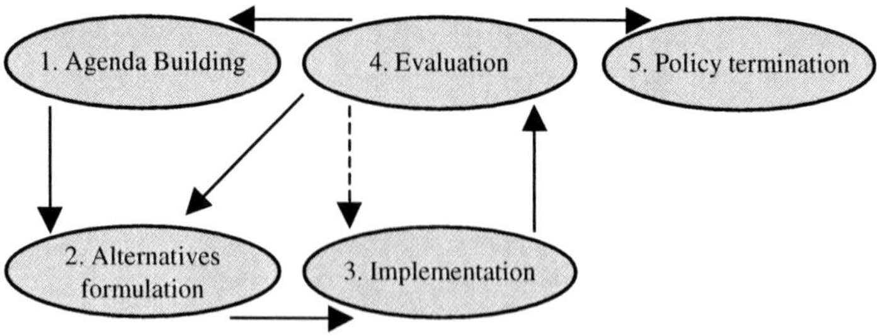

```
1. Agenda Building  →  4. Evaluation  →  5. Policy termination
      ↓                    ↓
2. Alternatives   →    3. Implementation
   formulation
```

The figure above shows also the feedback process (dotted lines) that results from the evaluation process, and the possibility of policy improvement derived from it. Even though being a useful analytical framework that systematizes the sub-phases of this process, rarely these stages are hermetic and clearly separated, and cannot be considered a synthesis of the political and administrative „life" of a policy. On the contrary, the policy-making process serves principally as a heuristic model to guide policy analysis in a systemic way.

Recognition of Public Demands and Agenda-Building

Agenda-building is the first stage of policy-making process. In this phase, the role of government is to identify relevant problems within the collectivity (political agenda) and transform them into a list of subjects deserving a government decision (institutional agenda). The recognition of a public problem includes clarification of its main characteristics, identification of causes and prediction of possible consequences.

As Regonini (2001) claims, the „problem" is the fundamental analytic category in policy studies. Public problem can be understood as the difference between what the collectivity has and what the collectivity would like to have. In other words, the difference between the reality and an ideal status. Public problems are the fuel for public administration actions. When a public problem emerges politicians and public managers have the opportunity to justify their existence and to demonstrate their real or rhetorical problem-solving capacities.

Accordingly to Cobb and Elder (1983), there are three conditions for the establishment of a problem in the institutional agenda:
i) The problem is peculiar to governmental entities;
ii) The social actors (politicians, citizens, interest groups, media, etc.) assume the status quo as an unsatisfactory situation;
iii) The problem is tractable.

When these three conditions are accomplished, formally or informally is held an *ex-ante* evaluation of the merit of the issue. In this way, potential impacts in terms of social, political and financial aspects are considered. In this stage of policy-making civic participation can be direct, through institutionalised deliberative channels, or indirect, through political representation, lobbying activities, social movements, etc.

In fact many scholars perceive a transition in the way the agenda-building process is undertaken in liberal democracies, translating from an almost complete indirect type to a hybrid framework that mixes direct and indirect participation. The appearance of policy networks (Börzel 1998; Klijn 1998) and several devices of deliberative democracy in liberal democracies are considered notorious trends in which citizens take part directly of the decision making of public policies through debate and direct exchange of ideas and perspectives (Pierre/Peters 2000). In fact these phenomena are related to a wider one: new patterns of governance.

Governance

The term governance receives many senses from the different disciplines that deal with it, and also from different theoretical approaches within these disciplines. Public administration, political sciences, international relations, private management are some of the disciplines that are concerned with themes of governance nowadays. In this paper we use the political view of governance as a process, as interactions between structures (government, market, policy networks) that are changing the way to steer society and public policy-making (Pierre/Peters 2000).

As Kooiman (1993) argues, our society and public problems are gaining more and more complexity (integration and interactions), dynamics (change) and diversity (specialisation and differentiation) so that new patterns of managing, guiding, producing and controlling public policies are suffering reconstruction. These new patterns tend to make more fluid the boundaries between state and market, and include new forms of cooperation between them.

Governance implicitly admits a trend towards a more pluralistic politic in which new actors and new arenas have access to policy decisions (Richards/Smith 2002). Other parallel phenomenon that can be perceived through the governance's lens is a more decentralised, transparent and integrative state model in order to pursue collective interests (Pierre/Peters 2000).

Since this paper focuses the analysis on a specific phase of the policy-making (agenda-building process), our assumption is that new patterns of governance correspond to the creation of new policy arenas for participation of a relevant number of non-state actors in order to accomplish the design of the institutional agenda.

Mechanisms for Public Problem Identification

Brazilian public administrations in the local level mix pre-bureaucratic, bureaucratic and post-bureaucratic models of public management (Pinho 2003; Bernardi/Secchi 2004). Due to this, the relationship and communication between public administration and citizen show paternalist practices in some situations, formalisms and rigid procedures in others. Sometimes, however, innovative initiatives to strengthen equal and systemic relationship between local government and citizens can be found in Brazilian reality.

A close relationship between local government and citizens is another characteristic of Brazilian reality, especially in small cities. Because of that, a part of public actions is focused on responding to individual demands or demands from specific groups (neighbourhood problems, interest group problems, etc.). These observations made us consider mechanisms for recognition of collective needs (previously defined) and also those mechanisms created by the local government to handle with needs from specific groups. In the conclusions of this paper we try to accomplish a distinction of mechanisms for recognition of public needs accordingly to the type of need (individual, specific group, collective).

The data analysis process basically showed that there are eight kinds of mechanisms used to identify demands in the investigated municipalities. The main mechanisms are: a) institutionalised policy network, b) public hearings for budgeting, c) participatory budgeting (in Chapecó), d) hearings during the election campaign, e) direct contact with elected officials, f) councillors' proposals, g) *Plano Diretor* (in Chapecó), and h) participatory strategic planning (in Chapecó).

a) The Institutionalised Policy Network

Policy networks are defined as a set of interrelated actors involved in the formulation and implementation process of policies in a specific policy area (Börzel 1998). Policy networks, in this sense, are considered concrete initiatives to promote governance as an alternative to traditional forms of regulation of public interests, as market and government hierarchy (Regonini 2005).

Municipal policy networks (*conselhos municipais*) were institutionalised as a tool for popular participation in the text of the Brazilian Federal Constitution in 1998. Since that time, public administrations of federal, state or municipal level are formally allowed and stimulated to create policy networks in order to support the public administration's decisions. The institutionalised policy networks are advisory bodies connected to the administrative structure, composed by representatives indicated from public sector, service providers, users/citizens, unions, NPOs. Some policy networks receive a deliberative status, depending on the specific law that created the network. Nonetheless, the specialised literature in Brazil perceives that a great part of „deliberative policy networks" are de facto advisory policy networks (Allebrandt 2003; Souza 2004). These networks have the responsibility to identify public problems, advise department managers and formulate and control programs within a specific policy area (Frey 2000). Each network is involved in a policy area, such as education, health, housing, economic development, childcare, transport and urbanisation, employment, agriculture etc. The meetings are held depending on the network's need, but generally more than four times a year.

In Brazil, policy networks on health, education and social assistance are recurrently found in the local level due to a federal law that incentives municipalities to create their own networks in these specific policy areas. However, municipal law can create other policy networks according to the city need.

In spite of being based on the principle of civic participation in the public decisions and decentralisation of political power, some negative evaluations can be made versus policy networks: limitations such as low participation culture within the population, scarce information delivered by the city government to civil society and low educational level of network's members. This kind of situation creates a difficulty in the recognition of communities' demand and reduces the effectiveness of this device.

Other operational limitations of the institutionalised policy network were identified. For instance in small municipalities like Cunhataí and Cordilheira Alta the number of people that are available to participate in the policy networks is limited, and sometimes one single person is indicated to participate in more then one network. Furthermore, network members can lose their motivation in participating because they do not receive immediate and selective incentives for it (i.e. financial retributions). It was reported during the research that members of policy networks use to complain because they have some difficulties to understand their influence on public administration's decisions. They complain that their participation has only procedural purposes and mostly what really counts is the government power to set issues in the institutional agenda. This kind of situation corroborates similar findings in Brazilian specialized literature (Allebrandt 2003; Souza 2004).

Nonetheless, a general consideration of the interviewed representatives during the research was that institutionalised policy network has a positive influence in the initialisation process of a participatory culture, and it tends to legitimate local government decisions. Policy networks allow a certain reduction in the hegemony of political criteria in the agenda-building process, opening space for technical debate in this arena.

b) Public Hearings for Budgeting

Plano Plurianual (PPA) is the instrument for budget planning instituted by the Federal Constitution of 1988 in all levels of the public administration. It includes guidelines and objectives for public action on a four years basis. PPA is elaborated in the first year of executive mandate and its implementation begins in the second year of mandate. In this logic, guidelines and objectives of PPA enforce actions in three years of the current mandate and the first year of the upcoming executive mandate. PPA foresees investments and operating expenditures that the executive power shall accomplish in the period.

Lei de Diretrizes Orçamentárias (LDO) deals with capital expenditures, orientates the elaboration of the annual budget and foresees alterations in the tax legislation to the upcoming fiscal period. Goals and priorities for the subsequent year are defined in LDO in harmony with priorities of PPA. LDO's objectives shall be observed in the annual budget (LOA) that lists programs, projects and actions to the executive power.

Brazilian Constitution and complementary legislation of Fiscal Responsibility Law, which deals with transparency and accountability aspects, prescribes the popular participation to the PPA, LDO and annual budget building.[1] Due to these normative aspects, the investigated municipalities accomplish specific public hearings with this aim, obeying (formally) the legal precepts. The participation is free for all citizens, but the introduction of issues in the institutional agenda depends on the government decision. These meetings (hearings) with the population occur in the neighbourhoods or communities with variable periodicity (annual, semestral). The executive power has the liberty to decide how to organize the public hearings.

One of the main problems of this kind of hearings refers the individuals' inclination to defend their own interests, leaving aside generic and public needs. Several testimonies were collected that indicated this evaluation. A possible reason of such inclination, according to the department manager for Economic Development of São Miguel do Oeste, could be a paternalistic perception of the public power and State within the society. Citizens think that the

---

[1] Congresso Nacional. Lei Complementar n. 101, de 04 de maio de 2000: Lei de Responsabilidade Fiscal. Brasília.

City Hall is a place for social care. Using the Department Manager's words: „One can find people coming here asking for jobs, asking for food or even asking us to find them a place to live."

Public hearings for PPA, LDO and annual budgeting in Chapecó, the largest city of the region, have been separately analysed in the next chapter. Participatory budgeting is an executive device that organises the processes of public hearings in municipalities administered by *Partido dos Trabalhadores* (Workers' Party) in Brazil.

c) Participatory Budgeting

Participatory budgeting (*Orçamento Participativo*) is a mechanism that stimulates citizens to participate in public budget decisions in an organised way. The public decisions derived from this mechanism deal with application of the municipal financial resources in capital investments (construction of schools, streets, health centers) and services. The decisions taken during plenaries and assemblies of participatory budgeting are the basis for PPA, LDO and annual budget in Chapecó.

Chapecó's local government instituted a specific organ in the administrative structure (*Executive Commission for Participatory Budgeting*) with representatives from executive power to organize public participation and to schedule assemblies. The executive commission organises community plenaries (more than 100 communities), sectoral policy plenaries, and regional assemblies (in the 10 great districts), for the final definitions of investments priorities to the next year. The access is free for all citizens and people have the prerogative to analyse investment proposal and take the final decisions.[2] The executive commission writes and disseminates printed materials to publicise decisions taken in the participatory budgeting process. Regional accountability assemblies of the public actions are organised as well.

Evaluations about this mechanism for problem identification are controversial. Those belonging to the opposition to the executive power criticize participatory budgeting, claiming that decisions are not accomplished by the executive power. Some considerations were also made that participatory budgeting is not able to reach discussions about municipalities' general interest. It is argued that the way the participatory budgeting is organised only incentive the discussion about neighbourhoods' and regions' needs. Such critics find support in the literature. Vaz (2002, pp. 276f.) claims that participatory budgeting „doesn't take into consideration the great investments, administrative costs of the public service and public policies".

---

[2] Prefeitura Municipal de Chapecó. Orçamento participativo 2002: Quem participa decide.

In spite of some limitations, participatory budgeting can be considered an innovative instrument emerged with the initiative of the local government (and not a mere federal law imposition) and serves as a mechanism for co-ordination of the public participation in public budgeting. Participatory budgeting can also be used as a device for democratic accountability.

d) Election Campaigns

Even before being elected, political parties and their candidates seek to identify demands from population through public hearings and visits to the municipal communities during the election campaign. It is the base for the design of political programs. According to the opinions of those interviewed, political program building is an important moment to identify public problems, and it becomes a political commitment with the population.

One limitation of public hearings during election campaigns as mechanism for problem identification is the weak possibility for enforcement of following administrative actions. Political programs have the capacity to identify demands from population in a specific chronologically moment, during the context of the election campaign. In many cases political programs are not updated across time and their objectives and actions usually become outdated. Political programs are not designed as a checklist of actions (like PPA and annual budget), and these programs are presented as a general notion of the city's needs.

e) Direct Contact with Department Managers and Mayors

During the research it was noticed that informal relationship between citizens and public managers is a natural mechanism for the reception of public demands, mainly in small cities.

Department manager for budget and public management of Cunhataí, the smallest investigated municipality, points out that direct contact is the principal mechanism for problem identification in the city. The following department manager's comment stresses out the informal procedure to request something to the public power: „Usually people come to the Mayor's office and ask for a tractor service."

Similar situations are noticed in Ponte Serrada, São Miguel do Oeste, Pinhalzinho and Cordilheira Alta, where civil servants and mayors are in permanent contact with population and they informally know problems of individuals. This informality allows public administration to solve problems quickly. In the smaller municipalities the interviewed people constantly emphasised the importance of this kind of mechanism. In their perception, direct contact is an alternative to excessive formalities and bureaucratic dysfunctions, such as depersonalisation of relationships.

Being the largest city of the studied region, Chapecó has an executive power with some difficulties to treat individual needs properly. Chapecó's executive power offers some mechanisms for problem identification dedicated to citizen groups or communities (participatory budgeting, institutionalised policy network, participatory strategic planning, etc.), but channels dedicated to treat individual needs are scarce. As a political and symbolic decision, Chapecó's mayor decided to reserve one afternoon during the week to receive individual requests in his office.

The contact of citizenry with representatives of the public administration, either informally or through hearings, can be described as a recurrent instrument to identify public problems in the investigated cases. Especially in the small cities, this kind of informal channel has an important role, allowing public administration to know the peculiarities of the citizens' needs. On the other hand, this practice can turn to clientelistic relations favoring those who are aligned to some political streams. Besides, this informality tends to maintain the personification of the public actions, illustrated in phrases like „the agriculture commissioner put limestone in my farming", or still „our mayor helped me to build a ranch in my property". The abuse of this kind of mechanism can suffocate the sense of collective demand and perpetuate paternalistic practices between the political class and citizens.

f) Direct Contact and Hearings with Legislators

Representatives of legislative power have a close contact with population and can fulfil an important role in the recognition of public demands. During the research, several testimonies stressed out the perception that council members are „spokespersons" of the population in the relationship with the executive power. Such perception can be considered a sign that council members priorise punctual demands. It also reveals a relationship with paternalistic inclinations, similarly to the related cases of direct contact with mayors and department managers.

Two main legislative's channels to identify public demands were observed: the public hearings (*audiências públicas*) and councillors' proposals to the executive (*indicações do legislativo*). In the case of public hearings, legislators in the city council receive complaints and advices from individuals or groups. In the specific case of Pinhalzinho one interesting initiative of deconcentration of the public hearings was identified, seeking to promote rounds of legislative sessions within communities and trying to increase the public participation in legislative sessions. In these sessions, the communities' member can expose their demands and problems directly to legislators. Councillors' proposals are requests of actions from councillors to the executive power. These proposals usually emerge from a group or community and involve budgetary actions that were not foreseen in PPA, LDO and annual public budget.

One crucial problem to the effective activity of councillors is the educational level of these representatives. Mainly in the smaller municipalities (Cunhataí, Cordilheira Alta, Ponte Serrada), a considerable part of legislators do not have a high school degree, causing some difficulties in elaborating bills, legal documents or policy proposals with minimum standard of quality. Different executive power members have similar interpretations that city councillors, in general, have little initiative to make bills, and their legislative role ends up as figurative approval or rejections of executive's proposals.

As positive aspects about the performance of the legislative power in recognising public problems we can stress out the closeness to citizenry and the capillarity and penetration of this institution in the society. On the other hand, negative aspects as the emphasis on punctual demands and legislator's educational deficits (especially in the small cities) seem like limitations that should be overcome.

g) Other Mechanisms for Problem Identification

Beyond the mechanisms described above, which are common to all the investigated municipalities (except participatory budgeting), some outstanding mechanisms are presented here.

In Chapecó, the interviewed people mentioned two further interesting tools: participatory strategic planning (*Congresso da Cidade*) and *Plano Diretor*. *Congresso da Cidade* was an event accomplished in 2001 in Chapecó that tried to integrate the population of Chapecó to develop strategies and a future vision for the city for the next 15 years. According to Chapecó's mayor, *Congresso da Cidade* had the role of elaborating objectives and strategies for the entire city, complementing participatory budgeting, which mainly focuses on neighbourhoods' and communities' demands. This opportunity was open to all citizens, and the issues introduced in the institutional agenda in this occasion started to be treated by local government. Examples of subjects treated during the participatory strategic planning process were the reformulation of urban transit in the central areas of the city, issues on economic growth and environment protection (soil and water).

Plano Diretor is an urban planning instrument that works on mapping preservation areas, urban expansion areas, etc. In spite of being basically a device that deals with territorial and urbanistic subjects, *Plano Diretor* handles with a wide range of communities's problems during the diagnostic phase. The public hearings were realised frequently (twice a month) with representatives from the government (40%) and from the civil society (60%). *Plano Diretor* was instituted as obligatory in the Federal Constitution for all municipalities that have a population of 20,000 or more, and the legislative power of Chapecó approved the new *Plano Diretor* in January 2004.

All the public agents were questioned about the use of internet for problem identification, but in none of the studied municipalities this device was found. Interviews and the search on the cities' websites indicated that the development of this instrument is still in its infancy. All of the studied municipalities can be ranked in the *presence phase* (basic information to the public), first stage of an electronic government development (Aoema 2004).

h) General Evaluation of the Mechanisms for Problem Recognition

All representatives from public administrations interviewed in this research stated that the present mechanisms of problem recognition are sufficient. An administrative commissioner from São Miguel do Oeste illustrated the situation with the phrase: „Problems arise naturally, we don't need to run after them." This reasoning could be considered an indication of a reactive behavior of the public administration. However, the number and level of public demands on municipal governments has increased significantly after the beginning of the administrative decentralisation instituted by the Federal Constitution of 1988.

A clear problem identified during the research was the low interactivity among the existent mechanisms for problem recognition. In other words, the public demands that are captured by the city councils, public hearings and policy networks do not suffer a systematic intersection and crossed analysis. This task is informally played by the department managers, who participate in meetings of their issues, receive city councillors and citizens in their office, participate in the budgeting process, etc. It was identified a lack of articulation of the presented mechanisms, which can cause a narrow vision of general situation of the municipal needs and problems.

The table below indicates the main mechanisms for problem identification used in the investigated municipalities, divided in groups according to the type of need (individual, community, collective) and according to who takes the initiative to start the communication process (citizen or public administration).

Table 1: Synthesis of the mechanisms for identification of public problems

		Type of need		
		Individual	**Community/ neighbourhood**	**Collective/city**
Initiative	*Citizen*	Direct contact with elected officials	Councillor's proposals to executive power	
	Public administration		- Participatory budgeting - Public hearings to PPA, LDO and annual budget - Hearings with legislative power	- Policy Networks - Election campaign - Participatory strategic planning - *Plano diretor*

The table shows that there are no channels created by the municipal administrations to assist specific/individual needs. In the same way, no examples of mechanisms to treat individual demands for collective subjects were identified. The first case can be considered a problem, since needs from individuals are treated without a systematic scheme of reception, analysis, treatment or rejection. This role is played by department managers, who personally evaluate whether a problem is important or not, using predominantly political (and sometimes clientelistic) criteria to decide. The second situation certainly is derived from that absence of participatory culture commented in the analysis. As individuals of the studied cases focus their claims mostly on individual demands, mechanisms to receive collective demands from individuals are considered unnecessary by the political class and by the population.

The public administration of Chapecó showed the highest development in creating and managing mechanisms to understand public demands. In fact, participatory budgeting and participatory strategic planning (*Congresso da Cidade*) are innovative devices that serve as models for other public administrations in Brazil (Pinheiro 2005).

Conclusions and Final Considerations

The citizens' contribution in the identification of collective demands was considered problematic in most of the studied cases. The lack of culture of participation within population, the prominence of particularistic demands in the spaces for collective discussion, the lack of information of public issues delivered to the population and a paternalist conception of state (for both politicians and citizens) were the main obstacles to the effectiveness of civic participation identified during this research.

The number of mechanisms for problem recognition was considered enough by city managers and councillors, specially because the number and the qualitative level of public demands has grown up significantly to the municipal power after 1988's Constitution. However, it was perceived a clear deficiency of coordination among present mechanisms. The role of synthesis and organisation of public demands remains centralised in the commissioner's person, who can bias the interpretation of public interest with her cognitive limitations and personal interests.

Regarding the treatment of individual demands, the data analysis concluded that a systematic tool of reception, categorisation, treatment or rejection of individual requests would be an important contribution. Such tool would contribute for an enlargement of democratic access to the public administration with a less clientelistic treatment of individual needs.

Chapecó, economic and political pole of the studied region, is a city in which civil society has shown an important development in the last years. In comparison with the other studied cities, Chapecó has a much larger number of associations, NGOs, universities, syndicates, etc. Using Kooima's (1993) terms, the diversity, dynamics and complexity of Chapecó is higher than the other investigated cities. These characteristics can be considered a valid explanation for the necessity of creation of plural mechanisms for public problem recognition. Although the criticisms addressed to the reach and the impact of mechanisms as participatory budgeting and *Congresso da Cidade* (participatory strategic planning), Chapecó's local government has shown initiative to create mechanisms and to enable citizen participation in the public decisions.

References

Allebrandt, Sérgio L. (2003): Conselhos Municipais: potencialidades e limites para a efetividade e eficácia de um espaço público para a construção da cidadania interativa. *Anais XXVII ENANPAD*, Atibaia-SP.

Almeida, Maria Hermínia Tavares/Carneiro, Leandro Piquet (2003): Liderança local, democracia e políticas públicas no Brasil, in: Opinião Pública 9 (1), pp. 124-147.

Aoema (2004): E-Government from a User's Perspective: Stages/Phases of E-Government. Accessed July 25, 2004. http://www.aoema.org/E-Government/Stages-Phases_of_e-government.htm

Bernardi, Esmael R./Secchi, Leonardo (2004): Modelos de gestão pública: estudo de casos em municípios do Oeste catarinense. *Research report (Unochapecó, Art. 170)*, Chapecó.
Börzel, Tanja A. (1998): Le reti di attori pubblici e privati nella regolazione europea. Stato e Mercato 54 (3), pp. 389-432.
Cobb, Roger W./Elder, Charles D. (1983): Participation in American Politics – The Dynamics of Agenda-Building. Baltimore.
Dye, Thomas R. (1987): Understanding Public Policy, 6th ed., Englewood Cliffs.
Easton, David (1973): Il sistema politico. Milano.
Frey, Klaus (2000): Políticas públicas: um debate conceitual e reflexões referentes à prática da análise de políticas públicas no Brasil, in: Planejamento e Políticas Públicas (21), pp. 221-259.
Heclo, Hugh (1972): Review Article: Policy Analysis, in: British Journal of Political Sciences, 2 (1), pp. 83-108.
Jones, Charles O (1984): An Introduction to the Study of Public Policy, Belmont.
Klijn, Erik-Hans (1998): Redes de políticas públicas: una visión general, in: Revista Hispana para el analisis de redes sociales. Accessed May 21, 2003. http://revista-redes.rediris.es/webredes/textos/Complex.pdf.
Kooiman, Jan [ed.] (1993). Modern Governance: New Government-Society Interactions, London.
Pierre, Jon/Peters, Guy B. (2000): Governance, Politics and the State, New York.
Pinho, José A. G. (2003): Inovação na gestão municipal no Brasil: a voz dos gestores municipais, in: Anais XXVII ENANPAD. Atibaia-SP.
Regonini, Gloria (2001): Capire le politiche pubbliche, Bologna.
Richards, David/Smith, Martin J. (2002): Governance and Public Policy in the United Kingdom, Oxford.
Souza, Celina (2004): Governos locais e gestão de políticas sociais universais, in: São Paulo em Perspectiva, (18) Apr./June.
Stake, Robert E. (1994): Case studies, in: Denzin, Norman K./ Lincoln, Yvonna S. [eds.]: Handbook of Qualitative Research, Thousand Oaks.
Triviños, Augusto N. S. (1987): Introdução à pesquisa em ciências sociais: a pesquisa qualitativa em educação. São Paulo.
Vaz, José Carlos (2002): Desafios para a incorporação da transparência em um modelo de gestão municipal, in: Spink, Peter/ Caccia-Bava, Silvio/Veronika Paulics [eds.]: Novos contornos da gestão local: conceitos em construção, São Paulo.

Wenting Fei

Local Public Participation in Government Legislation and Decision-Making in China
The Case of Shanghai

Legitimacy basis is a pivot in ensuring the existence of a government and of approaching the effective implementation of government policies. Therefore, setting and strengthening the legitimacy basis become fundamental political tasks for a government and the pre-condition for developing other political functions.

China has experienced a thirty years' economic system reform which has transferred the planned economy into a market economy progressively from the late 1970s. During the first twenty years of that period, the Chinese government established legitimacy on the basis of economic development, and then enjoyed wide-spread political acceptance through the great success of the economic reform. The government enhanced the public support by improving the population's living standard, and completed the transformation by shifting the legitimacy basis from historical materialism and traditional political culture to political achievements.[1] However, after twenty years of sustainable economic increase with high speed, promoting the economic development in the market-oriented reform encountered obstacles due to the existence of *core* in the original political system. This resulted in meeting the bottleneck of the economic reform, slowing down of the economic increase and emerging of economic polarization. As a result, the Chinese government had to seek for a new legitimacy basis again.

So, the end of the 1990s saw the start of the government modernising reform with *administration according to law*[2] as its core, and Chinese leaders and the social elite have realised that the Chinese government would eventually establish legitimacy on the basis of democracy and rule by law.[3] If we treated the political achievements

---
[1] See, Kang Xiaoguang, 1999.
[2] After amendments to the Constitution adopted by The Congress in 1999 put forward that administration according to law is included in the framework of rule by law.
[3] The plenum of the Central Committee held in Sep. 2004 put forward to construct a society of „democracy and rule by law", which signifies a strategic improvement from to emphasising the synchronisation of economiy and society for sustainable development.

legitimacy as gaining in public acceptance by increasing output-legitimacy, the Chinese government is paying more and more attention to strengthening input-legitimacy now in order to expand the legitimacy basis of the political system.[4] The government hopes that it can provide more institutional channels for diverse interest groups to participate in political activities.[5]

With the above background, this article mainly focuses on the status and development trends of citizen participation in the legislation[6] and policy-making processes of government in Shanghai[7]. It conducts investigation on the following institutional arrangements of two different levels: i) open government information as the precondition for public participation and ii) preliminary practices of public participation in government legislation and policy-making during recent years, with a focus on the quantifiable analysis on the implementation of public hearings. In part 3, we will give a prospect of the development trends, which is the key component for the development of citizen participation.

1. Open Government Information

Access to information is the prerequisite of public participation in legislation and policy-making of any government. The quality of public participation primarily depends on whether the government can provide the public with adequate, all-encompassing information they need in advance to make judgments. Due to the culture of secrecy shaped by the historical and cultural traditions in the past,

---

[4] In the Implementation Outline for the All-round Advancement of Administration by Law promulgated by the State Council on April 20, 2004, establishing and improving the democratic and scientific mechanism, and extending the citizen participation in government legislation have been regarded as one of the major tasks and measures.

[5] The major institutional channels for political participation in China are the system of the People's Congress and the system of the Political Consultative Conference. The government also provides non-institutional channels, such as the letters and visits, leaders reception, etc. These non-institutionalised systems need to be improved. It becomes necessary to seek for an institutionalised system in public participation.

[6] According to Article 73 of *Legislation Law of the People's Republic of China*, the governments of provinces, autonomous regions, municipalities, and other bigger cities may formulate regulations.

[7] Shanghai is one of the four provincial-level cities directly under the central government, which are called municipalities in China, and a major economic center of the country. By the end of 2003, the city had a total area of 6,340.5 square kilometers, and its population of long-term residents reached 17.11 million.

the Chinese government still has a long way to go in the field of open government information compared with western democratic countries. But this situation is being improved. While the central government mulls over a draft of China's freedom of information legislation, all levels of governments are conducting the relevant legislation. Among them, Shanghai's legislation and practice played an important rule in promoting the open information course of the Chinese government.[8] The Shanghai government adopted the *Provisions of Shanghai Municipality on Open Government Information* (the Shanghai Provisions)[9] on January 20, 2004, which was China's first provincial-level open government information legislation. The Shanghai Provisions claimed the protection of „right to know" and represented the most comprehensive framework to date in China for accessing government-held information, containing more details than the pioneering *Guangzhou Municipal Open Government Information Provisions* and other lower-level local Chinese legislations to date.[10] The Provisions came into effect on May 1, 2004, by which Shanghai launched its transparent government program. It was also taken as the new basis for citizen's better participation in government policy-making process. So it is important to learn its legislative contents and the implementation situations in order to understand the status of citizen participation in the city.

1.1 Content of Legislation

– *Principle*: As those of most of developed countries, the Shanghai Provisions establish a presumption of disclosure, making secrecy the exception rather than the rule. The Provisions also direct governments to implement the open government information policy conveniently, effectively, and in a timely manner.
– *Scope of Application*: The Provisions apply to administrative agencies and organisations that carry out administrative powers in Shanghai.
– *Management System*: A Joint Conference comprised of the relevant government departments shall be responsible for research and coordination of major policy issues involved in promoting open government information. The Shanghai Information Commission is designed to be in charge of organising, guiding and promoting the implementation of the Provisions.

---

[8] Since Shanghai promulgated its Provisions, there were four cities, Hangzhou, Wuhan, Ningbo, and Chongqing, which have promulgated provisions for open government information.
[9] http://www.shanghai.gov.cn/shanghai/node8059/Bulletin/node11244/node13068/userobject26ai1464.html
[10] See, Horsley 2004.

- *Ways of Openness*: The Provisions stipulated that government information is to be made public in one of two ways: i) disseminated on the government's own initiative, or ii) provided in response to a specified request. The Provisions also specify a broad category of information that must be disseminated on their own initiative by the government. The general public may apply to the relevant government agencies for all the information listed in the scope of openness except for the information that shall be disseminated on the government's own initiative.
- *Scope of Information Disseminated on the Government's Own Initiative*: Administrative agencies shall, on their own initiatives, make known to the general public the following government information: a) government management documents, plans of economic and social development and city plannings; b) with respect to major issues that are closely related to the general public, including but not limited to contingencies, disasters and epidemics, social security, land requisition and housing demolition and relocation; c) with respect to the use and supervision of public funds; d) with respect to government organisations and personnel affairs.
- *Making Known of the Draft of Major Decisions to the Public*: „Government Information" in the Provisions refers to resulting information. As for the information which is in the course of being investigated or discussed, such information shall be included in the scope of open administrative procedure rather than open government information. However, since there is no specific legislation stipulating that major decisions related to the major public interests shall be made known to the public before they being executed, and in consideration of the protection of the right of the public to know and to participate and promotion of science and democracy in government policy-making, such information is also regulated in the scope of open government information in a temporary manner. The Provisions stipulated that „If the decisions to be made, the regulations to be formulated, or the plans and programs to be drawn up by government agencies involve important interests of citizens, legal entities and other organizations, or have major social impact, the drafting agencies or the decision-making agencies shall make them known to the general public in the course of their formulation, and fully solicit opinions from the general public." This creative provision opens a door, which provides possibilities for the public to participate in government legislation and major policy-making processes.
- *Scope of Exemption*: a) state secrets; b) commercial secrets; c) an individual's private information; d) related to a matter that is in the course of being investigated, discussed or processed; e) related to an administrative enforcement action that might in-

fluence the enforcement activities or endanger an individual's life or safety; f) otherwise exempted from disclosure by laws or regulations. In consideration of balancing the protection of individuals' information and the protection of the public interest, in case of the following situations, government information listed in items b and c is not subject to the restrictions of exemption from being made known to the public: The owner of the right agrees to its being made known to the public or the benefits of making it known to the public outweigh the detriment that may result. Government agencies may decide to make known to the public government information listed in items d and e, provided its being made known to the public has obvious benefits for the general public and will not cause substantial detriment.
– *The tools:* Governments shall through one or several forms, including government bulletins, government websites, government news briefing, and public reference rooms etc., disseminate information on their own initiative. The public also can request the acquisition of government information by such means as letters, telegrams, faxes and e-mails.

1.2 Implementation of the Provisions

Despite of the comparatively late commencement of the construction of the open government information system, the government attached great importance to it, as one of the core tasks of the Shanghai government in building itself into „a government of services, responsibilities, and law ruling", and made unprecedented full preparations to drive it with great efforts, achieving fairly good effects among the public, where government information is largely demanded. With the implementation period reaching eight months by the end of 2004, the government made a conclusion on its implementation situation and formed the annual report published to the public.[11]

According to the statistics in the Annual Report, various government agencies took the initiative to disseminate information totaled up to 106,730 items with a rate of 95.7% of such information in electronic version, where 14.3% for information on policies, laws and regulations, 3.0% for information on planning and program, 57.3% going for business, and 25.4% for organisation structure and others. There are 146 million persons looking up government information in the Open Government Information Columns of the government websites on the internet. There established totally 287 numbers of public looking-up sites around the whole city, accommodating the public looking-up of 23,814 persons. The government bulletins

---

[11] http://www.shanghai.gov.cn/shanghai/node2314/node2319/node12344/userobject26ai3216.html

published two times periodically totaling 200,000 copies in each month, arriving free in charge at the public through archives, libraries, post offices, newspaper booths, and bookstores, etc. In the whole year, there convened 25 municipal press conferences, releasing 62 items of important news and answering more than 500 questions raised by journalists.

Government agencies at all levels got in total 8,799 requests for government information, with 56.5% applying by personally presence, 37% through the submittal of electronic forms or sending e-mail on the government websites, 2.8% via posting letters and 3.7% by other means. The contents of these requests mainly involve such aspects as introducing of talents, reform of public institutions, wages and welfare, management of civil servants, social security, labor employment and relocations of residents. For such requests, 79.3% were wholly accepted, 5.5% were partially provided the information and 15.2% were not provided.[12] The total costs for the copy and delivery of government information according the requests is RMB 4,306 Yuan and the costs invested by the government for the implementation of the Provisions is 25.78 million Yuan. On the aspects of relief, government agencies at various levels totally received 38 pieces of applications for administrative reconsideration of concerning open government information, and the courts accepted and heard six cases for administrative lawsuits.

2. The Initial Practice of Citizen Participation

The promulgation of the Provisions renders Shanghai Government find the breakthrough opportunity to push forward the modernisation reform for itself and drive forward the course for local democracy. The improvement of governmental transparency that it implemented and promoted sparing no efforts makes the public have much more clear expectations while making the decisions on their own affairs, which is favorable to strengthen their trust in the government and makes the relationship between the government and citizens get better. However, in open government information, the relationship between the government and the public is a one-way process, where the information generated and delivered by the government is used by the public[13], based on which, in order to further close the gap between the public and the government, Shanghai starts to seek more

---

[12] Among the information un-provided, 28.6% didn't exist, 35.4% were not under the jurisdiction of addressee of the requests, 9.0% were applications with unclear contents, and 6.5% were within the scope of exemptions according to the Provisions, 20.5% went for other reasons.

[13] See Organization for Economic Co-operation and Development 2001, p. 23.

institutional channels for the public to more directly participate in government decision-making in more extensive aspects, building the two-way interaction between the public and the government. Besides the indispensable pre-requisite of establishment of the open government information system, state and local legislations also offered institutional support for public participation, rendering the scope of the substantiality expanded continuously and the ways for participation diversified. In this part, the elaboration and analysis will be made mainly against the law systems of the two major tools for participation in practice as well as their application conditions.

2.1 Public Consultation in Government Legislation

In law, the clear expression of the right to participate in government legislation begins in *The Legislation Law of People's Republic of China*.[14] Article 58 of the Legislation Law specifies that the State Council shall, in the process of drafting out administrative regulations, extensively consult the opinions of concerned government agencies, organisations and citizens through various means as symposiums, demonstrative meetings, and hearings, etc. The Legislation Law authorises the State Council to promulgate special administrative regulations to formulate the lawmaking procedures in the local governments. Subsequently, *The Regulations on the Procedure for Making Rules and Regulations* issued by the State Council in November of 2001 specified that local governments shall, in the process of drafting out regulations, make deeply investigation and research, summarise the experience of practices, and largely consult the opinions of concerned government agencies, organisations and citizens through various means as enquiring opinions in written, symposiums, demonstrations, and hearings, etc. Afterwards, related provisions for the implementation procedures issued by Shanghai government followed these expressions. From the legal system above, we can see that the substantive right to participate in government legislation was reiterated and ensured, and the means for participation were also dealt with in general, but the procedures for participation have not taken shape. Before the issuance of the Shang-

---

[14] The Constitution specifies: The people, under the laws, through various ways and forms, manage national affairs, economic and cultural tasks and social affairs. It's a generalised expression of sovereignty in people. Before the issuance of *The Legislation Law of the People's Republic of China*, there were no other laws that externalised the rights to participate directly in the legislative activities of legislatures and administrative authorities. Article 5 specifies: The legislation shall embody the will of the people, develop democracy of socialism and ensure the people to participate in the legislative activities through multiple ways.

hai Provisions, the practice for government to hold public hearings in law-making was pretty much limited. Except of comparatively large cases, where public opinions will be heard through such formal way of hearing, which will be dealt with in the next paragraph, generally only such informal and non-institutional means as symposiums were applied to acquire the opinions from the associations, administrative authorities, and specialists in specific fields, which took some positive effects in balancing the interests of various groups and listening to different opinions. However, government had, in the process, very broad administrative discretion, including the selection of objects for consulting, means to be taken for acquiring opinions, adoption or reject of opinions heard and so on. The key is that the process of legislation was not open to public, which lower the actual public participating rate.

The turning of such situation begins from the innovative attempts of public participation in the constituting process of the Shanghai Provisions. To draft out a regulations to protect the rights to know, the procedure itself shall be known by the public. And in order to make the system design broadly accepted and convenient for its future implementation, the government, when drafting this regulation in 2003, firstly published the whole draft in the two major newspapers issued openly in the whole city and on the municipal website on internet to acquire openly public opinions besides consulting and demonstrating with various legal specialists, government agencies, foreign specialists, enterprises and non-governmental organisations. The public may send their opinions to the government legislative office through e-mail, letter or fax, etc. After the issuance of the Shanghai Provisions, such means as consulting public for opinions have been followed afterwards in the government legislation in accordance with the article concerning opening the important decision-making drafts. From May 2004, every draft of the government regulation and every proposal of local statutes submitted to the local congress by the government have been published on the municipal government website to acquiring public opinions. By the end of March 2005, such cases added up to 31. After one year's practice, this procedure somewhat similar to the *Notice and Comment* in *Administrative Procedure Law of the United States* was set down into another government regulation at the end of 2004, systemised, standardised and crystallised[15], which symbolized the externalisation of the procedures

---

[15] In August 2003, governments at various levels carried out a new round of reform with far-reaching significance surrounding the subject of *Administration According to Law*, and cleaned up administrative regulations, with a view to expediting the withdrawal of government from the market, and restricting administrative authorites. In Shanghai a half of the 203 items of administrative licensing items was canceled. This, what we refer to as openly consulting public opinions, is written into

of public participation originally controlled internally by the administrative authorities. Now the public not only can know the rules of using such channels for interests expressing, but also can supervise whether governments implement such procedure legally and fairly. This procedure consists of the following elements:
a) To publish the information on the government websites on internet for acquiring public opinions is the legal way. Supplementary publishing channels through other media are encouraged.
b) The contents of the notice must be in details with provisions of sufficient and effective information, attached with explanations of the government regulation drafts so that the public can understand better.
c) Clearly indicate the ways for feedback opinions and disseminate the ways of contact.
d) The period left for the public giving feedback opinions shall be not less than 20 days.
e) Government must sort and analyse the public opinions and shall state the results of opinion-enquiry when submitting the drafts to the highest decision-making level of the government. Meanwhile, it shall give feedbacks to the public about the adoption/rejection of opinions with related reasons clearly stated.

2.2 Public Hearings

The system of public hearings, as the core element of due process of law, was introduced into China firstly in the field of administrative penalty, subsequently extending into the field of law-making and other government decision-making on important affairs. *The Price Law of the People's Republic of China* implemented from 1 May, 1998 prescribed that hearing system shall, in setting down such government guided and determined prices as public utility price, common weal service price, prices of commodities of nature monopoly, which involves the direct interests of the public, be established, presided over by the competent government departments of price to acquire the opinions of customers, operators, and concerned parties, demonstrating its necessity and feasibility. It was the first that the decision-making hearing system is established in law in the field of decision-making. The Legislation Law issued in March 2003 mentioned legislative hearing system. Subsequently, the State Council issued *The Regulations on the Procedure for Making Rules and Regulations*, externalising the legislative hearing system[16], the most

Provisions of Shanghai Municipality on the Procedure of Creating Temporary Administrative License.

[16] See Article 15 of *The Regulations on the Procedure for Making Rules and Regulations*. It crystallised the procedures of hearing systems specified by the Legislation Law, but it is still in a broad-brush way.

outstanding function of which is to outline the scope applicable for holding hearings – regulations drafted out directly involving the personal interests of citizens, legal persons or other organisations, or concerned authorities, organisations or citizens have significant different opinions on it. Although this expression still went out of focus, and administrative departments still enjoy fairly large discretion whether or not to take opinions through hearings for decisions-making, which thus objectively results in such occurrence as necessary hearings may be neglected, it after all put forward a rule, which lay the exercisable foundation for further practices.[17] Concurrently, no law at national level has made a unified specification on the specific operation proceedings of decision-making hearings yet, while such exploration at provincial level has been undertaken unceasingly.

From the practice in Shanghai, we can see, regarding price hearing, from the implementation of the Price Law in 1998, 13 price hearings have been held successively in Shanghai, including public house rentals, tap water price, waste water price, bus/tube ticket price, public high school tuition fees, higher education fees, planned liquefier price, inter-provincial road transportation tickets price in spring, municipal pipe gas price, etc. Regarding legislative hearing, from the effectiveness of Legislative Law in 2000 to now, totally seven legislative hearings has been held in Shanghai. Four were organised by the Shanghai People's Congress – the local legislature – and three were organised by administrative authorities, including five local statutes and two government regulations as the disposal of injury accidents of elementary and middle school students, employment contract, protection of customers' rights, residence property management, protection of historic and cultural scenery zone and building, etc. Based on the practice, the Shanghai people's congress and the Legislative Affairs Office of Shanghai Government established respectively in May 2001 and February 2003 the internal operation norms for legislative hearings, specifying the scope, organization, determination of participants and general procedures for legislative hearings and promoting the legislative hearing activities in Shanghai moving toward normalisation and institutionalisation. Besides,

---

[17] The identification of the scope applicable to hearing is recognised in our country as one of the difficulties in the practicing of decision-making hearings. Currently, laws at national levels in our country seldom dealt with decision-making hearings, besides the Price Law above mentioned, as well as *Environment Influence Evaluation Law* and *Law of the People's Republic of China on Administrative Licenses*. On one side, we need the general principle to guide the practice, on the other side, the applicable scope of decision-making hearings is subject to further defining through the accumulation of experience in practice.

Shanghai also probes into in somehow the decision-making hearings in the implementation of related local statutes and regulations matching with the state laws, gradually expanding the applicable range of decision-making hearings.

3. Development Prospect

As it were, it is too early to make an all-round evaluation to legal system of public participation in government legislation and decision-making, which is still in the groping stage. However, it is still necessary for us to probe into the measures for the perfection and development of this system from its current operation effect.

Generally speaking, at present the public participation rate in our country is still comparatively low with the scope of items for their participation in decision-making is pretty much limited. And due to the restriction of technical conditions and culture degree, the institutionalised level of interests expressing is subject to improve with comparatively narrow aspects and few channels and tools for participation concurrently.

To be specific in microscopic view of the system itself, it emerges the following defects: In the system design, the lack of penalty on failing to perform responsibilities or in other words the ambiguity of responsibilities on the government side renders the great randomness of the rules of this system, evolving into a unilateral controlling pattern that is driven and guided by one party (here referring to the government), instead of legal and institutional controlling pattern. The key to the perfection of the public consultation system is at the link connecting public participation and the final decision-making of the government. Although the system design requires the response of the government to public participation, in practice, except when the issuance of the Shanghai Provisions, the government gave its feedback through websites and newspapers to the public opinions it heard and adopted and made detailed explanations about the rejected opinions, no other legislations that once consulted with public opinions have ever followed this step. Due to the absence of such an effective supervising mechanism, the sense of responsibility in the administrative authorities is weak, resulting in random negligence on the side of the public opinion.

At the same time, in a procedure where the government and the public should interact with each other, the public will finally lose their confidence in the government since the unresponsiveness to their opinions and will then reveal indifferently to the participation activities, even finally forming into a vicious circle. Regarding policy-making hearing system, many scholars and practicers see the hearings concurrently in our country as actually symposiums with considerable randomness in respects of the selection of events for hearings, determination of participants, organisation of the hearing procedures, and the effectiveness of the hearing results and without sufficient recognition to the value of the hearing procedure itself. Such cases as the results of hearing may breach public opinions often occur.

Such occurrence as the above problems is no doubt due to the irrationality of the system design itself in somehow. However, it is also undeniable that the deep reasons are closely in connection with the soil where this system locates – the background of the politics, economy and culture of a country. Public participation is on the foundations of representative democracy, which is the outcome of the development of democratic politics. Some system arrangements are directly transplanted from western democratic countries and there must be a course of accommodation, adjustment and localisation in China.

At the initial stage of development, it is inevitably restricted by such elements. And also some systems provisionally haven't been introduced into due to the shortage of suitable soil and environment. For example, in many western countries, citizen participation in legislative activities firstly reveals in the right to table legislative proposals, which can be launched in case of obtaining signatures of constituencies in the amount legally specified. In the same way, obtaining of signatures of constituencies in the amount legally specified could also launch a referendum to determine whether or not to abolish a law or some clauses of a law. In our country, since the Constitution and the Legislation Law doesn't deal with the public's direct raising legislative proposals, this very powerful public participation institution provisionally can't be applied. In this part, we trie to probe, from such basic social perspectives as public internal demand for participation in development and its external conditions, into the key elements driving the public participation system within the concurrent systematic frame in future.

3.1 Development of Social Organisations

One of the important functions undertaken by government legislation and decision-making is to coordinate and balance the diversified interests of the society which could be expressed and displayed through institutional arrangement of public participation, or we can also say that the diversification of interests is the driving force and requirement of existence and development for public participation system. Along with the transforming from planned economic system to market economic system of China, „the rapid economic growth benefits most social members but to varied extent among different individuals and groups. Social hierarchy is thus quickly and obviously resulted and followed by different interest requirements and ways of presentation", and „more and more people begin to dissociate from formal social organizations such as lots of rural surplus labor force and urban self-employed etc."[18]. Independent interests and notions would require a way to present and realize the interests such as obtaining legal protection and favorable public policy through exerting influence on policy-making.

However, dispersive individuals stand in a vulnerable position compared to government or other entity organisations and thus their voice is subject to be ignored or counteracted, which requires the individuals of the same interests gather together as an organisation to make a higher consistent voice for their interest while utilising the gathered resources to influence the policy making of the government. This serves as a necessary social basis for the development of public participation system. The emergence of multi-interest pattern depends on the level of market economic development to a great extent. We have established the market economic system in China but our market economy is still government-oriented at present. Therefore, social organisation, the „third department" of our country, is still not mature. Many organisations bear intense administrative color and are called „the second government" since they are established with the assistance of government. So these social organisations could not make interest presentation completely on behalf of the interest groups.

As the economic center of China, Shanghai put forth the local regulation of *Provisions of Promoting the Development of Trade Association* in 2002 given the key importance of social organization development to the market economy. Meanwhile, the government tries to transform its functions to give the power back to the society on affairs that could be managed by the organisations and associations on their own. Almost all the industries in Shanghai have set up their own trade associations and are playing a more and more important role in political participation as benign interaction with the government. If the momentum is kept along, there would be much more ordered and powerful participation with the improvement of social organisation and development of political and cultural groups after economical groups as well as a larger scale and range of participation.

3.2 District Government Democracy and Community Autonomy Re-building

Shanghai is a super large city with over 13 million permanent population and more than four million floating population. Such a giant

---
[18] See, Ge Yanfeng.

population causes a high cost of public participation on municipal level, a limit to optional tools, more difficulty to organise the activities and achieve the expected results. It is seen from the experience of foreign countries that public participation system tends to be much more developed on lower level governments since they are more connected to the public in their range of responsibilities which are specific and targeting to people's daily life. For the public, they have more intense desire to ask for their interest since they could get effect instantly by participating in relevant administrative management to improve the situation directly. Moreover, the population under district government jurisdiction is easier and more proper to conduct public participation of various forms. Shanghai municipality has 18 districts and one county under it, each having set up their official website on internet as a channel for public information. Some even have arranged columns for public participation related to government events collection and administrative quality review in the precinct etc. Seen from the development trend, the key to promote public participation system lies in district and county government level as the most important stage for people to be part of broader range of events in more channels and ways and to stipulate procedures rules.

There are also 3,293 residential councils and 1,991 villagers' councils in Shanghai. According to the constitution, residential/villagers' councils are grass roots organisations of autonomy yet they were extension of district government under planned economic system since personnel were to be appointed and dismissed by the government and they implemented administrative orders given by the government. With the transforming of government functions, residential / villagers' councils come back to their original functions gradually with direct election currently in Shanghai. With the upgrading of autonomy of these communities, democracy on internal affairs should be promoted on one hand and political functions have to be displayed to restructure interests of all parties as a channel of interest presentation especially in aspect of participation in district and lower level government management.

3.3 Procedure Institutionalisation

Procedure building falls into problems on technical level compared to the above-mentioned two key factors for development. Yet lack of procedure institutionalisation has become the bottleneck for further development of public participation in China. The state has not yet stipulated uniform procedure regulations on some key systems due to inadequate practical experience, which leads to mis- or non-operation of some local governments, impairing the creditability and enthusiasm from the public and even injuring the participation system. Generally the public opinions have no binding on the government and thus the participation procedure stands out with independent value to protect the right to participate. The Shanghai government is working on regulations of hearing procedure in the process of government legislation and decision-making so as to come up with unified and specific regulations on the policy-making hearing in the municipal administrative system and to restrict the power of administrative authorities.

3.4 Development Trend of Public Participation

The above discussion is based on the scope of executive branch and this section turns to new explorations in public participation by legislative bodies, which is not within the study range of this article though. As background information closely related to the theme of this article, we think it necessary to provide readers with an overall perspective. As mentioned before, representative democracy serves as the foundation of direct participation since public views are realised by election system and the legislators might lose certain votes if they refuse to adopt the public views. The political function of election system has not totally realised in China and legislative organs have no powerful driving force to hear public voices at the beginning. An expression becomes rather popular recently: Open Legislation, which means that many provincial and municipal legislation organs open the door of legislation to the public by adopting various forms to absorb and represent their views. Apart from conventional practices such as legislative hearing and entrusting experts for drafts etc., it is worth noticing that People's Congresses of Ningbo, Liaoning city and some other places collect legislative proposals from the public and also have set up five-year legislative items database of projects suggested by the public, thus ensuring science and democracy of the legislation from the very source.[19] Compared to the legislative procedures of western countries mentioned above, our practice is not conducted in a system with much freedom and random but it has obvious advantages: highly efficient and easy to collect as many as opinions and wisdom. When the current constitution and laws have no specific public legislation procedure, it is rather recommendable for local legislative organs to make such attempts to provide the public with channels of direct participation.

After finishing this article, a piece of news attracted the author's attention. The State Environmental Protection Administration held the Public Hearing on the Lake Bottom Seepage Proof Project of Old Summer Palace, reputed as the first real state-level hearing in

---

[19] See, The People's Daily, 25 Mar., 2005.

China by authoritative media.[20] Though the overall process of the hearing was a bit out-of-control, more like a passionate debate without focused and ordered view presentation and discussion. However, this also shows that it's not a hearing controlled by government but real public participation. Moreover, over 40 media and more than 100 reporters witnessed this over five-hour event and two websites broadcasted live in the internet. Many people came from afar and all directions for the hearing with their files and materials had to stand outside the site to watch the live broadcasting due to the limited number of places. Those common people with an attitude of active participation in government decision-making are the real hope and cornerstone for the future development of public participation system in China which would transform from a top down model led by government to bottom up model dominated by society. To sum up, the democracy in China is proceeding in orderly steps but never in the reversed way.

References

Blair, Harry (2000): Participation and Accountability at the Periphery – Democratic Local Governance in Six Countries, in: World Development 28 (1), pp. 21-39.

Gabriel, Oscar W (1999): Democracy in Big Cities: The Case of Germany, in: Gabriel, Oscar W./Hoffmann-Martinot, Vincent/Savitch, Hank V. (eds.): Urban Democracy, Opladen, pp. 187-259.

Ge Yanfeng: The Social Life Conformation Has Changed Greatly in China. http://www.ccrs.org.cn.

Irvin, Renée A./Stansbury, John (2004): Citizen Participation in Decision-Making – Is It Worth the Effort?, in: Public Administration Review, Jan/Feb 2004.

Horsley, Jamie P. (2004): Shanghai Advances the Cause of Open Government Information in China, 20 Apr. 2004. http://www.freedominfo.org/news/20040420.htm

Kang Xiaoguang (1999): Economic Increase, Social Justice, Democracy and Rule by Law, and Legitimacy Basis – Changes since 1978 and Choices for the Future, in: Strategies and Management, 4/1999.

Luo, Changqing (2003): The Indigenous Situation of the Public Hearing System, in Local Legislation in China. Unpublished manuscript.

---

[20] See, The Old Summer Palace Hearing Had a Great Demonstrative Meaning, in: The Weekend in South, 21 Apr., 2005.

Organization for Economic Co-operation and Development [OECD] (2001): Citizens as Partners – Information, Consultation, and Public Participation in Policy-Making. E-Book: http://www.oecdbookshop.org.
The People's Daily, 25 Mar., 2005.
The Weekend in South, 21 Apr., 2005.
Vetter, Angelika/Kersting, Norbert (2003): Democracy versus Efficiency? Comparing Local Government Reforms across Europe, in: Vetter, Angelika/Kersting, Norbert (eds.): Reforming Local Government in Europe – Closing the Gap between Democracy and Efficiency, Opladen, pp. 11-28.
Vetter, Angelika (2004): Modernizing German Local Government: Bringing People Back in Direct Communication.
Wollmann, Hellmut (2002): The Civic Community ('Bürgergemeinde') in Germany – Its Double Nature as Political and as (Civil) Societal Community, in: German Journal of Urban Studies, 2/2002.
World Resources Institute (2003): Public Participation and Access, in: World Resources 2002-2004: Decisions for the Earth: Balance, Voice, and Power. E-Book: http://pubs.wri.org.
Yao, Yuerong (2004): The Studies of the Issues of Public Participation in Legislation Process, in: Xu, Xianghua (ed.): The Review of the Legislation in China in the New Era.

Anzeige

Potsdamer Textbücher PTB 2/8

Das moderne Polen

Wissenschaftler aus Polen und Deutschland bieten eine exzellente Analyse über die Entwicklung von Demokratie, Staat, Gesellschaft, Wirtschaft und Außenpolitik in Polen von Anfang der 1990er Jahre bis 2005.

Bestellungen beim Universitätsverlag Potsdam

ubpub@uni-potsdam.de

Taghi Azadarmaki

Good or Bad Government – The Case Study of Iran

Recognising the degree of people's contributions in the political field more than anything else depends on the understanding of their judgment on the government and the political system. If people in a country have a good picture of their political system, the nature of their contribution will be different from that of those whose judgment on the government is negative or ambivalent about their government. In the first section of this paper we will try to pin down theoretically the difference between good and bad government based on definitions given by theoreticians concerning the state and the influence it could have on innovation processes. In the following pages of the paper report, based on information obtained during an experimental survey, we will focus on the following questions: Do Iranians have a good or bad judgment about their government? If they perceive the state to be good, what are their standards and criteria for that conclusion?

The questions above will be studied according to an experimental survey conducted in Iran with a sample size of 2,535 nationwide. In this paper, while considering people's judgment on the government, we will present the degree of their contribution to the government.

1. Theoretical Place of Government

The claim that the concept of government is the same as that of the state is not agreed upon among theoreticians. Some thinkers, like Wincent, consider the concept of state to be broader than the concept of government. In his view, state is not only a set of institutions but an indicator of the existence of ideas and behavioral methods that are called „civilization" and is part of it. The state has made its way into our daily affairs and will continue to do so. Our life starts and ends within the framework of the state (Wincent 1990: 17-18).

Contrary to the above view, some writers have used the concept of state as a whole and have given limited definitions. Cool defines

---

* This paper has been presented at the conference „Social life, Civil Society, and Governance. Comparing Local Political Participation in a Global Society - Interdisciplinary Views" in November 4-6, 2004, in Potsdam.

government as a „National Machine" (Cool 1920: 86). Laskey believes that the definition of the government as „action of the state" is the same as that of government (Laskey 1919: 30). Rice believed that „the word state means government as an institution (Rice 1969: 216). In the view of Weber, the state represents the united institutions that claim legal rule on a specific geographical area and is thus the most important source of strength.

When the role of the state and its share in the development of countries is discussed, the conflict becomes more serious and many different views are expressed.

In view of the development of theoreticians, the central issue in that theory is the concept of „modern state" versus „traditional state" that is rooted in tribal and familial structures. A state with a political, legal and executive system is a certain tool for a country's development. This idea is synonymous to the definition of the World Bank:

> „World Bank defines three legislative, executive, and judicial bodies as main elements in a state. In this case state in general means a governing institution that protects national interests and consists of a collection of institutions that are formed above society and shaped to control a country's affairs." (Evans 2001: 36, quoted by Bay-Salami 2004: 42)

After World War II, many tried to limit and undermine the role of state in development theoretically and empirically; however, in the two recent decades „Return to State" and the importance of its role in development have been emphasised. In other words, changes in the recent two decades made states the focus of theoreticians and scientists. If in the past we undermined the importance of the existence of a state or spoke of a small state with limited responsibilities, in the new era many development theoreticians speak of various roles a state could play. This view, that has been interpreted as „Return to State", is based on a positivistic view and tries to establish a good state against a bad one. According to „Return of State", to serve its citizens, institutional independence and capabilities as a major element for the realisation of development objectives are emphasised. In this way, the necessary requirements blossoming in society are achieved.

Experimental study

In this part, we tried to use collected information from the survey on world values to answer the main question of the study. The study was conducted with a sample size of 2,535 nationwide. The method of the study was face to face interview with questionnaires. The

collected information has been analysed statistically. In this survey, several important points must be considered:
- How important are political institutions when compared to other institutions and affairs from people's point of view?
- What sort of political system and with what specifications is important in people's view?
- How high is people's participation in political matters and parties?

2. The Importance of a Political Institution

Important issues and facts in the life of people within society may determine the norms and their objectives. In the survey, as a starting point, it was tried to identify important and noticeable matters in people's view to determine the place of political institutions among other institutions and matters. The most important indicators, that most people chose, were: family (94.2 %), religion (79 %), job (77.3 %), help and contribution to others (61 %), friends (29.1 %), free time (28.5 %), and politics (16.8 %). Therefore, we could see that politics is the least important factor in Iranian people's view.

Contrary to these figures, 20.6 % of people considered politics, 5.6 % free time, 2.3 % friends, 1.5 % the job, 1.3 % contribution to others, and less than 1 % family as totally unimportant. On the other hand, among those who chose somehow important or less important options, 24.2 % and 3.1 % picked politics, 39.7 % and 21.8 % free time, 49.7 % and 16.4 % friends, 31.7 % and 4.2 % help and contribution to others, 15.9 % and 3.6 % work, 14.9 % and 3.3 % religion and 4.5 % and less than 1 % family. Therefore, it is possible to draw the conclusion that the order of important issues in their lives is the following: family, religion, job, helping others, friends, free time, and politics.

Table 1:
Percentage of the importance of different matters %

Issues/Degree of Importance	Important	Unimportant	No Response
Family	98.7	0.9	0.4
Friends	78.8	18.7	2.5
Free time	68.2	27.4	4.5
Politics	41.0	51.7	7.4
Work	93.2	5.1	1.7
Religion	93.9	4.4	1.7
Helping others	92.7	5.5	1.7

The Friedman Test – for studying inner case single factor data – shows that there is a meaningful difference between important issues. The amount of Kay square in this test is X2=5490, and the calculated meaningful level is p = 0.000, making the data useful. Thus, we can conclude that there is a noticeable difference among the importance of each of the cases.

3. Specifications of a Political System

The main issue, that has been put into the three following options, is to study the idea of Iranian people about a good political system:
(1) a strong head of state,
(2) a strong government, and
(3) a democratic political system.

3.1 A strong Head of State

To understand the judgment of Iranian people on a strong head of state, we should first consider the following option, that is „having a strong head of state that has no need to waste his time with parliament and election". Among those questioned, 4.5 % considered this way of governing „very bad". However, 17.6 % of people called this method „to some degree good" and 11.9 % of people even called this a „very good" method („Good" 29.5 %, „Bad" 25.9 %, „No Response" 44.6 %).

There is no considerable difference among male and female participants in this respect, and a few differences would not result into a meaningful statistical relation in this field.

Those questioned differ in their marital status: 33.4 % and 31 % of those married and 31.2 % and 25 % of those who were single, respectively, called a strong state „to some degree bad" and „absolutely bad". Considering this difference, the correctness of this relation is confirmed. Therefore, we can conclude that single people see a strong state more as a necessity rather than married ones.

With increasing age the number of people who called this way of governing a „very good" one and „to some degree good" becomes less and less. The number of people who see a political system based on a strong state as „somehow bad" and „very bad" increases. In other words, young people when compared (18 % and 25.6 %) to older people (12.6 % and 19 %) have more positive views in this respect. The number of coefficients of gamma examination is equal to 10, and the amount of alpha is acceptable.

Findings show that when knowledge of people increases, the number of those who view a strong state as „good" and „to some extent good" increases, too. 9 % of uneducated people selected the

„very good" option, and 31.8 % of them selected the „very bad" option, whereas 19.5 % of educated people chose „very good" and 24.4 % „very bad". Gamma statistical exam in this respect shows a meaningful relation on an acceptable level.

In respect of the relation of the level of earnings of those questioned, with way of governing based on a strong state, there is no meaningful relation. However, some small differences show that most people with low income and high income find this way of governing proper and good, but those who have an average high or low income, find that somehow improper.

Table 2:
Percentage of the relationship between having
a strong head of the state with other variables %

Issues/Views	Good	Bad
Gender:		
Male	37.9	62.1
Female	40.5	59.4
Marital Status:		
Married	35.7	64.4
Single	43.9	56.2
Age Groups:		
15-24	43.6	56.2
25-34	38.0	61.0
35-44	38.2	61.9
45-54	32.0	68.0
more than 55	31.6	68.5
Education:		
illiterate	33.5	66.3
elementary	32.2	67.7
high school	49.2	60.7
diploma	38.5	61.6
university degree	43.3	56.9
Family Income:		
very low	41.2	58.8
low	36.9	66.0
average	39.7	60.2
high	42.5	56.5
very high	43.3	56.8

3.2. Strong Government

On the point of strong government, the survey shows that 42.8 % find it „very good" and 24.4 % find it „good". Also, 8.3 % called it „to some extent bad", and 4.9 % described it as „very bad". In summary: „Good" 67.2 %, „Bad" 13.2 % and „No Response „ 19.6 %.

In a survey conducted among male and female voters, there is no clear difference of opinion on the issue of powerful political system, and therefore the calculated relation is not meaningful. Conducting a statistical sample among married and single voters on the issue of having a powerful government, there is no meaningful relation. Therefore the relation between the two variables in question is rejected.

The information collected through the study shows that 53.7 % and 31 % of people between 15-24 and 55, and 30.6 % of people between 25-34, and 32.6 % of people between 35-44, 54.2 % and 30.4 % of people between 45-54, and 29.6 % of 55 or older selected „very good" and „to some extent good" for having a powerful government. Thus, there is no noticeable difference among age groups.

On the question of a powerful political system, we can say that uneducated people – when compared to educated people – see a powerful government more as a necessity. 58.4 % of uneducated people in comparison to 51.3 % of highly educated people find this way of governing „very good". On the other hand, 5.8 % of highly educated people and 3.4 % of uneducated people described it as „very bad". Considering the existing differences, there is no meaningful statistical relation.

The collected information does not show a meaningful statistical relation between the two variables; however, it must be considered

Table 3:
Percentage of the relationship between
the strong government and other variables %

Issues/Views	Good	Bad
Gender:		
Male	83.5	16.4
Female	83.6	16.4
Marital Status:		
Married	84.2	15.8
Single	82.8	17.3

Age Groups:		
15-24	84.7	16.9
25-34	85.6	14.3
35-44	82.3	17.7
45-54	84.6	15.4
more than 55	79.6	20.4
Education:		
illiterate	89.9	10.1
elementary	82.6	17.5
high school	85.3	14.5
diploma	82.9	17.1
university degree	83.3	16.8
Family Income:		
very low	70.6	29.2
low	85.5	14.5
average	84.5	15.5
high	79.2	20.6
very high	83.4	16.6

that people with low level and average income, have a negative idea about this matter and in comparison to people with low income or high and upward income who described this method very good.

3.3 Democratic Political System

Findings show that 33.6 % of those questioned described a democratic political system as „very good", and 21.6 % described it „to some extent good". However, 5.8 % and 3.5 % respectively described it as „somehow bad" and „very bad". Among the opinion of female and male voters on the question of having a democratic political system there is no noticeable difference, and the relation of these two variables – a from statistical point of view – is rejected. In Summary: „Good" 55.2 %, „Bad" 9.3 % and „No Response" 35.5 %.

Single and married voters have different views with respect to democracy based governance. In other words, 54.5 % and 33 % of married people and 48.7 % and 34 % of single people, respectively, chose „very good" and „to some extent good" with regard to a democratic political system. 10 % and 7.2 % of single voters and 8.3 % and 4 % of married voters, respectively, described a democratic political system as „to some degree bad" and „very bad". Therefore, the meaningful relation between the two variables is confirmed (P = 0,83).

Table 4:
Percentage of the relationship between having a democratic political system with other variables %

Issues	Good	Bad
Gender:		
Male	87.3	8.8
Female	83.4	16.8
Marital Status:		
Married	94.5	12.4
Single	82.7	8.2
Age Groups:		
15-24	81.2	18.7
25-34	85.3	14.7
35-44	88.3	11.8
45-54	92.5	7.6
more than 55	88.1	11.0
Education:		
illiterate	92.0	8.0
elementary	87.7	12.3
high school	39.4	20.4
diploma	86.4	13.7
university degree	87.5	12.5
Family Income:		
very low	74.2	25.9
low	86.4	13.6
average	86.1	14.0
high	85.1	15.0
very high	79.1	20.5

4. Political Participation

We have measured political participation with regard to two major indicators: (1) the scale of political discussion and (2) level of familiarity with political parties and their support.

4.1. Scale of Political Discussion

Political discussion is the first step toward political action and could be different considering the different cultural and economic levels in different societies. Findings show that 52.6 % of people, when meeting with their friends, „sometimes" have political discussions.

In this respect, about 30.5 % of people have „never" had political discussions. Among those questioned 16.8 % said that they „always" have political discussions on different political matters.

Table 5:
Percentage of discussions on different political matters %

Discussion on political matters	Always	Sometimes	Never	No response
Percentage	15.8	49.5	28.7	5.9

Now we study the relation of the scale of political discussion of voters with major variables in this research. Among those questioned, the political discussion is more prevalent among men than women. In other words, the option of „sometimes" was chosen by 54.8 % of men and only 50.1 % by women. In the second stage, „always" was picked by 19,7 % of men and 13.5 % of women. With respect to the option „never", the percentage of women that have never had political discussions is higher than that of men (36.4 % and 25.6 %). Therefore, we can conclude that the tendency of men toward political discussions when being with their friends is stronger than among women. This difference is confirmed in 5 % alpha.

The scale of political discussion among unmarried people compared to married ones is different. Therefore, a meaningful statistical relation could be seen. 17.7 % and 58.8 % of single people, respectively, „sometimes" and „always" have political discussions, compared to 16.3 % and 48.5 % of married people. The percentage of those people who discuss political matters in company of their friends is higher among married people (35.3 % vs. 23.5 %).

The percentage of people of 15-24 years of age is higher than that of 55 year old and upward. In this indicator, parallel to age growth, the scale of political discussion among people is reduced. The number of those people who never participate in political discussions increases with growth of age. Therefore, we can conclude that younger people – when compared to older people – have more political discussions among themselves. The relation of these two variables – from a statistical point of view – is meaningful.

The scale of political discussions is increased when the level of education is increased in the following way: „always" and „sometimes" is picked 8,1 % and 26.2 % by uneducated people and 25.3 % and 61.1 % by educated people. Therefore, the calculated meaningful relation is confirmed in an acceptable range.

People with high level of income have different political discussions. 19.5 % and 40.9 % of people with a very low level of income and 24.6 % and 42.1 % of those with a high level of income, respectively, do „always" and „sometimes" have political discussions.

The amount of gamma coefficient in respect of the relation of these two variables in level of 5 % of alpha is acceptable, and the above relation is confirmed.

4.2. Taking Part in Elections and Voting for Political Parties

One of the features of political participation among people within society is taking part in national elections. In this respect, we asked three questions about the participation of people in the future elections of the country. In reality, in the first question we were to find which political party the voters are going to vote for. The final result is that 44.2 % of those questioned would vote for independent parties. In this stage, 31.8 % voted for a left-wing party and 23.9 % voted for a right-wing party. Among those people, 37.1 % did not mention any specific political party which could be interpreted as unwillingness to take up political positions or early judgment about their participation in the future election.

Table 6:
Distribution of responses in terms of voting for parties %

Voting on the first level	Right Parties	Left Parties	Independent
Percentage	23.9	31.8	44.2

In another question on which political party the person questioned would vote for as second choice, 39.8 % of people answered independent party, 32.2 % said left party and 28 % voted for a right party. The number of undecided voters was as high as 41.5 %.

Table 7:
Distribution of responses in terms of voting for parties %

Voting on the second level	Right Parties	Left Parties	Independent
Percentage	28	32.2	39.8

In the third and last question on which political party the person questioned would never vote for, half of those questioned had no opinion. However, 56.4 % answered independent party, 30.6 % right wing party and 13 % said that they will never vote for a left wing party.

Table 8:
Distribution of responses in terms of voting for parties %

Which party would you never vote for?	Right Parties	Left Parties	Independent
Percentage	30.6	13	56.4

Table 9:
Distribution of responses on the importance of the political system (percentage) %

Components of Political system	Good	Bad	No Response
1. Having strong head of the state	29.5	45.9	24.6
2. Strong state	67.2	13.2	19.5
3. Having a democratic political system	55.2	8.3	35.5

5. Conclusion

As mentioned in the introduction, the situation in the world and Iran caused both political rhetoricians and analysts to emphasise a powerful state vs. a weak state. This emphasis has been interpreted as „Return to the state". Therefore, in social, economic and political developments, a further emphasis has been put on the role of the state along with other actors. Thus, for us as Iranians, the question was to figure out whether people's judgment on the „Return to the state" is positive or not. In order to answer this question, an experimental study was conducted to measure importance, nature and place of the state. The result of the study shows some major points:
(1) It is true that Iranian people see a powerful state as an important factor, but in comparison to other issues – such as religion and family – it is of second importance in their daily life.

(2) People are somehow familiar with politics but they do not care much about it.
(3) People want a powerful head of government but a democratic one.
(4) The head of government should act along with parliament.
(5) He should respect people's and parties' rights.
(6) He should be decisive and determined.
(7) He should be able to handle the system democratically and pave the way to establish democracy permanently. In this case, contrary to the claims made by many in the fields of politics, Iranian people are not in favor of a totalitarian regime. However, they would support a head of state that – while respecting democracy – could fulfill his responsibilities through legal means and prevent anarchy.
(8) Iranian people, while they are not willing to have widely political participation, are in favor of independent, left wing and right wing parties. However, they are more in favor of left wing parties.
(9) Although Iranian people in ordinary condition care little about political participation, they expect politicians and other people with important responsibilities to bring maximum growth and development to the country.

References

Bay-Salami, Ebrahim/Gholam-Haydar (2004): The Role of State on Machine Industry, Doctorate Dissertation, Tehran, The University of Tehran, (1383).

Evans, Peter (2001): Development or ... – The Role of State on Industrial Changes, translated by Abbas Zandbaf and Abbas Mokhbe, Tehran, Tarhe No, (1380).

Gary, Joun (2002): Liberalism, translated by Mohammad Savoji, Tehran, Foreign Affairs Ministry, (1381).

Goldtorp, J, A. (1990): Sociology of Third Countries – Unequal Development. Mashhad, Astane Ghods Publisher, (1370).

Rice, Mickel (2002): Society and Politics – Introduction to Political Sociology, translated by Manuocher Sabouri, Tehran, Samt Publisher, (1381).

Weber, Max (1992): The Protestant Ethics and the Spirits of Capitalism, translated by Abdolhamid Ansari, Tehran, Samt Pub, (1371).

Winest, Andoro (1989): The Theories of the State, translated by Hossain Bashirieh, First Edition, Tehran, Nashre Nay, (1369).

World Bank (1999): The Role of the State in Developing Countries, translated by Hamid Reza Shoraka and others, Tehran, The Institute for Studies and Research in Marketing, (1378).

Jochen Franzke

Representation and Participation in New Unitary Municipalities
Cases from the German Federal State Brandenburg

The debate on the size, scale and scope of local government, amalgamation or secession of municipalities is an evergreen in political science discussions. Nevertheless, the process of re-mapping the territorial structure of local government is taking place in some European countries, among them Germany. It has a strong influence on the process of democratic renewal at the local level in the affected states. It may be useful, therefore, to have a look at some new developments in this field. In fact, little attention is paid to the sub-local level in studies on amalgamated municipalities. Hence, in this paper I will concentrate on newly amalgamated municipality and its sub-local districts in the German Federal State Brandenburg.

In this contribution, for the first time, results from a research project evaluating the local territorial reform in Brandenburg (2000-2003) are presented. The sample contains 11 cases of new unitary municipalities, differing in their ways of establishment (voluntary or by law), their location within Brandenburg (urban capital-near area or rural area) and the dominant actors in the political decision-making process (political parties or civic associations). The following questions are at the centre of interest: How has amalgamation influenced the democratic legitimacy? Who is dominating the policy process in the new municipalities: political parties or civil associations? Which role does the new districts play in the local decision-making structure? Are these new institutions strengthening local legitimacy or weakening it by taking on a veto player's role? What are the consequences for the local identity of the citizens?

I. Local Territorial Reform in the Federal State Brandenburg – Concept and Results

Reform Concept

Reforming the territorial map of municipalities was one of the most important reform projects of the new federal state government,

---

* Paper presented at the study group Local Governance and Democracy at the EGPA Annual Conference 2006 (August 31st – September 3rd), Milan, Italy

coming to power in Brandenburg at the end of 1999. Previous municipal territorial reforms had failed (see Buechner/Franzke 1999: 175, Wollmann 1996). The state government of the „Great Coalition", formed by the Social Democrats and the Christian Democrats, was able to count on 62 of 89 deputies (70 %) in parliament (*Landtag*). Facing this overwhelming majority, major conflicts during the reform were not expected within parliament, but rather between state politicians, pushing reform, and (mostly) local politicians refusing it.

The state government's reform concept consisted of the following elements:

The amalgamation of municipalities by forming unitary municipalities was regarded as the best solution by the government for increasing efficiency and effectiveness of local governments. These were supposed to have at least 5,000 inhabitants.[1]

Associations of municipalities were to remain in the rural peripheral areas only. To make them more effective, a minimum of 5,000 inhabitants was designated. The number of municipalities, belonging to an association, was to be reduced to three to six.

A third way within the local territorial reform provides the opportunity to incorporate municipalities, situated in suburbs, into the neighboring city.

In order to promote unitary amalgamations, financial incentives were specified. However, these were limited until March 2002.[2]

The reform concept of the state government was based on learning from mistakes occurring during former reforms of this kind in other German states, with a particular concern for the establishment of sub-local district councils, which were supposed to help retain the identity of all municipalities, that would lose their independence during the reform. New districts rights were introduced as well, including the right for hearings, proposals and applications as well as for hedge clauses.

Districts could choose between two models of representing their interests: They could directly elect a district mayor, who bore the responsibilities of the district council in personal union („Single Fighter"); or they could elect a district council, consisting of several members electing a district mayor (who would be the chairman of the district council at the same time) and its deputy („Team Variant"). The number of members of district councils differs from three (in districts up to 500 inhabitants) to nine (in districts with more than 2,500 inhabitants).

---

[1] This way, it was sought to target the problem of 93 % of the municipalities in Brandenburg having less then 5,000 inhabitants while 58 % have even less than 500.
[2] Voluntary amalgamation was supported by Federal state subsidies with 200 to 300 DM per inhabitant.

Reform Process

The reform process consisted of the following phases: First, the federal state government decided upon guidelines for the local territorial reform on September 20, 2000. On July 11, 2000 the *Landtag* affirmed this concept. In February 2001, the *Landtag* adopted the respective legal regulations. Until March 2002, municipalities were able to amalgamate voluntarily (as 63 % of them did). The remaining municipalities were forced to amalgamate by six laws, adopted by the *Landtag* in March 2003. These laws were implemented by October 2003.

With its comfortable majority in Parliament, the government was able to push its original concept forward with very few changes. The reform was completed with the local election on October 26, 2003, the first of its kind within the new municipal structure. Finally, the municipalities were able to complain to the state's constitutional court about the amalgamation with other municipalities by law.[3] 255 of them did so; however, by June 2006 all complaints had been rejected. The state's legal regulations were confirmed. Only two municipalities[4] succeeded. The original legal decision had to be cancelled because of material errors in the consideration.[5]

Results

In October 2003, after three years of controversial discussion, the process of reforming the territorial structure of the municipalities in Brandenburg was finished. Their number declined dramatically from 1,479 (1999) to 421 (2004). The state government regarded this as an impressive success. In comparison with reforms of this kind in Germany, Brandenburg carried out a very thorough reform, cutting the number of municipalities by more than 76 %. The number of unitary municipalities rose from 66 to 148; the number of the „asso-

---

[3] Originally, 30 municipalities succeeded with their constitutional complaints because of hearing errors in the legislative procedure. However, the legislator issued a new law, with which it held in the result to its reorganisation conceptions, concerning the population, after a hearing in July 2004. Thus, some of the municipalities affected by the confirmation turned to the state's constitutional court a second time, but they remained unsuccessful.

[4] VfGBbg 63/03 and VfGBbg 138/03.

[5] Originally, the legislator had intended to integrate them (Königsberg and Herzsprung) into the municipality (Wittstock/Dosse). After the decisions of the constitutional court in the year 2004, they were able to obtain their amalgamation with another municipality of their choice (Heiligengrabe).

ciations of municipalities" sank from 152 to 54 (with 272 municipalities).

However, a more precise view of the reform results shows that the reform only changed the local territorial structure in the urban parts of the state, situated near the German capital Berlin, according to the government's plans, . In this area (called „narrow integration area"), a new structure with unitary municipalities was established.[6] With only four exceptions, all municipalities now have more then 5,000 inhabitants. Thus, in this area the government's plans lead to an even outcome.

As for the sparsely populated rural areas of the state (called „outer development area"), the dominance of the „associations of municipalities" remained. At the end of the municipal territorial reform 284 municipalities are now part of 54 associations, and 87 unitary municipalities now exist. More than 300 municipalities have less then 5,000 inhabitants. So in this part of the state, the reform was less successful, finding its limits in the specific demographic situation. It may be the result of the local territorial reform in this area that the existing system of „associations of municipalities" becomes more effective (with fewer actors).

To conclude, as a result of the reform, Brandenburg has now been split into two different areas of local governments: The urban capital-near areas with unitary municipalities and the rural areas, where „associations of municipalities" are still dominant. The majority of municipalities (64.3 %) is still a part of these associations; the minority (34.0 %) is organized as unitary municipalities. The rest belongs to county-free municipalities.

One of the quantitatively measurable consequences of the territorial reform for local democracy is the sinking mandate density, i.e. the number of local councillors per inhabitant. Now, 282 eligible voters can elect a councillor (in 1998 the number was 109). The number of elected local councillors has decreased from 13,550 to 6,295 (see table 1). However, the consequences of this development can not be evaluated, even if the qualitative aspects of this process are considered. In the past, local councillors often criticised their real influence in local affairs because of financial restrictions. In the new unitary municipalities they have won a wider scope of influence.

II. New Unitary Municipalities in Brandenburg

Cases

During the local territorial reform, 82 new unitary municipalities were founded. This paper's sample covers 11 of them (13 %), which

---

[6] In this area only one association of municipalities still exists.

Table 1
Number of Local Councillors in Brandenburg

	Local Elections 1993	Local Elections 1998	Local Elections 2003	Variance 2003 to 1998	Variance 2003 to 1993
Eligible Voters	1,591248	1,703386	1,777438	+74,052	+186,190
Elected Local Councillors	14,664	13,550	6,295	-7,255 (-53.6 %)	-8,369 (-57.1 %)
Eligible Voters per Elected Local Councillors	108.5	125.7	282.4	+156.7	+173.9

Source: State Election Supervisor
(http://www.wahlen.brandenburg.de/cms/detail.php/lbm1.c.295931.de)

is not representative, but gives a good insight in the consequences of this kind of reform for local democracy and identity (see table 2).

Most of the cases, which are to be analysed in the following, are based on the findings of an ongoing research project at the *Institute of Local Affairs* at Potsdam University, evaluating the consequences

Table 2
Basic Data of the Cases

	Inhabitants (Number June 2005)	Inhabitants (Per qkm)	Core Municipality (% of inhabitants)
1. Nuthetal	7,500	185	Bergholz/ Rehbrücke (80 %)
2. Altlandsberg	8,700	82	Altlandsberg (63 %)
3. Groß Pankow	4,600	18	No core municipality
4. Gumtow	4,000	19	No core municipality
5. Wustermark	7,500	143	Two[b] (together 80 %)
6. Michendorf	11,100	160	No core municipality
7. Rheinsberg	9,100	28	Rheinsberg (84 %)
8. Karstaedt	7,100	28	No core municipality
9. Stahnsdorf	13,100	266	Stahnsdorf (79 %)
10. Zehdenick	14,700	66	No core municipality
11. Schwielowsee	9,600	165	No core municipality

of the local territorial reform in Brandenburg.[7] The cases were chosen to find out the influence of the following variables on the establishment of a new municipality: firstly, the manner of their establishment (voluntary or by law), secondly, their different location in the state (urban capital-near area or rural area) and thirdly, the dominant actors in their political decision process (political parties or civic associations).

Local Actors Strategies

Establishing new unitary municipalities is a deep cut into the history of local self-government in the respective territories, both for the political elite and the population. In the selected cases during this reform, 95 municipalities, which governed themselves within an „association of municipalities" (called *Ämter* in Brandenburg), lost

---

[7] Within the framework of this project, student research seminars have been held since October 2003, directed by Dr. Christiane Buechner and myself. The analysis of the cases 3, 4, 5, 6, 7, 9 and 11 of the sample of this paper are based on interviews and reports made during this seminar in the winter term 2003/2004 (cases 3 to 7, 9) and the summer term 2005 (case 11). All other cases are based on my own research carried out in summer 2006.

Table 2 (cont.)
Basic Data of the Cases

Number of Districts	Founded	Manner of Foundation	Area
6	10/2003	Voluntary	Urban capital-near
6	1/2003	Voluntary	Urban capital-near
18[a]	12/2002	Voluntary	Rural peripheral area
16	6/2002	Voluntary	Rural peripheral area
5	12/2002	Voluntary	Urban capital-near
6	10/2003	By law	Urban capital-near
17	Finally 10/2003	6 voluntary; 11 by law	Rural peripheral area
13	10/2003	By law	Rural peripheral area
4	1/2002	Voluntary	Urban capital-near
13	10/2003	5 voluntary; 8 by law	Rural peripheral area
3	1/2003	Voluntary	Urban capital-near

[a] Combining 39 villages.
[b] Elstal and Wustermark, with nearly the same number of inhabitants.

Source: Own compilation based on data from the Brandenburg Ministry of the Interior, the Brandenburg Ministry of Infrastructure and Regional Development and the State Statistical Enterprise

their independence and finally found themselves as a district within a new municipality. 12 districts won a new status because they obtained district status without any representation before the reform. Now they are able to establish a district council and elect a district mayor.

As mentioned previously, the final decision in the local territorial reform belonged to the *Landtag*. Therefore, the choices for the local political elite were rather limited: either organise the amalgamation themselves, according to the framework set by the state, or allow it to be organised by the state without any influence at all. Obviously, some of the local elite hoped to block any decision and to prolong the status quo. However, this was a deep misperception of the nature of this kind of reform and ultimately failed.

The strategies of local elite during the local territorial reform can be described by two models: the contract and the confrontation model. In the contract model, the municipalities voluntarily agreed, according to the defaults of the state, among themselves by signing a contract.[8] It was allowed to contain stipulations on all important questions of future municipal politics on a long-term basis (up to five years).[9] This way of regulating amalgamation by local actors was, however, limited to the time between July 2000 and March 2002.

A strong argument for the contract model was additional money from the state (known as an „amalgamation bonus" or more ironically „head money"), given only to those municipalities, that voluntarily agreed in time. This model was typically used when the local elite was already consent-oriented. Since a refusal would have only led to an amalgamation by law, many of the local elites decided – not completely voluntarily – on the financial advantages. This indicates a consent-oriented decision-making process in the new unitary municipality. Under these circumstances, the new district councils received additional local legitimacy and effectiveness resources. These are good preconditions to change from the contract to the co-operation model, when the contract runs out.

---

[8] The State Ministry of the Interior drew up a model contract for the establishment of new unitary municipalities in June 2001. (see http://www.mi.brandenburg.de/sixcms/detail.php?id=12606) In nearly all cases, the standard contract was used. Some contracts (e.g. in the case of Gumtow) additionally secured the control over the amalgamation bonus as well as over the incomes from the enterprise of wind-powered devices, for the districts – whenever the financial situation of the municipality allowed for it.

[9] The contract regulates various questions, from the order of the future investments through the assumption of the administrative workers to the rate of assessment of the taxes on land.

The second model – the confrontation model – arose whenever some influential parts of the local elite opposed amalgamation according to the conditions of the state. They were not at all interested in agreeing to a contract. Thus, the decision to establish a new unitary municipality was taken by the *Landtag*. All hopes of the local elite were in vain, the state constitutional court was able to annul the law. When the law came into force, the local elite found themselves, nevertheless, in a new unity municipality.

When the new municipalities were established in October 2003, a new situation was created and the models had to be generated. The contract model lasts for a maximum of five years. It would probably not be a problem to replace it with a co-operation model after this period of time. However, this can only happen if all contract stipulations are fulfilled. Unfortunately, the way back to confrontation is also imaginable, should the contract stipulations not be fulfilled. Despite all its advantages, the contract model includes two risks: Firstly, the contracts are continuously attached to a financial reservation, i.e. their regulations can be abolished if the financial situation of the municipality gets worse. Secondly, it is uncertain whether the new local council, elected in 2003, will adhere to the contractual regulations in the long run as they limit its room for making decisions. This particularly applies when the political majority in a municipality changes as a result of the election. It is certainly not easily to quit the contract. Nevertheless, the new political majority will try everything to overcome it in the long run and to change single regulations step by step. It can be expected, however, that this kind of confrontation will only occur in some rare cases. In general, one can still say that contracts pave the way for long-term cooperation.

To overcome the confrontation model would be much more difficult. To change over to cooperation, all the local elite would have to accept the results of the territorial reform. The primary task of the local council would then be to find a new consensus by deciding on a new municipal statute. The districts are not able – in view of their limited rights – to play the role of a veto player in this process; however, they can support or obstruct it. After a transition period, it is to be expected that most new unitary municipalities, established by law and against the resistance of some parts of the local elite, will find the way to a more cooperative form of self-government. At the same time, however, in some cases confrontation cannot be overcome rapidly.

Institutional Arrangements

After the final decision on the establishment of unitary municipalities was taken and their local councils and mayors were elected in October

2003, the political elite in these municipalities had to find new institutional arrangements. Naturally, they had a lot of experience from the past, when all local councils and mayors worked together within the *Ämter* structure. After hierarchy changed, however, only one local council and one mayor are now responsible. On the other hand, these actors had to learn to cooperate with new district councils and district mayors, who represent the interests of the districts but had only a few competencies. This will most definitely be a long lasting learning process. In this paper, we can only present preliminary results of this process.[10]

Political Representation in the New Unitary Municipalities

Two models of political representation in the new unitary municipalities can be described: On the one hand, we found networks with party dominance in the local councils (in the cases of *Karstaedt* and *Wustermark*); on the other hand (in the cases of *Groß Pankow* and *Gumtow*), networks with civil associations dominate in the local councils, in which parties hardly play a role.[11] Such associations are primarily the auxiliary fire brigades and the sports clubs as they dispose of an own organisational structure in nearly all districts.[12] Other institutions, such as culture clubs, social help organisations and churches were also mentioned. In the other cases, both forms are mixed (see table 3).

Under these circumstances, the role of the mayor in the local decision process was strengthened by the reform. In the full-time position, he gained control over greater financial and personal resources than before.[13] It became easier for him to find support in a smaller local council. The councillors were also strengthened as their number was reduced and they won more influence and more room for local self-government decisions. Hopefully, their professionalism will increase as a result.

The districts (former municipalities) lost influence, because their rights were dramatically limited. According to institutional arrangements, they may only play a limited role in the local political decision process of the new unitary municipalities. As a new institution, in most of our cases, regular meetings of the mayor with the district mayors were introduced.

---

[10] Reflecting the situation in February 2004 (cases 3 to 7 and 9), in summer 2005 (case 11) and summer 2006 (cases 1, 2, 8 and 10).
[11] Both models can be dominated by strong personalities.
[12] In many cases, the auxiliary fire brigades even took part in local elections.
[13] In the former municipalities the post of the mayor was often an honorary position.

Representation in New Unitary Municipalities 163

Citizens' Engagement and Participation

During the local territorial reform, fears were widespread that it could weaken the democratic legitimacy of local government and damage the citizens' engagement and participation. Actually, some indicators seem to prove this proposition: loss of mandates in the local councils and the decreasing voter turnout in local council elections. In fact, the number of local councillors had been significantly reduced as a result of the local territorial reform. In the cases considered, between 52 % and 84 % of local mandates were lost. In all but one case, the loss of mandates in the local councils was higher than the state average of minus 53 %.

The voter's turnout in the local councils elections in Brandenburg in October 2003, immediately after the end of the local territorial reform and for the first time in the new local municipal structure, dramatically decreased from 77.1 % (in 1998) to 46.9 % (- 31.2 %). This was the most dramatic decrease ever seen in a German state since unification. One may interpret this result as a clear vote against territorial reform.

However, there are also some indicators for another version of the story. Our case studies show, that most councillors, who were not re-elected, found other ways to participate in local affairs. The majority of them (the same goes for the mayors) turned over to other forms of engagement and participation in local social life. Firstly, they were elected in the newly established district councils or in the new function as district mayors, or they took over line functions in local civil organisations. Secondly, the remaining councillors won a stronger role in local politics . Thirdly, the voter's turnout for the local council elections in all German states dramatically declined over the last ten years from an average of 70.9 % (1994) to 52.6 % (2004), in the East German states even to 46.1 %. This holds for states with local territorial reforms just as for states without this kind of reform. Thus, the result in Brandenburg reflects a general trend. Certainly, the denial of the results of the local territorial reform played a role in the decline of the voters turn out. Nevertheless, further research is necessary to define this more precisely.

However, some damage to local democracy could be noted, surprisingly because of the use of instruments of local referenda during the local territorial reform. It was legally intended to use these instruments in order to become acquainted with the majority opinion of the local population on the ways of territorial changes. However, it was not made clear enough to the population that these local referenda – in contrast to the „usual" local referenda in all other cases – were not obligatory. Furthermore, the Ministry of the Interior – responsible for carrying through the local territorial reform – only in a few cases changed its original territorial allocation according to

Table 3
Political Representation in New Unitary Municipalities

	Local Councillors (Election 2003)[a]	Local Councillors (Election 1998)	Local Councillors 2003 on Party Lists
1. Nuthetal	18	54 (-67 %)	12 (67 %)
2. Altlandsberg	18	48 (-62 %)	11 (61 %)
3. Groß Pankow	24	96 (- 75 %)	3 (14 %)
4. Gumtow	16	90 (- 82 %)	1 (6 %)
5. Wustermark	18	45 (- 60 %)	18 (100 %)
6. Michendorf	22	64 (- 66 %)	13 (59 %)
7. Rheinsberg	26	152 (- 83 %)	16 (62 %)
8. Karstaedt	18	114 (- 84 %)	18 (100 %)
9. Stahnsdorf	22	46 (- 52 %)	17 (77 %)
10. Zehdenick	28	100 (- 72 %)	22 (79 %)
11. Schwielowsee	18	42 (- 59 %)	11 (61 %)

Table 4
Political Representation in the New Municipal Districts

	Number of District Councils	Number of District Councillors[a]	District Councillors on Party Lists	Number of District Mayors
1. Nuthetal	5	17	5 (29 %)	5
2. Altlandsberg	6	...	...	6
3. Groß Pankow	18	57	1 (2 %)	18
4. Gumtow	16	79	2 (3 %)	16
5. Wustermark	5	18	17 (94 %)	5
6. Michendorf	6	34	20 (59 %)	6[b]
7. Rheinsberg	17	54	15 (28 %)	17
8. Karstaedt	13	55	21 (38 %)	13
9. Stahnsdorf	3	11	3 (27 %)	3
10. Zehdenick	13	32	4 (13 %)	13
11. Schwielowsee	3	23	...	3

Table 3 (cont.)
Political Representation in New Unitary Municipalities

Mayors	Mayors as Party Member	Parties' Influence in Municipal Politics
1 (Prev. 6)	Yes	High
1 (Prev. 5)	Yes	Medium
1 (Prev. 12)	No	Low
1 (Prev. 14)	No	Low
1 (Prev. 5)	No	High
1 (Prev. 6)	No	Medium
1 (Prev. 16)	Yes	Medium
1 (Prev. 13)	Yes	High
1 (Prev. 4)	Yes	High
1 (Prev. 13)	No	Medium
1 (Prev. 3)	Yes	Medium

[a] The first election in the new unitary municipalities took place on October 23, 2003, in the new municipality Schwielowsee on January 21, 2003.

Source: Own compilation on the basis of data from the State Election Supervisor and the student research project

Table 4 (cont.)
Political Representation in the New Municipal Districts

District Councillors as Local Councillors	Districts Represented in Local Council	Parties' Influence in District Politics
5	...	Low
...	...	
20	16 of 18	Low
6	7 of 16	Low
9	5 of 5	High
14	5 of 6	Medium
8	...	Low
6	3 of 13	Low
5	3 of 3	Low
7	4 of 13	Low
...	...	

[a] Including the district mayors.
[b] All are members of the same party.

Source: Own compilation on the basis of data from the State Election Supervisor and the research project

the majority vote of the municipalities' citizens in these local referenda. Hence, the respective citizens often regarded this decision as „undemocratic". In this way, the instrument of local referenda was damaged permanently in the eyes of the population of many municipalities in Brandenburg.

Districts in New Unitary Municipalities

In most of the interviews from our research project, the establishment of district councils and/or district mayors was described positively. At least for a transition period, these institutions will make it possible to advance the citizens to new territorial structures without losing well-known partners. The rights of these district councils are by nature clearly smaller than the rights of local councils. This fact was – at the time of their election and even later on – not always noticed by many of their members as well as the population.

Under these conditions, the way of including the district councils into the new local decision-making process depends on the more powerful local actors, especially the new mayor and the local council. As a veto actor, the district councils and/or district mayors are legally too weak, although they can strengthen local legitimacy and effectiveness. In all our cases, the districts decided upon electing a district council and a district mayor („Team Variant").

Our cases show that the interests of the new districts in a unitary municipality can be represented best, when the district councils and/or district mayors operate actively and when the districts are represented in the local council. This hold for most of our cases. In the seven cases, where data is available, 31 densely populated districts are not represented in the local council (42 % of all districts); however, in some cases not the district council members, who are elected as local councillors, but other district representatives. This demonstrates possible new forms of inner-district conflicts.

The two models of political representation are also to be seen in their districts. The influence of political parties in the districts is even more limited than on the municipal level. Accordingly, the role of civil associations is higher than at municipal level (see table 4). As such, possible conflicts between the local and district councils are not due to different political orientations but rather express different opinions on factual issues.

Some further problems even limit the given possibilities of district councils to participate in local politics. Many of them meet irregularly without any order. Nevertheless, many local decisions had to be made within a certain period of time. One local councillor from *Michendorf* described the problem as follows: „The requirement of some district councils to be included in the decisions is often greater than their commitment to actually bringing themselves into the political processes." On the other hand, the possibilities of co-operation between the district councils have, so far, not been explored enough.

Identity

The next research question regards the identity of the citizens during the territorial reform. Can local identity be damaged by the amalgamation? Surprisingly, we found few indicators for an emotional loss of the local residents as a possible consequence of their municipality having lost its historically grown self-governing status. The point of reference for citizens' identity remains their town, regardless of its political-administrative status. In contrast to its limited political influence, the district council plays an important role with regard to identity. The readiness of the citizens to identify themselves with the new unitary municipalities is (with the exception of the core municipalities) rather less developed.

This result differs from other findings (Wollmann 2004). Obviously, this is the result of governments learning from negative developments in previous territorial reforms. With the district council they formed an institution, which could attract the identity of the residents. Additionally, the government avoided changing any signs of identity during the territorial reforms. In particular, the municipality names were retained as part of the new name of the unitary municipality (visible on the local entrance nameplates).

In all cases, the interviews show, that local identity has not been affected by changes in the political-administrative structure. Different identities developed during a historical process and are not changeable at short notice. Only some municipalities, outside of our sample, form exceptions, in which the population changed dramatically after 1989. In some of these cases the new inhabitants now form the majority. The political majority in the local council has changed. In this way, identity will also change in the long run, or the new inhabitants will form a significant minority with their own civil-social structures. In this kind of municipality we find a split identity.

At any rate, this result shows that the strong emotional identity discussion in many municipalities during the territorial reform was initially determined politically by the local elites to resist certain decisions. The greatest challenge to local identity now is the loss of public institutions in many small municipalities, especially where schools are concerned. They have been closed because of a decrease in population. However, the existence of a public infrastructure is one of the core elements of identity.

III. Conclusions

The results of the case studies of new unitary municipalities in the federal state Brandenburg can be summarized as follows:

Firstly, amalgamation undoubtedly influences the legitimacy of the new municipalities. The number of the councillors has dropped dramatically, sometimes up to 84 %. The new posts of district councillors, due to their limited rights, are not able to compensate for the loss of so many mandates. The voter's turnout in the local election, which took place immediately after the reform for the first time in the new structures, decreased strongly. Nevertheless, a positive affect can be seen in that the new councillors were able to gain more political influence. There are also signs for a higher level of professionalism in the new local councils. However, a final answer to the question of the consequences of the local territorial reform for local democracy obviously needs further research.

The establishment of the new district councils and district mayors can be seen to be positive. At least for a transition period, these institutions will make it possible to advance citizens to the new territorial structures without losing well-known partners. As a veto actor, the district councils and/or district mayors are legally too weak, but they can strengthen local legitimacy and effectiveness. The interests of the districts in the new unitary municipality are represented best when active district actors (no matter whether district councillors or mayors) are represented simultaneously in the local council. Due to the decrease in population and migration, particularly of active young people, recruiting problems for district councils are to be expected in the future. This problem could get even worse, if the present district councillors were to gain the impression, that their participation is seen as being not very attractive, partly frustrating, labour intensive and promising little success.

Local identity has not been damaged by amalgamation. There is no indication of an emotional loss to the local residents because their municipality has lost its historically grown self-governing status. The point of reference for citizens' identity remains their town, despite its politically-administrative status. In this respect, two elements of the government's policy were helpful: With the district council it formed an institution, which could attract the identity of the residents. Additionally, the government avoided changing any signs of identity during the territorial reform. This holds especially for the names of the municipalities, which were retained as part of the new name of the unitary municipality. Nevertheless, there will be new challenges to local identity in the future. Many of the small municipalities will lose further public institutions, especially schools, because of the decreasing population. Yet, the existence of a public infrastructure belongs to the core elements of identity.

References

Bogumil, Jörg (2001): Modernisierung lokaler Politik – Kommunale Entscheidungsprozesse im Spannungsfeld zwischen Parteienwettbewerb, Verhandlungszwängen und Ökonomisierung, Baden-Baden.
Büchner, Christiane/Franzke, Jochen (1999): Kommunale Selbstverwaltung in Brandenburg, in: Büchner, Christiane/Franzke, Jochen (eds.): Kommunale Selbstverwaltung – Beiträge zur Debatte, Berlin, Berliner Debatte Wiss.-Verl., Potsdamer Textbücher 5, pp. 175-192.
Franzke, Jochen (2001): Kommunale Gebietsreformen im Spannungsverhältnis zwischen Demokratie und Effizienz, in: Priebs, Axel/von Saldern, Adelheid/Scholl, Rose (eds.): Junge Städte in ihrer Region, Garbsen, Schriftenreihe zur Stadtgeschichte 10, pp. 129-147.
Gern, Alfons (1997): Deutsches Kommunalrecht, Baden-Baden.
Nassmacher, Hiltrud/Nassmacher, Karl-Heinz (1999): Kommunalpolitik in Deutschland, Opladen.
Reuber, Paul (1998): Raumbezogene politische Konflikte – Geographische Konfliktforschung am Beispiel von Gemeindegebietsreformen, Stuttgart.
Seibel, Wolfgang (2001): Administrative Reforms, in: König, Klaus/Siedentopf, Heinrich (eds.): Public Administration in Germany, Baden-Baden; Nomos, pp. 73-89.
Wagner, Frido/ Blümel, Willi (2001): State Structure and Administrative Territories, in: König, Klaus/Siedentopf, Heinrich (eds.): Public Administration in Germany, Baden-Baden, Nomos, pp. 93-105.
Wollmann, Hellmut (1996): The Transformation of Local Government in East Germany – Between Imposed and Innovative Institutionalization, in: Benz, Arthur/Goetz, Klaus (eds.): A New German Public Sector? Aldershot, Dartmouth, pp. 137-163.
Wollmann, Hellmut (2000a): The Development and Present State of Local Government in England and Germany – a Comparison, in: Wollmann, Hellmut/Schröter, Eckhard (eds.): Comparing Public Sector Reform in *Britain* and Germany – Key traditions and Trends of Modernisation, Aldershot, Ashgate, pp. 107-131.
Wollmann, Hellmut (2000b): Local Government Systems – From Divergence Towards Convergence? Great Britain, France and Germany as Comparative Cases in Point, in: Environment and Planning C: Government and Policy, vol. 18, pp. 33-55.
Wollmann, Hellmut (2004): The Two Waves of Territorial Reforms of Local Government in Germany, in: Meligrana, John (ed.): Fighting Over Local Government Boundaries – An International Study of Politics, Procedures and Decisions, UBC Press. http://www2.rz.hu-berlin.de/verwaltung/down/Two_waves_ofterrit_reforms.rtf

Christoph Reichard

From Public Management to Public Governance

A Changing Perspective in the German Public Sector

The Starting Position: NPM Reforms in Germany

Germany is a late mover in the context of New Public Management (NPM) reforms. It is only since about 1990 that German municipalities have started considerable efforts to modernise their administrative structures and to introduce modern management concepts and instruments. Reforms started at the local level; they concentrated primarily on internal administrative structures and on financial management (Reichard 2003). These reforms were labelled with „New Steering Model" (NSM) and they were heavily supported by the KGSt[1], an association and a think tank of municipalities for managerial reforms. The reform movement was quite lively through the mid-1990s and it spread-out over the whole local level. At the moment, almost all of the (larger) German municipalities claim to have implemented at least some elements of the NSM. Some few years later, most of the German state governments (*Landesregierungen*) followed with similar, although less comprehensive concepts of NPM. In contrast, the federal government so far has been quite reluctant to implement major elements of the NPM. It was only active in some selected fields of modernization, e.g. in e-government, in cost accounting, in de-bureaucratisation etc. (Jann/Reichard 2003).

The conceptualization of the NSM at the German local level has gone at least through two different phases: In its early years it mainly consisted of the following elements (KGSt 1993) and it may be called „NSM 1.0":
– detailed product descriptions
– internal management contracts based on defined products and on flexible budgets
– integrated decentralised responsibility for results and resources
– flexible and product-based budgeting

---

* An earlier version of this paper was published in: R. Mussari (ed.): Dal Management Pubblico alla Governance Pubblica. Series „Dottorati di Ricerca in Economia Aziendale" Quaderno Nr. 11, Università di Siena 2005, 31-45.

[1] KGSt = Kommunale Gemeinschaftsstelle = Association of Local Authorities in Germany for Public Management Reforms.

- cost accounting (usually still based on cameralist bookkeeping style)
- monitoring and evaluation of results and related costs (in Germany usually called „controlling")

After several years of practical experience, „NSM 1.0" was extended, and some new elements were added to the original NSM framework. Some of the major elements of the second generation NSM („NSM 2.0", from about 1998 onwards) were:
- some tools of quality management (customer surveys, etc.)
- concepts and instruments of human resource management (e.g. with recruitment and evaluation methods, personnel development concepts, performance-related pay, etc.)
- activities to strengthen market forces and competition, based primarily on non-market competition (in few cases also on market testing of internal services)
- increasing activities to change the financial management system from a cash to an accrual base

After ten years of heavy reform work it is time to look back and to take stock (Jann et al. 2004): What has been achieved? What have been the strengths and weaknesses with regard to concept and to implementation? If we ask the practitioners in the municipalities, we will hear on the one side that considerable efforts have been made, and that a remarkable part of the NSM program has been on the agenda. On the other side, we will hear a lot of frustration, and we will learn that the enthusiasm of the beginning has disappeared. „Reform exhaustion" is a dominant observation. There is, however, not much empirical evidence about the „real changes" in the public sector. We have to rely so far to anecdotical and case-based findings. Neutral empirical surveys are rare (for an actual example of an informative survey of all larger municipalities in Germany see Knipp 2005).

If we take stock with regard to some own empirical investigations, we can conclude that there are some limited positive effects in numerous municipalities after ten years of NSM:

a) institutional changes:
   - some practice with management instruments
   - some restructuring (reduction of hierarchy, result centers, devolution)
   - some experiences with internal contracting
   - but not much emphasis on process redesign, on personnel development, on quality management
b) changes of the performance of public sector:
   - cost reductions (primarily because of budget ceilings)
   - more transparency (because of performance measurement and accounting)
   - faster responses to citizen demands

c) impact and outcome for the constituencies:
   – stronger customer and citizen orientation (one-stop offices etc.)
   – higher citizen satisfaction

In summary, the last decade of NPM reforms in Germany has shown some specific features: The reforms concentrated largely on intra-administrative issues, they dealt primarily with organisational and financial affairs. The focuses were on efficiency, on service and quality improvements, on performance and resource allocation, on more discretion and freedom for managers. The impact for the citizens and for the society in general was rather limited.

Because of these limited results and the mixed experiences with NPM-type reforms in Germany, there is a growing academic debate about the appropriateness of the NPM-concept. Several scholars argue for a change of the perspective: from a pure „public management" view (more) to a „public governance" view.

The Governance Perspective

The term „governance" is widely used, but there is still no clear and homogenous understanding of the underlying perception. However, the following definitions may help to find some orientation:
- Governance is about regimes of laws, administrative rules, judicial rulings and practices that constrain, prescribe and enable governmental activity, where such activity is broadly defined as the production and delivery of publicly-supported goods and services (Lynn et al. 2002).
- Governance is a self-organising mode of coordination and cooperation in interorganisational networks composed of political-administrative organisations, corporations and private non-profit organisations (Jann 2003).

If we look more deeply into the new field of governance, we will identify several variants of „governance" in the scientific discourse:
- *public governance:* intra- and inter-organisational steering and controlling in the public sector, covering single public sector organisations as well as whole governmental structures, based on a mix of different modes of steering and controlling (market, hierarchy, network structures), including multiple actors (government, enterprises, civil society)
- *corporate governance:* adequate structures and mechanisms for supervision and control of (private and public) corporations, particularly of joint stock companies
- *good governance:* framework conditions for effective government and administration, based primarily on accountability, rule of law, transparency and public sector management (introduced by the World Bank in the early 1990s; World Bank 1992)

If we are using the term „governance" in the following, we will concentrate on the perception as public governance. Although corporate governance issues are also important for the public sector (e.g. the corporate governance of municipalities or of public enterprises) they are more narrowly related to well-known aspects of public management and they can be tackled within that context. The version of good governance may be interesting for debating about adequate framework conditions and structures of the modern state, but they are more about good government, and do not directly touch the sphere of governance in the version of public governance.

One of the unsolved research questions is about the relation between public management and public governance. Is the latter a sharp contrast of the first or is it an extended version of public management? There are good arguments for both versions: If we are contrasting the two terms to each other, the difference between the two concepts will come out more clearly (Table 1). If we perceive public governance as an extension of public management, the evolutionary character of the concept of public governance becomes more plausible. From this view, public governance is a broader and more pluralistic perception of public management.

The public governance perspective seems to be quite adequate to deal with some actual features and trends of governing and steering the public sector. The following examples may demonstrate the relevance of the governance perspective for understanding and interpreting recent trends in the public sector:

a) In most countries of the world we are observing an increasing differentiation and fragmentation of the public sector. *Autonomisation* and *corporatisation* are the most obvious trends at all governmental levels[2], but particularly at the local level. Supported by the decentralisation doctrine of NPM, many public sector organisations have increased the managerial discretion and the autonomy of their service providing units. They have introduced cost or result centers and they have delegated decision-making competencies to those centers. At local level, municipalities have separated their utilities more and more from the core administration. They established corporate holding structures and they transformed their local enterprises into companies with an own, private-law based legal status („corporatisation"). According to actual empirical findings, each German municipality currently has in average about 20 separated entities (utilities, corporations, etc.). Nearly 75% of all separated entities have the legal status of a limited company (*GmbH*). More than 50% of the workforce at the local level is employed in the autonomous

---

[2] This tendency is well-known in many countries of the world; it is partly discussed under the heading of „agencification". See, Pollitt/Talbot 2004, OECD 2002, Verhoest et al. 2004.

entities – with a growing tendency. In fact, the public sector today is no more a uniform body, but a patchwork of very different forms and variants of public sector organisations. The borderlines between the public and the private sector are more and more blurring.

Table 1:
Differences of Public Management and Public Governance

	public management	*public governance*
focus of analysis	managing inside organisations	managing inside organisations and interorganisational coordination
level of analysis	single organisation	a) single organisation b) (policy) networks, societal subsystems
underlying logic of steering and control	a) old public management: hierarchy, rules, inputs b) new public management: results, competition	the same but additionally: - bargaining - exchange - trust, solidarity
dominant rationality	efficiency (+ legality)	effectiveness legitimacy (+ legality)
example for typical phenomen	result-oriented management of single PSO unit	policy management in a local or regional setting including multiple actors like local authorities, welfare associations, voluntary groups, enterprises

b) The interfaces between the public and the private sector have remarkably increased. The state is heavily relying on the private provision of numerous public services. The state is no more the unique producer of services; it is more the guarantor and coordinator of the services. *Public-Private Partnerships* (PPP) are one example of the collaboration between public and private actors. PPP activities – which seem to be another world famous fashion in the recent times – are of growing significance also in Germany (Budäus 2003). They are relevant in two different variants: As contractual PPP which can be found primarily in the fields of project financing, and as institutional PPP. With regard to the second variant, we have found that about 40% of all companies owned by local government have at least some private shareholders, i.e. they can be considered as being institutional PPP (Edeling/Reichard 2003).

c) Contracting-out and privatization is another trend in most of the countries. In Germany, during the last years municipalities and other public sector organisations have extended their efforts to transfer the production and delivery of services to private for-profit and not-for-profit suppliers. Municipalities are withdrawing from direct service provision and are concentrating more on their role as the ensuring and guarantying institution. Private providers can be found in many sectors of public services, e.g. in maintaining infrastructure, in housing, transport, waste disposal, energy, but also in internal services like office cleaning or IT-services. Similar trends can be observed regards to *material privatisation*, i.e. the total transfer of certain tasks and services to private companies, including the granting responsibility. Although privatisation activities in Germany have been less comprehensive as in some other European countries, there have been considerable activities at all levels of government, including the local level.

In several policy fields we are finding nowadays clear *network structures*. Private companies are collaborating with private non-profit organisations, with semi-public organisations and with public sector organisations in providing certain services or in maintaining infrastructures in the social, the health, the cultural or the security sector. The state or a local authority carries new and different roles in such a network setting: it is the initiator of a specific program, it is the coordinator of the different activities within such a network, it is – at least partly – the financier of the program, but also the qualifier of other actors, the moderator of planning and production processes, the democratic controller of the whole program and perhaps the multiplier aiming to initiate additional networks.

We can, however, approach the issue of governance from a more technical point of view: Recent developments of information and communication techniques demonstrate that we can enjoy new opportunities and potentials of e-government in the public sector. One example are service networks where the production is centralised in one back office, and where the distribution of services is highly decentralised to a series of „one-stop" front offices. Such networks are demanding for new and different modes of steering. Traditional hierarchical modes are no longer adequate, contractual modes and trust-based relations between different network partners will become more important in the future. Consequently, e-government is another driving force asking to look for new modes of governance in the public sector.

Last but not least, the actual debates about the *corporate governance* are also of relevance within the public sector. The originally private sector based issue seems to become more important also in the public sector. At first, the corporate governance of public enterprises is a relevant and controversial issue in some countries (basic question: How can we set up adequate structures and regulations which allow a proper control and oversight of public enterprises by the public owner?). Secondly, the corporate governance debate is approaching also the core administration: Questions of proper control and supervision but also of ethical behavior (e.g. public corporate governance codex) become more and more relevant at state and local government levels. In conclusion, the governance perspective of the public sector has quite different dimensions and aspects.

The German Debate about the „Ensuring State"

The concept of the „ensuring state" (*Gewährleistungsstaat*) has been an issue in the German-speaking countries for about ten years (Mastronardi/Schedler 2004, Reichard 2004, Schuppert 2000, 933ff.). The debate seems to concentrate at large to Germany, Austria and Switzerland, although there are also some notions in the Anglo-Saxon world. The basic idea behind this term is the assumption that the modern state is not any more the quasi-monopolistic producer of public services but the guarantying and ensuring institution which decides on certain policies and which ensures the delivery of services to the citizens according to certain standards and budgetary restrictions. The role of the state according to this doctrine is as follows:
- The state is deciding on certain tasks and services (granting a service level based on a contractor/provider split).
- The state is deciding on the institutional setting (Who should deliver a service?).
- The state is tendering the service; service providers may be public or private (make or buy decision).
- The state is monitoring and controlling the service delivery.

The paradigm of the ensuring state is partly related to some other actual versions of perceiving the state (Table 2). If we speak about the enabling or the activating state (the first was an important phrase of the Blair regime in the United Kingdom; the latter was part of the mission of the Red-Green federal regime in Germany in the late 1990s), or if we focus of the new bargaining options between state and society (particularly the industry sector), it is a similar perception of the soft roles and functions of the modern state. The paradigm of the ensuring state can also be seen as an alternative to the neoliberal perception of the minimum state at the one side and to the traditional welfare state at the other side which is no more affordable. Based on the respective ideological doctrine, the paradigm of the ensuring state can be interpreted in a more market-oriented version (more weight to private provision of public services) or in a more state-centered view (more emphasis to a public production regime). This makes it a politically flexible concept.

Table 2:
The „Ensuring State" and Similar Perceptions

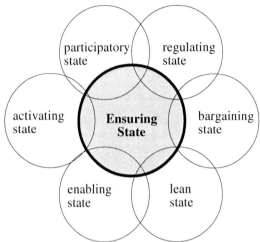

An important aspect of the paradigm of the ensuring state is the *concept of distributed responsibilities*. Instead of one single aggregated responsibility for a „public task", the proponents of the ensuring state argue for the distribution of responsibilities (Schuppert 2000, 400ff.):
– granting responsibility: ensuring the delivery of politically desirable and affordable services to the public
– providing responsibility: production of such services and delivery to the public

Additionally, it may be appropriate to include two more kinds of responsibilities:
– the financing responsibility, i.e. the responsibility of certain actors to carry the costs of investment or the current costs of a service
– the rescuing responsibility, i.e. the responsibility to step in for delivering services in case of insolvency of a private provider.

The idea of distributed responsibilities is that the allocation of each of the responsibilities to a certain actor is a matter of the context and is depending on the type of the respective task. Following a rough differentiation, it is possible to distinguish three different types of tasks:

- *public core tasks*: From a governmental view there are highly relevant tasks, e.g. military or security tasks. Such tasks are strategically important for the survival of the public community. Both variants of responsibilities should therefore be with the state.
- *public granting tasks*: These are services of general (public) interest, e.g. education, social or health care services, infrastructure maintenance, etc. While the granting responsibility remains with the state, the providing responsibility can either be allocated to a public or a private provider of such services, largely depending on the effectiveness and efficiency of the service provision.
- *private core tasks*: These are all other tasks and services without a clear character of a public good or of a common concern. Both responsibilities lie with actors in the private sector.

There is no clear analytical distinction between the different types of tasks and there is no definite rule for allocating the providing responsibility to a certain actor. It is rather a case-by-case decision which must be taken by the politically responsible institution (parliament, government).

The paradigm of the ensuring state has organisational consequences. If we try to restructure the patterns of the public sector but also of single public sector organisations, we have to distinguish between two different roles:
- the *contractor*: The core government unit is the buyer of a certain service and is ordering the service according to political targets and within the framework of a given budget.
- the *provider*: Services can be produced either by the own public production units, by other public entities or by private for-profit or not-for-profit organisations, depending on costs and quality of the offers.

The *contractor-provider-split* is well-known from the experiences with NPM reforms. Several countries have introduced it and have replaced traditional hierarchical modes of steering with contract-based modes (Table 3). The contractor and the respective internal or external provider are agreeing upon a contract which includes the description of the service to be produced and provided, the budget or price for the service and the necessary rights and duties of the contract partners. The contractual logic is relevant not only for the transactions between a public sector organisation and a private provider but also for the intra-organisational relations between buyers and suppliers of a certain service. As a result, we are observing new modes of governance in the public sector (and within public-private networks) which are more and more based on contractual agreements and on partnership relations.

Table 3:
Contractor-Provider Split (Local Government Case)

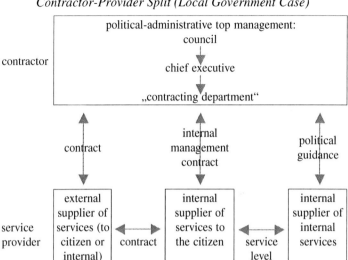

Marketisation and competition have set additional impulses for the governance issue. Influenced by the NPM movement, many governments made efforts to introduce market-type mechanisms and to increase competition in the public sector (Reichard 2002). One variant is the introduction of internal markets in public sector organisations by setting up competitive mechanisms (service level agreements, internal pricing, and termination of obligations to buy services exclusively from internal providers). Another variant is the „make-or-buy" principle which derives from the ensuring state concept and from the contractor-provider split: There is considerable institutional choice with regard to each public service. In every case it must be decided whether the respective service should be provided by the own public production units or by external providers. Thus, the level of competition among the different providing actors is remarkably increasing. This trend is again leading to new and different modes of governance (e.g. concerning the coordinating and ensuring role of the state as a „smart buyer").

Conclusion

As we have seen, the issue of governance has become more important during the last decade. Although it is not a new phenomenon in the real world, we are facing new and different features of governance in the public sector. The landscape of actors being involved in the production and the delivery of public services has become more complex. The interfaces between the public and private sphere have increased and the borderlines have become blurred. The styles and modes of governance have changed; traditional hierarchical modes have been replaced by market-type or contractual variants of governance. All these developments in the real world resulted in a change of the scientific analysis and interpretation of the institutional settings in the public sector. In the administrative sciences, we have therefore moved from the perspective of „public management" to a broader, interdisciplinary and more complex view on the complex world of the public sector: to „public governance". We have enlarged the focus of our analysis. Instead of a primarily intra-organisational and efficiency-oriented view on single public sector organisations we are now looking to the whole pattern of connected public and private units which are involved in the politico-administrative processes and which are contributing to the community. The new focus is broader and multi-disciplinary. It comprises issues of efficiency as well as of effectiveness, legitimacy and legality. The enlargement of the focus does not mean that genuine issues of public management like accounting, budgeting, performance management or human resource development are becoming less important. Such issues remain still relevant. But we should not restrict our research interests exclusively on topics of internal management, we should open it up to some of the challenging new problems and trends of „public governance". Such an extension of the analytical perspective will have consequences for the future teaching and research in public sector management. But this is another story...

References

Budäus, D. (2003): Neue Kooperationsformen zur Erfüllung öffentlicher Aufgaben. Charakterisierung, Funktionsweise und Systematisierung von Public Private Partnership, in: Harms, J./ Reichard, C. (eds.): Die Ökonomisierung des öffentlichen Sektors – Instrumente und Trends, Baden-Baden, pp. 213-233.
Edeling, Th./Reichard, C. (2003): Kommunale Betriebe in Deutschland – Ergebnisse einer empirischen Analyse der Beteiligungen deutscher Städte der GK 1-4, Abschlußbericht eines Lehrforschungsprojekts der Universität Potsdam in Kooperation mit der KGSt, Potsdam.

Jann, W. (2003): Governance, in: Eichhorn, P. et al. (eds.): Verwaltungslexikon, 3rd edition, Baden-Baden.
Jann, W./Reichard, C. (2003): Evaluating Best Practice in Central Government Modernization, in: Wollmann, H. (ed.): Evaluation in Public Sector Reform – Concepts and Practice in International Perspective, Cheltenham/Northampton (Elgar), pp. 36-55.
Jann, W. et al. (2004): Status-Report Verwaltungsreform – Eine Zwischenbilanz nach 10 Jahren, Berlin.
KGSt (1993): Das Neue Steuerungsmodell, KGSt-Bericht No 5/1993, Köln.
Knipp, R. (2005): Verwaltungsmodernisierung in deutschen Kommunalverwaltungen – Eine Bestandsaufnahme, Berlin.
Lynn, L. et al (2002): Studying Governance and Public Management: Why? How?, in: Lynn, L./Heinrich, C.J. (eds): Governance and Performance, Washington.
Mastronardi, Ph./Schedler, K. (2004): New Public Management in Staat und Recht – Ein Diskurs, 2nd edition, Bern.
OECD (2000): Distributed Governance, Paris.
Pollitt, C./Talbot, C. (eds.) (2004): Unbundled Government, London/New York.
Reichard, C. (2000): „Kontraktmanagement" – Experiences with Internal Management Contracts in German Local Government, in: Fortin, Y./van Hassel, H. (eds.): Contracting in the New Public Management, Amsterdam, pp. 127-141.
Reichard, C. (2002): Marketization of Public Services in Germany, in: International Public Management Review, vol. 3, no. 2, pp. 63-79.
Reichard, C. (2003): Local Public Management Reforms in Germany, in: Public Administration, vol. 81, no. 2, pp. 345-363.
Reichard, C. (2004): Das Konzept des Gewährleistungsstaates, in: Gesellschaft für öffentliche Wirtschaft: Neue Institutionenökonomik, Public Private Partnership, Gewährleistungsstaat – Publikation der Jahrestagung 2003, Berlin, pp. 48-60.
Schuppert, G. F. (2000): Verwaltungswissenschaft, Baden-Baden.
Verhoest, K. et al. (2004): The Study of Organizational Autonomy: A Conceptual Review, in: Public Administration and Development (24), pp. 101-118.
World Bank (1992): Governance and Development, Washington (DC).

Abstracts

Ireneusz Pawel Karolewski: Civil Society and its Discontents
The concept of civil society faces methodological challenges, particularly when applied to different cultures. This is due to specific cultural roots that pose obstacles to a trans-national analysis. The article discusses the problems that occur in that context while departing from the discussion of the sources of the broad interest in civil society and proceeding to the functional expectations about it. It addresses the issue of what constitutes civil society, its autonomy and impact as well as the challenges for the state. The interest of scholars and political decision-makers in civil society as a new instrument of governance is tracked back with respect to the debate on the defective state. Three objects of analysis are recommended by the author for the examination of the impact of civil society on governance and democracy: the structure and functions of civil society, the type of state co-existing with it and the character of the the relationship between state and civil society.
Keywords: Civil Society, Governance, Defective State

Sebastian Braun: Die Wiederentdeckung des Vereinswesens im Windschatten gesellschaftlicher Krisen – Konzepte, Kontroversen, Perspektiven
„In seinem Verein, da richtet man sich's gemütlich und behaglich ein." Wie behaglich es in Deutschland zugehen müßte, lassen aktuelle Schätzungen nur erahnen: Beinahe zwei Drittel der Bevölkerung sind Mitglied in einem der rund 700.000 existierenden Vereine. Allerdings legt dieser Beitrag dar, dass es nicht die Behaglichkeit, sondern vielmehr das Unbehagen über längerfristige Entwicklungstendenzen in Deutschland ist, das in der gesellschaftspolitischen und sozialwissenschaftlichen Diskussion der letzten Jahre zu einem erheblichen Bedeutungsgewinn der assoziativen Lebenswelt beigetragen hat. Die Entwicklungstendenzen werden zumeist als Krisen etikettiert; Vereinen wird in all diesen Krisendiskursen eine alternative und multifunktionale Steuerungsfunktion zur Bewältigung dieser disparaten, zugleich aber wechselseitig aufeinander bezogenen Phänomene zugeschrieben. Der vorliegende Beitrag führt in aktuelle Ansätze ein, in denen Vereine als Hoffnungsträger zur Linderung von Krisenphänomenen diskutiert werden.
Keywords: Vereinswesen, Deutschland, Bürgerpartizipation

Lahouari Addi: La culture politique en pays d'islam: le cas de l'Algérie (Religion und Politik im Orient)
Die Kritik am Ethnozentrismus ist Allgemeingut geworden. Auf der anderen Seite ist es in den Sozialwissenschaften in Mode gekommen, kulturelle Variablen, also z.b. „das arabische Patriarchat" oder die Religion des Islam, als ursächliche Faktoren für Differenz auszugeben. Gegen diese Erscheinungsform des „Kulturalismus", die häufig vergleichende Untersuchungen durchzieht, wendet sich Addi. Diese Ansätze – argumentiert der Autor – verführen zu sozialpsychologischen Erklärungen, essentialistischen Deutungen und kulturrelativistischen Irrwegen. Wer im vermeintlich typisch arabischen Patriarchat die Unfähigkeit zur Demokratie beschlossen sieht, verliert sich in einer kulturalistischen Ethnologie des Orients. Addi warnt vor dem exotisierenden Blick, der fast unvermeidlich die Differenz zur Kultur des Beobachters überbetone und die Aufgabe, die diagnostizierte Kulturdifferenz zu beseitigen, der anderen Kultur auferlege. Diesen Vorwurf führt er an dem Universalismus der Demokratie vom westlichen Typ etwa bei Almond/Verba, der im systemtheoretischen Rahmen von Parsons radikalisiert worden ist, aus. Aus einem solchen Blickwinkel könne die islamische Zivilisation im Hinblick auf die zivilgesellschaftliche Norm der westlichen politischen Kultur nicht anders als defizitär erscheinen.
Addi verteidigt die bestimmende Kraft historischer Bahnungen und sozialer Rahmungen. Er folgt frankophonen Autoritäten wie B. Baczko, B. Badie, Denys Cuche, J.-P. Rioux und J.-F. Sirenelli. Kulturalistischen Ansätzen wirft er einen kurzsichtigen Empirismus vor. Am Ende ergibt sich, daß in der Ausblendung geschichtlicher Kontextbedingungen der Orientalismus der Wissenschaft und der Islamismus der blutigen Tat sich treffen. Addi diskutiert die Grundbegriffe „politische Kultur", „politische" und „kulturelle Ressource", sowie das Begriffspaar „Kultur"–*„imaginaire social "* (das Inventar gesellschaftlicher Sinnangebote) und die spezifischen Thematiken von Politologie, Soziologie und Ethnologie.
Die Kultur ist in den arabischen Staaten mit den politischen Institutionen verkuppelt, was einen Unruheraum schafft, in dem gesellschaftliche Utopien eine Eigendynamik eröffnen können. Hier holt der Autor zu einer Erklärung des Islamismus, der die Religion in seine Politik einbaut und sich anschickt, den Gläubigen alles andere als erst im Jenseits eine bessere Welt zu versprechen, aus (Abschnitt II). Die Modernisierung hat in den arabischen Gesellschaften die lokalen und tribalistischen Sozialbeziehungen weitgehend zerstört. Parallel dazu ist aus dem Ende des Kolonialismus in dieser Region der Zentralstaat als Sieger hervorgegangen. Addi geht auf das Interessenbündnis zwischen den alten Kolonialmächten des Westens und den neuen Eliten in den arabischen Staaten ein. Hier steht die Gesellschaft fragmentiert neben ihren Regierungen, von Mißtrauen

erfüllt und opportunistisch in dem herrschenden System von Katzbuckeln und Vorteilsnahme. Die Opposition bedient sich, da die Sprache der Stammesgesellschaft im allgemeinen nicht mehr funktioniert, verstärkt seit den 1960er und 1970er Jahren anderen politischen Ressourcen, v.a. der religiösen Einkleidung. Ihre Utopie der Einheit und der Reinheit artikuliert das Versprechen einer gerechten Ordnung, die endlich auf göttlichem Recht beruhen soll.

Im letzten Abschnitt geht der Autor auf die Widersprüche ein, in die sich kulturalistische Ansätze verstricken, wenn sie das Phänomen der Gewalt in den arabischen Gesellschaften erklären wollen. Im Gefälle seines sozio-politischen Ansatzes konstatiert er dort indes einen erbitterten Kampf um die Macht und eine Konkurrenz widerstreitender Legitimitäten in einer Situation, in der eine institutionalisierte Legitimität nicht vorhanden ist, am allerwenigsten die der parlamentarischen Demokratie mit Elitenwechsel. Somit wurzelt die Gewalt, die durch Muslime ausgeübt wird, auch wenn sie als Bestandteil ihrer Kultur erscheint, in politischen Konflikten, für die institutionalisierte Formen der Lösung in diesen Gesellschaften nicht entwickelt sind.

Keywords: Demokratie, Politische Kultur, Kultur, Arabische Gesellschaften

Benjamin Stachursky: Globale Normen, lokaler Aktivismus – *Advocacy* **NGOs und die Sozialisierung der Menschenrechte von Frauen am Beispiel Ägyptens**

In diesem Beitrag wird auf die mögliche Rolle ägyptischer *advocacy* NGOs und ihrer transnationalen Netzwerke bei der Sozialisierung internationaler Frauenrechtsnormen eingegangen. Gefragt wird hierbei, ob diese NGOs als Vermittler zwischen internationalen Normen einerseits und den lokalen Werten und Normen andererseits fungieren, ob und in welchem Ausmaß sie hierdurch sozialen Wandel auf einer breiten gesellschaftlichen Ebene beeinflussen können, und ob sich Prozesse der Transnationalisierung eher fördernd oder hemmend auf ihre Arbeit im Bereich der Menschenrechte von Frauen auswirken. Hierzu werden einige zentrale Merkmale internationaler Frauenrechtsstandards hervorgehoben. Exemplarisch wird auf Aktivitäten ägyptischer *advocacy* NGOs im Bereich der Frauenrechte eingegangen. Die Strukturen dieser NGOs und die zentralen Debatten über ihren gesellschaftlichen und politischen Status werden beleuchtet sowie rechtliche und soziale Rahmenbedingungen für deren Arbeit diskutiert. Hierbei werden Möglichkeiten und Grenzen der NGO-Arbeit in Ägypten genannt.

Keywords: NGOs, Menschenrechte, Ägypten, Frauenrechte

Heidi Wedel: The Role of Civil Society Organisations for Democratisation – Lessons from Turkey

Great hopes were pinned on civil society as a means of liberation from authoritarian regimes. Fed by developments in Eastern Europe in the wake of the collapse of the Iron Curtain, a debate on whether or not the Eastern European case could be a model for liberalisation and democratisation in the Middle East arrose. This contribution points at the role of political Islam as a major factor distinguishing Middle Eastern societies from Eastern European societies. It analyses the potential contribution of civil society to a deepening of democratisation and peace within society in the Middle East by focusing on civil society in Turkey – the most secular country in the Middle East –, which is already in the process of transition from authoritarian rule to democracy.

Keywords: Democracy, Civil Society, Middle East, Turkey, Citizen Participation

Leonardo Secchi: Agenda Building in Brazilian Municipalities – When and How Citizens Participate

This contribution is based on an exploratory-descriptive research, which had the objective of analysing the policymaking process in municipalities located in Santa Catarina state (Brazil). It contains conclusions concerning the first phase of the policymaking process in those municipalities: the process of agenda building and identifying public problems. The investigated municipalities use institutionalised policy networks, public budget hearings, participatory budgeting, direct contact between executive power and citizens and participatory strategic planning. Despite the presence and dissemination of these mechanisms, there is low integration, and the agenda building remains centralised in the hands of executive power's members. This contribution attempts to provide a picture of the agenda building process in Brazilian municipalities and illustrates some aspects of the relationship between politicians and citizens in the countryside.

Keywords: Brazil, Local Government, Public Policymaking, Agenda Building, Citizen Participation

Wenting Fei: Local Public Participation in Government Legislation and Decision-Making in China – The Case of Shanghai
Legitimacy basis is a necessary pillar for ensuring the existence of a government. Therefore, establishing such basis is the fundamental political tasks for a government, and the precondition for political functions. Since the end of the 1990s, the Chinese government is reforming to *administration according to law* – Chinese social elite has realised that the government would establish legitimacy on the basis of democracy and rule by law. This article mainly focuses on the status and development trends of citizen participation in the legislation and policy-making processes of government in Shanghai. It conducts investigation on the institutional arrangements of open government information as the precondition for public participation and preliminary practices of public participation in government legislation, with a focus on public hearings. It also gives a prospect of citizen participation.
Keywords: Citizen Participation, Administration according to Law, Democracy, China, Shanghai

Taghi Azadarmaki: Good or Bad Government – The Case Study in Iran
The main objective of this contribution is to present the situation of the Iranian government theoretically and empirically. According to the sociological literature, there are three perspectives on government: (1) autonomous government, (2) dependend one, and (3) back to the first stage, good and autonomous government. Many social and political thinkers have thought that the only way of improvng society is sticking to a strong and centralised government and state. The article projects the situation of the government in terms of a national survey conducted in Iran (1999-2002) with a sample size of 2,535. In that survey, questions concerning the situation of the Iranian government were raised regarding Iranian identity, effectivity and the institutional position of the government. The data has shown that most of the people in Iran prefer to support a strong and efficient government rather than having a weak and autonomous one.
Keywords: Government, Political Participation, Parties, State, Democracy, Iran

Jochen Franzke: Representation and Participation in New Unitary Municipalities – Cases from the German Federal State Brandenburg

In this contribution the changes in the framework for local representation and participation of the citizens after amalgamation of municipalities are analysed. The sample contains 11 new unitary municipalities, established during the local territorial reform in the German federal state Brandenburg. Amalgamation undoubtedly influences the legitimacy of the new municipalities. The number of the councillors has dropped dramatically. At the same time, the new councillors gained more political influence. The establishment of the new district councils and district mayors can be seen as a positive outcome. At least for a transition period, these institutions will make it possible to advance citizens to the new territorial structures without losing well-known partners. As a veto actor, the district councils and/or district mayors are legally too weak, but they can strengthen local legitimacy and effectiveness. Local identity has not been damaged by amalgamation.

Keywords: Amalgamation, Local Government, Democracy, Germany

Christoph Reichard: From Public Management to Public Governance – A Changing Perspective in the German Public Sector

The issue of governance has become more important during the last decade. We are facing new and different features of governance in the public sector. The landscape of actors being involved in the production and the delivery of public services has become more complex. The interfaces between the public and private sphere have increased, and the borderlines have become blurred. The styles and modes of governance have changed; traditional hierarchical modes have been replaced by market-type or contractual variants of governance. The perspective in administrative science has moved from „public management" to a broader, interdisciplinary and more complex view on the complex world of the public sector: to „public governance". It comprises issues of efficiency as well as of effectiveness, legitimacy and legality.

Keywords: Public Management, Governance, Germany

Autoren

Addi, Lahouari – Soziologe, Professor am Institut d'études politiques der Universität Lyon. E-Mail: iep.info@univ-lyon2.fr

Azadarmaki, Taghi – Soziologe, Professor, Sozialwissenschaftliche Fakultät der Universität Teheran. E-Mail: tazad@ut.ac.ir

Braun, Sebastian – u. a. Soziologe und Sportwissenschaftler. Prof. Dr. Dr., Department Sport & Gesundheit an der Fakultät für Naturwissenschaften der Universität Paderborn.
E-Mail: Sebastian.Braun@uni-paderborn.de

Fei, Wenting – Mitarbeiterin im Rechtsamt der Provinz-Regierung von Schanghai (VR China). E-Mail: tealf@hotmail.com

Franzke, Jochen – Politologe, Hochschuldozent, Wirtschafts- und Sozialwissenschaftliche Fakultät der Universität Potsdam. E-Mail: franzke@uni-potsdam.de

Karolewski, Ireneusz Pawel – Politologe, Wissenschaftlicher Mitarbeiter, Lehrstuhl für Politische Theorie an der Wirtschafts- und Sozialwissenschaftlichen Fakultät der Universität Potsdam. E-Mail: karole@uni-potsdam.de

Reichard, Christoph – Ökonom, em. Professor, Wirtschafts- und Sozialwissenschaftliche Fakultät der Universität Potsdam. E-Mail: reichard@t-online.de

Secchi, Leonardo – Politologe, Professor, Department für angewandte Sozialwissenschaft in Unochapecó (Brasilien).
E-Mail: leosecchi@hotmail.com

Stachursky, Benjamin – Doktorand, Graduate School of Modern Governance an der Universität Potsdam.
E-Mail: b.stachursky@gmx.net

Wedel, Heidi - Dr., Leiterin des Referats Nahost, Nordafrika, DAAD Bonn. E-Mail: wedel@daad.de